Oxford Studies in European Law

General Editors: Paul Craig and Graínne de Búrca

ESTABLISHING THE SUPREMACY
OF EUROPEAN LAW

Establishing the Supremacy of European Law

The Making of an International Rule of Law in Europe

KAREN J. ALTER

OXFORD
UNIVERSITY PRESS

OXFORD

UNIVERSITY PRESS

Great Clarendon Street, Oxford OX2 6DP

Oxford University Press is a department of the University of Oxford.
It furthers the University's objective of excellence in research, scholarship,
and education by publishing worldwide in

Oxford New York

Auckland Bangkok Buenos Aires Cape Town Chennai
Dar es Salaam Delhi Hong Kong Istanbul Karachi Kolkata
Kuala Lumpur Madrid Melbourne Mexico City Mumbai Nairobi
São Paulo Shanghai Taipei Tokyo Toronto

Oxford is a registered trade mark of Oxford University Press
in the UK and in certain other countries

Published in the United States
by Oxford University Press Inc., New York

© Karen J. Alter 2001

The moral rights of the author have been asserted
Database right Oxford University Press (maker)

First published 2001
First published new in paperback 2002

British Library Cataloguing in Publication Data
Data available

Library of Congress Cataloging in Publication Data
Data available
ISBN 0-19-924347-6
ISBN 0-19-926099-0 (pbk.)

Printed in Great Britain
on acid-free paper by
Biddles Ltd, Guildford and King's Lynn

For Brian

With gratitude for your intellectual contributions,
support, and encouragement over the years

GENERAL EDITORS' PREFACE

While scholarly work on the European Union has often tended, over the decades since the initiation of this powerful instance of regional integration, to remain relatively confined within disciplinary boundaries (primarily those of law, politics, economics, and their various subdisciplines), a more comprehensive understanding of the nature of the transformation taking place is inevitably aided by analyses which go beyond particular disciplinary approaches and methodologies. Within the field of legal scholarship, the focal points of interest for many years were the complex doctrine emerging from the rulings of the European Court of Justice, the nature of the law-making processes, and the substantive body of legislative and other measures resulting from those processes. To contrast this emphasis—admittedly in a simplified way—with that of much of the political science research on the EU, it can be said that while legal scholarship has largely focused on the norms which have been created and on their implications, political science scholarship has concerned itself more with how and why events have occurred, interests have been formed, and decisions have been taken. Primarily legal approaches have tended to concentrate on procedures and the substantive content of norms, while political science research has focused more on understanding the reasons for their adoption, acceptance, and impact in practice.

Karen Alter, in this lively and provocative book on the impact of the European judiciary in creating an 'international rule of law' in the EU, brings her training as a political scientist to bear on that quintessentially legal subject. Whereas the story of the 'constitutionalisation' of EC law is very well known to lawyers and numerous accounts of the articulation of the famous doctrines of direct effect and supremacy have been retold and refined, the primary focus of this book is on aspects of that story which have remained relatively neglected by legal scholars. Although she does consider how and why the European Court of Justice developed these important legal principles, her concern is more significantly with how and why this doctrine and the authority of European law took hold across the EU. In seeking to explain the impact of the doctrine of the ECJ on national legal and political systems, she investigates the functioning of the preliminary ruling mechanism and considers how the relationship between the European Court of Justice and various different levels of the national judiciary has evolved. In addition to proposing her own account of why the ECJ's authority over national law and policy was to a large extent accepted, by national governments as well as courts, her examination of the responses of the French and German judical systems respectively provide interesting and more detailed case studies of the gradual phenomenon of conditional acceptance.

The book discusses what the author considers to be both the positive and the negative implications of the emergence of this strong form of an international rule of law in Europe. On the positive side she considers the benefits of holding states and political actors firmly to their commitments, and less positively she discusses the implications of limiting political autonomy by legally privileging certain trade norms and of increasing the nature and range of actors using the legal process for particular ends. By emphasising the 'international' dimension of her subject, she draws attention to the continuities between developments in Europe—which are so often categorised by lawyers without further explanation as 'sui generis'—and other international and global fora where bodies of a judicial nature are given an increasingly central role.

This book will provide legal scholars with fresh and challenging perspectives on an important and familiar story, and politics scholars with a highly accessible and stimulating account of a subject and a set of legal institutions which too often is told in the specialised language and discourse of lawyers. We are delighted to launch the new series of *Oxford Studies in European Law* with this lively and ambitious work.

May 2001   Paul Craig
                                                                Gráinne de Búrca

PREFACE

My interest in the European Community's legal system was piqued by two talks given in 1989 and 1990 at the Center for European Studies at Harvard University. European Court Judge Federico Mancini told an amazing tale about how the European Court had constructed a constitution for the European Community through its legal decisions, convincing national courts to accept these decisions during champagne lunches at the Court of Justice in Luxembourg. The second talk, by Joseph Weiler, offered a similar account, but saw compelling legal reasoning, quasi-religious reverence for courts, distracted politicians, and judicial empowerment as the key to national acceptance of the ECJ's revolutionary decisions. The implication of these talks was that judges talking to judges built an international legal institution. Judges agreed to what politicians could not, trading state sovereignty for the ideal of a supranational legal system where fundamental conflicts of interest seemingly did not exist.

Every account of the European legal system I read supported the arguments of Professor Weiler and Judge Mancini—the ECJ had made bold and revolutionary legal declarations that were accepted by national judges and politicians. Missing was a compelling explanation of *why* national judges and politicians accepted the ECJ's bold legal assertions. Weiler and Mancini had offered their best intuitions, but in the end these were not much more than intuitions. Not only did few accounts venture beyond Weiler and Mancini's intuitions, but most subsequent writings cited Weiler's and Mancini's talks (now articles) as their source for why there was national support for the ECJ's legal pronouncements. I was left unsatisfied with the answers (as were Weiler and Mancini, whose encouragement to investigate this question helped launch this study).

Explaining national support interested me because it is the key to understanding larger questions raised by the European experience. The European Community's legal system is everywhere cited as the best example of an authoritative international legal system that actually works. Ask European law specialists, and they point to the direct effect and supremacy of European law as the basis of the European system's success. But why did national acceptance of the supremacy of European law elevate the influence of European law in European politics? And given the European system's tremendous success, why weren't more judges following the ECJ's lead? Why weren't judges everywhere getting together to grant themselves new authority in the name of strengthening respect for law and building a more workable legal system? These are the questions motivating this study.

At the time I did not fully appreciate how asking these questions would lead me far into a world of law about which I knew little. It must have been my naivety that gave me the strength to begin. For over a year I grappled with *how* to investigate this subject. After false starts coding European law decisions and analysing reference patterns in an attempt to discern judicial preferences, it became clear that what I needed to do was explain why national courts changed national legal doctrines to accommodate the supremacy of European law. Comparative political analysis was the obvious means to investigate this issue.

The European experience lent itself well to such analysis. Membership in the European Community alone did not produce change in national legal doctrine. Indeed, the national and European legal texts regarding the issue of supremacy stayed largely constant from 1958 to 1993: similar contexts, non-changing texts, yet variation in the timing in which member states' national legal doctrine regarding the issue of European law supremacy evolved. I used well-tried political science methods to proceed. I searched through legal and political science scholarship to find alternative hypotheses that could explain why legal doctrine changed when it did, and selected two countries where these hypothesized factors (the independent variables) varied and where there was temporal variation that could help sort through alternative explanations (see p. 28–9 for an explanation of my case selection). I then traced the process of doctrinal change at the national level, using changes in the reasoning in legal decisions to chart the evolution of legal interpretation. I embedded the changing legal reasoning into scholarly debates of the time.[1] I also used articles written by the judges, lawyers, and *Commissaire du Gouvernement* involved in the cases to gain insight into why interpretation evolved. I supplemented this textual analysis with interviews with key participants in the

---

[1] According to a major text on comparative legal traditions, 'a critical case note by a leading author, is, in effect, like an important dissenting opinion, indicating where controversy exists and the possible future direction of the law' (Glendon *et al.* 1985: 162–3). Indeed, national judges and the in-house lawyers who prepare legal analyses for the court to consider (*avocat-général, Procureur-Général*, and *Commissaire du Gouvernement*) cite scholarship in their reasoning and adopt an interpretive language that appears in the legal doctrine. Since my objective was to look at doctrinal interpretation over time, my use of the legal literature is intentionally dated. I avoid current summaries of the meaning of certain legal decisions, since these examine older decisions in light of subsequent rulings and do not necessarily reflect how a decision was understood (and meant) at the time. Instead I rely on literature written when the debates were unfolding.

process, including national court judges, legal scholars, lawyers who brought European law cases, government officials in charge of European legal issues, Commission officials, ECJ judges, and the founders and leaders of academic associations of European law.[2] The interviews directed me towards important contemporary events (parliamentary debates, statements by government officials, controversies over policies, academic conferences, developments in national legal and political systems, etc.) that shaped legal interpretations. Where possible, I found a paper trail of these events and used them instead of interviews. I have, however, also relied on the memory of these participants.[3]

The methodology I have used has proven to be surprisingly controversial among legal audiences. I say 'surprisingly' because these methods, however flawed and problematic, are extremely common in political science. They are well accepted means to examine an uncertain world where the evidence we would most like to see is usually unavailable (King et al. 1994: 885).[4] This book is not intended to be a legal study of the European legal system. I hope that legal audiences will make the effort to understand the perspective and the enterprise of political science that it represents.[5]

One final choice needs to be explained. Given that the European Court acts in many respects as a constitutional court for Europe, in what ways should it be considered an international court? Most specialists of European law prefer the label 'supranational' to characterize the European Union's legal system. For some, this terminology indicates a significant contrast between the European legal system and most other international legal systems, namely the fact that private litigants can bring cases to the ECJ via

---

[2] My primary field research was conducted from 1992 to 1995, and I was able to interview participants in the legal and political debates of the time. I also used interviews with actors involved in the European legal process in the 1960s, 1970s, and 1980s to get a better sense of the legal and political context in the early years of the European legal system.

[3] To facilitate free discussion, I promised anonymity to the people I interviewed. I cite each person by their functional role, since it was this role that led me to interview them, and by the date and location of the interview.

[4] I cannot help but observe that most people are willing to impute political motivations to politicians and interest groups even though they rarely come out and say, 'I endorse this policy to get re-elected, to earn campaign contributions, to satisfy special interests, and because I care about my own power.' While judges do not openly declare their motives, at least they defend their rulings (in the body of legal decisions) so as to convince legal and political audiences, and the litigants of its validity. Moreover, European judges write scholarly articles analysing their decisions, and participate in direct dialogue with scholars and practitioners. They are also quite willing to speak to researchers. Indeed, in many respects there is more information available regarding the motivation of judges than one tends to have with respect to other political actors.

[5] I have written on the difference in legal and political science approaches to studying European law in an essay in the forum section of *European Union Politics* slated to be published in 2002.

national courts (Helfer and Slaughter 1997: 692).[6] For others the term 'supranational' is the most appropriate way to indicate that the EU is more than a typical international organization, yet less than a state (Mancini 1998: 25; Ladeur 1997: 859; Weiler 1981: 65).

My goal is not to quibble with these valid distinctions. Yet it is impossible to escape the paradigm of international law when considering the national reception of European law, at least in the countries examined in this book. The legal authority of the EU and ECJ comes from international treaties ratified by domestic parliaments. For this reason most national debates about the supremacy of European law were conducted within the framework of international law, with the basis for European law supremacy being found in national constitutional provisions regarding international law.[7]

It is also undesirable to walk away from the more general paradigm of international law. The EU's legal system may today be more 'supranational' than 'international'. But this was not always so. To forget the European Community's origins as an international legal system would miss an important opportunity to learn lessons from the European experience that are potentially valuable for other international legal systems.

I was fortunate in having significant financial and intellectual support for this research. The MacArthur Summer Research Grant (administered by the Center for International Studies at MIT) and a Doctoral Dissertation Fellowship from the European Communities Study Association (ECSA) funded exploratory research for this topic. The Deutscher Akademischer Austauschdienst, the Chateaubriand fellowship, and the Program for the Study of Germany and Europe at the Center for European Studies, Harvard University, supported my field research. The Program for the Study of Germany and Europe also supported me while I wrote my dissertation, and Smith College provided follow-up research support and time for revisions.

The mistakes are all mine, but any strengths in this work deserve shared credit. At the European Court of Justice, the library staff and the Research and Documentation Division provided access to key materials that would otherwise have been difficult to find. I thank especially Carlos Correia, Maria Rodriguez, Maria Martin-Hardt, Timothy Millett, and Luigia Maggioni.

---

[6] While this system is unusual, it is not unique to the EU. Indeed, this special institutional feature is seen as creating a 'transnational' as opposed to inter-state legal system (Keohane *et al.* 2000: 809).

[7] In some countries such as Luxembourg, governments altered their ratification processes for the EC treaties in order to escape the paradigm of international law. For these countries it might not make sense to consider European law as a subset of international law.

I also thank the late Justice Mancini, who hosted me at the Court and spend many hours talking with me about different aspects of the European legal process. Thanks to the seventy some judges, academics, government officials and lawyers I interviewed for sharing their memories and experiences with me, and especially to Gert Meier, the lawyer behind the *Cassis de Dijon* ruling and many others, who invited me to watch a legal proceedings and shared his thirty years of EC legal experience over beers and dinners. Thanks to Christian Tomuschut, Ulrich Everling, and Marie-France Buffet-Tchakaloff for helping me to learn about their national legal systems, and to Hjalte Rasmussen for early support and an opportunity to try out my raw ideas. Thanks to the Deutsche Gesellschaft für Auswärtige Politik, the Centre d'Études et de Recherches Internationales, Sciences Po, the Center for European Studies, and Smith College for providing hospitable places to work.

My intellectual community has been my constant base of support and constructive prodding. The Department of Political Science at MIT provided an unusually open, tolerant and non-hierarchical intellectual and professional environment. Thanks to Suzanne Berger, the chair of my dissertation committee, who taught me how to think and write about politics and encouraged me though my work was far from her interests. Thanks to Anne-Marie Slaughter, whose patience with me is a sure sign of her dedication to interdisciplinary work and contributed fundamentally to whatever merit there is in this book. Thanks to Joseph Weiler and Federico Mancini, for believing in me when others questioned if I even had a topic, and for patiently answering my hopelessly naive questions. Thanks as well to Ken Oye and to scholars at the Center for European Studies, especially Peter Hall, Stanley Hoffman, Lisa Martin, Andy Moravcsik, and Paul Pierson. My graduate student colleagues were perhaps the greatest assets of both MIT and the CES. For helpful comments, critical prodding, commiseration, and support, thanks to Erik Bleich, Brian Burgoon, Mark Duckenfield, Erin Flynn, Virginie Guiraudon, Brian Hanson, Wade Jacoby, Kevin Leppmann, Sophie Meunier, Mary O'Sullivan, Mark Pollack, Tim Snyder, Andy Tauber, Inger Weibust, and Todd Wilson.

Deep appreciation to Brian Hanson, Simon Hix, Wade Jacoby, Sophie Meunier, Harm Schepel, Claire Kilpatrick, Erika Noebel, and the anonymous reviewers who read the manuscript and gave me very helpful comments. Thanks to Erika Noebel and Stephanie Carnes for their valuable research support in finishing the manuscript. I know there are others I am forgetting who read chapters as well—thanks to you too!

My greatest debts go to my parents, for their encouragement; my grand-parents, who supported my education and made it possible for me to pursue the profession of my choice; and most of all to my husband, Brian Hanson. His intellectual contributions, support, and encouragement over the years have made this work possible.

Karen J. Alter
Evanston, Illinois

CONTENTS

ABBREVIATIONS

Institutions

BFH	*Bundesfinanzhof*, Federal Tax Court
BVerfG	*Bundesverfassungsgericht*, German Constitutional Court
BVerwG	*Bundesverwaltungsgericht*, Federal Administrative Court
EC	European Community
ECJ	European Court of Justice
EEC	European Economic Community
ENA	*École Nationale d'Administration* (National College of Administration)
ECSC	European Coal and Steel Community
EU	European Union
FG	*Finanzgericht*, Tax Court
GATT	General Agreement on Tariffs and Trade
VWG	*Verwaltungsgericht*, Administrative Court
WTO	World Trade Organization

Legal journals

AJDA	L'Actualite juridique: Droit administratif
AWD	Außenwirtschaftsdienst des Betriebs-Beraters
CMLR	Common Market Law Reports
CMLRev.	Common Market Law Review
D. Jur.	Dalloz Jurisprudence
Doc. Parl.	Documents Parlementaires
DS Jur.	Recueil Dalloz Sirey
EFG	Entscheidungen der Finanzgericht
EuGRZ	Europäische Grundrechte-Zeitschrift
EuR	Europarecht
EuZW	Europäische Zeitschrift für Wirtschaftsrecht
EWS	Europäisches Wirtschafts- und Steuerrecht
FAZ	Frankfurter Allgemeine Zeitung
Giur. It	Giurisprudenza italiana
Il Foro It.	Il Foro italiana
JDI	Journal de droit international
JO Ass. Nat. Deb.	Journal officiel, Assemblée Nationale Debates
NJW	Neue juristische Wochenschrift
RDI	Rivista di diritto internazionale

RDP	Revue du droit public et de la science politique en France et en étranger
Rev. gen. droit int. public	Review générale de droit international public
R. Fr. D. Admin.	Revue française de droit administratif
RIW	Recht der Internationalen Wirtschaft
RJC	Recueil de jurisprudence constitutionnelle
RTDE	Revue trimestrielle de droit européen

TABLES AND FIGURES

LEGAL DECISIONS CITED

Danish

ECJ

French

Conseil Constitutionnel

German

Italian

The Making of an International Rule of Law in Europe

The European Union's legal system has become the most effective international legal system in existence, standing in clear contrast to the typical weakness of international law and international courts. Unlike most international legal systems where international tribunals hear few cases, where most state violations of international rules are not pursued through legal means, and where most legal disputes are resolved out of court, in Europe the legal process is a key element inducing compliance with European law. There is an international rule of law that works in Europe. It works much like a domestic rule of law, where violations of the law are brought to court, legal decisions are respected, and the autonomous influence of law and legal rulings extends to the political process itself.

The European legal system was not always so effective at influencing state behaviour and compelling compliance. The system designed at the founding of the European Community in 1957 was inherently limited and weak. It was a system where few cases would make it to the Court, and in which the largest infractions could easily and without repercussion persist until a political will to rectify the situation emerged. Indeed, in the 1960s and early 1970s the European Court heard few cases of political significance, and its most important doctrines were not widely accepted in national legal and political communities.

The transformation of the European legal system was orchestrated by the ECJ through bold legal interpretations. The critical change involved the preliminary ruling mechanism that allows a national court to stop domestic legal proceedings and send a legal question to the ECJ for interpretation. In key decisions the ECJ took this relatively obscure legal mechanism and turned it into a means to ensure that states respect their European legal obligations. It did this by empowering individuals to raise violations of European law in national courts, and making European law hierarchically supreme to national law. In the transformed European system, private litigants challenge national policies that violate European law in national courts; national courts send these challenges to the ECJ as preliminary ruling references; and national courts apply European law over conflicting national law, thus holding European governments accountable for implementing and complying with their European obligations.

The European Court's actions in transforming the EC's legal system were extremely controversial. The ECJ based its provocative interpretations on the 'special' and 'original' nature of the Treaty of Rome.[1] But nowhere did the Treaty of Rome actually say that individuals had standing to raise state violations of European law in national courts. Nowhere did it say that national courts were to enforce European law over national law. Few politicians or legal scholars saw the Rome Treaty as anything more than a traditional international treaty. Indeed, the whole idea that the Treaty of Rome created a 'new legal order of international law'[2] was really nothing more than an assertion of the European Court. The Court's radical jurisprudence had to be accepted by national judiciaries and national governments in order for the 'new legal order' to become a reality. Yet both had significant reasons to reject the Court's edicts.

This book explains why national courts took on a role enforcing European law against their governments, and why national governments accepted an institutional change that greatly compromised national sovereignty. It then shows how harnessing national courts to funnel private litigant challenges to the ECJ and enforce European law supremacy contributed fundamentally to the emergence of an international rule of law in Europe, extending the shadow of law into the political process itself.

For those interested in the European Union, this study provides a revisionist explanation of the growth in influence and power of the European Court. Traditional European law scholarship looks predominantly at the European level, using legal exegesis to explain (and defend!) the ECJ's legal interpretations and national judicial acceptance of these interpretations. These analyses tend to minimize if not ignore the fact that legal interpreta-

---

[1] *Van Gend en Loos v. Nederlandse Administratie Belastingen*, ECJ Case 26/62, [1963] ECR 1, [1963] CMLR 105. *Costa v. Ente Nazionale per L'Energia Elettrica (ENEL)*, ECJ Case 6/64 [1964] ECR 585. [1964] CMLR 425.

[2] Ibid. *Van Gend en Loos* decision, p. 12. The ECJ later dropped the label 'of international law'.

tions which differ from those of the ECJ are equally plausible, and deny a role for political factors in shaping which legal interpretation wins out. Neo-functionalist accounts of European legal integration have also tended to minimize the role of political factors in the process, assuming a harmony of interest in support of further integration. Mutual interest, whether it is an interest in European integration, self-empowerment, greater efficiency, or the rule of law, is seen as driving national courts and the ECJ to promote European integration through legal interpretation. The facts that not every-one likes the ECJ's efforts to advance integration, and that integration creates both winners *and* losers, are conveniently glossed over.

This study shows how contestation between supporters and opponents of the ECJ's doctrine and authority drove the evolution of the European legal system. Seeking advantage, European law and the ECJ are invoked by private litigants and national judges to arbitrate domestic and European disputes. Private litigants use the European legal system as a venue where deals made at the national or European level can be reopened. National judges use the EC legal system to escape national hierarchies and the constraints of national law. The legal cases raised by private litigants and referred by national courts are used by the ECJ to advance integration by expanding the reach and scope of European law, filling in lacunae in European law, and crafting compromise positions in legal confrontations. The effects of this interaction reverberate through national legal systems, shifting the national legal and political con-text. So far this account may seem consistent with neo-functionalist assump-tions of interests aligning in support of integration.

But the very success of the actors advancing integration triggers a counter-reaction. When the ECJ implies that national rules must change, those actors preferring national solutions or the flexibility of legal lacunae lose out. The losers may well lack the political strength to change European legislation, and thus find themselves forced to accept a legal and political reality defined by European law and the ECJ. But they do not concede defeat and join the winners, nor do they become supporters and proponents of further integra-tion. At best the losers *and* the winners remain opportunists, ready to use the European system when it suits them and to challenge European authority when a national solution is preferable. One also sees learning occur. Recognizing that European law has undermined their influence, independ-ence, and authority, national courts, administrators, parliamentarians, and citizens have demanded for themselves more input and influence over future European policy-making. They use their greater influence to write new European law more carefully, to protect cherished national policies, and to argue more effectively on behalf of national autonomy and the repatriation of political authority to the national level.

The European experience offers lessons about what might contribute to making international law more authoritative in other contexts. The transformation of the European legal system shows us how the design of a legal system can enhance or undermine the ability of law to shape state or individual behaviour. Because of the way the European legal system was originally designed, in the 1960s the ECJ had few cases to hear, its decisions were unenforceable, and states were largely left to interpret the law on their own, in a self-interested way. In harnessing private litigants to monitor compliance and national courts to enforce European law, the transformation of the European legal system helped shift the interpretation of the law from states to courts, facilitating the emergence of a coherent and dense web of precedent that guides state decision-making, and creating the expectation of undesirable consequences for violations of European law. With private litigants ready and able to draw on European law to challenge national policy, and with national courts enforcing European law against their own governments, national and European actors are forced to take European legal concerns into account during policy-making and political negotiation.

There are also cautions in the European experience. It is not unusual for the expansion and exercise of power by a supreme or federal authority to create unhappiness among those actors whose independence and political power is undermined (states, local officials, individuals, etc.); indeed, there are many parallels in the European experience to domestic struggles in federal polities.[3] But the Treaty of Rome is an international treaty, not a constitution, and the European Union is still an international organization, not a federal polity. Because there is as yet no democratic process to legitimate policy-making at the European level, the public status of the supreme European authority is more precarious, and the potential for backlash leading to disintegration is higher. Indeed, the very success of the ECJ in helping European law penetrate the national political system has led the European Court to be a principal target of Euro-sceptics and opponents of European integration. While these groups remain relatively small and weak, their sentiments towards European law resonate in the larger public and cannot be ignored. Despite its success, the European experience serves as a reminder that as long as international legal bodies lack popular legitimacy, their growing strength and influence can

---

[3] This similarity has been explored in Goldstein (1997), Rasmussen (1986), Cappelletti and Golay (1986), Hartley (1986), Jacobs (1986).

contribute to popular opposition to international law and international institutions, and even encourage nationalist backlash.

The rest of this introduction explains in more detail how the ECJ used legal interpretation to transform the European legal system. Section I explains how the European legal system was originally designed to function, and how it worked *before* the transformation of the European legal system. Section II explains how the ECJ transformed the European legal system, embedding the Court's provocative legal interpretations into the political and legal context of the period to give a sense of exactly what was needed to turn the ECJ's audacious declarations about a transfer of national sovereignty into a real transfer of national sovereignty. Section III outlines the structure of the rest of the book.

I. The establishment of a limited European legal system, 1950–1964

How did the ECJ's transformation of the European legal system change the role of the ECJ in the European political process? To answer this question, one must first understand the role of the ECJ in the original design of the European legal system. Member states created the European legal system to serve three functional roles: (1) to help ensure that the Community's supra-national institutions did not exceed their authority; (2) to help resolve inter-pretive questions about European treaties and secondary legislation, and (3) to work with the Commission and member states to ensure compliance with European law. The transformation of the European legal system sought to enhance the last of these three functional roles: policing compliance with European law. But the original European legal system was intentionally weakest precisely in this area.

Keeping the European Community's supranational institutions in check

The Court was created primarily as a check on the powers of the supra-national institutions. The European Court was created in 1951 as part of the European Coal and Steel Community (ECSC). The model was the French *Conseil d'État* (Haas 1958: 44; Robertson 1966: 150), an institution that in its judicial function is designed to ensure that the government stays faithful to parliamentary law and does not exceed its authority (Rendel 1970). In the

ECSC, the High Authority (the predecessor of the Commission) had broad authority to decide on production levels for coal and steel, and to levy fines on firms or states that violated ECSC rules. The ECJ was created primarily to protect member states and private firms from excesses by the High Authority. If a firm or a member state felt that the High Authority was exceeding its mandate, taking an illegal action, or failing to act, it could challenge the action (or inaction) before the European Court. Indeed, all the treaty articles about the Court's jurisdiction under the ECSC treaty are about enabling private litigants, member states, and other European institutions to keep the Community's supranational institutions in check.[4]

In negotiating the Treaty of Rome, negotiators started with the blueprint of the ECSC (Pescatore 1981: 165). The ECJ's role was changed somewhat, but keeping the Community's supranational institutions in check remained central to the ECJ's mandate. The ECJ can review the validity of Commission decisions and European directives and regulations passed by the Council. It can hear challenges by private litigants, member states, and other European institutions to the legality of acts by European institutions. It also adjudicates the separation of powers between the Council, the Commission, and the Parliament[5] to ensure that each body follows proper decision-making procedures, that it does not go beyond its political mandate, and that it does not encroach unduly on member state prerogatives.

The emphasis on the ECJ's checking role is revealed in the Treaty of Rome itself. Most of the Treaty articles regarding the ECJ's mandate in the Economic Community are about this checking role, and the only place in the Treaty of Rome where 'natural persons' were granted direct access to the ECJ is in challenging the validity of Commission or Council actions.[6] The most significant expansion of the Court's authority by national governments since the Treaty of Rome also facilitates the ECJ in its checking role. In creating the Tribunal of First Instance in 1989, member states allowed for

---

[4] In the limited realm of the ECSC, the ECJ continues to play the same role.

[5] Originally the European Parliament could not raise cases or be challenged in front of the ECJ. As the Parliament's role grew, it was granted authority by the ECJ and through Treaty amendment to have its actions challenged and to raise cases before the European Court. (This change was enshrined in the European Treaties in an Amendment to Article 173 (now 230) made in the Treaty on a European Union.)

[6] While Article 173 (now 230 EEC) grants natural persons direct access to the Court to challenge decisions by European authorities or regulations that are of direct individual concern to them, because of the European Court's narrow interpretation of this clause, private litigants rarely have legal standing to use Article 230 to challenge European policy. For more on the ECJ's doctrine regarding Article 173 see Micklitz and Reich (1996: 39, 42–53).

greater oversight of the Commission. The Tribunal is able more carefully to review Commission decisions in the highly technical areas of ECSC and competition policy, and the ECJ is freed from these highly technical cases to focus its energies elsewhere.[7]

Filling in contracts

A second role of the Court is clarifying lacunae in the legal texts and resolving disputes over interpretation—or, in the words of Garrett and Weingast (1993: 198), filling in incomplete contracts. It is impossible when drafting laws or international agreements to anticipate all the situations that may occur. Usually administrative agencies are delegated the task of adapting the rules on a case-by-case basis and courts review the interpretations of administrative bodies (Lowi 1969: 128–56). This is also how it works in the European Union. The Commission is the primary body responsible for interpreting and applying European rules, and thus for completing contracts in delegated areas. National administrations also fill in the principles of European regulations and directives as they administer them on a national level. The ECJ's jurisdiction may be invoked in the event of a disagreement between member states or private litigants, on the one hand, and the Commission or national governments, on the other, about how the Treaty or other provisions of European law have been interpreted. Since the ECJ is essentially reviewing interpretations of administrative actors, its role in filling in contracts is hard to separate from its larger 'checking' role. But this role is still distinct. Member states wanted the ECJ to arbitrate interpretive disputes. And when the Court resolves the disagreement by interpreting disputed legal clauses, it contributes to filling in contracts.

Co-monitoring defection

Monitoring and enforcing the Treaty was *not* the Court's primary role. This has always been the Commission's responsibility. In the ECSC's the High Authority could enforce Treaty rules on its own through decisions and recommendations backed up by penalties. The fines could be collected by suspending payments to states in breach of their obligations or by authorizing injured member states to take measures to correct for breaches by another state. The Court was an appellate body hearing challenges to High Authority decisions.

---

[7] Based on an interview with the German representative negotiating the possibility of creating a Tribunal of First Instance, 2 Nov. 1995, Bonn. On the Tribunal of First Instance, see Millett (1990).

The monitoring and enforcement system was changed in the Treaty of Rome, weakening the High Authority's considerable power. The Commission's first task is still 'to ensure that the provisions of [the] Treaty and the measures taken by the institutions pursuant thereto are applied' (Article 165, now Article 211 EEC) [8] The Commission enforces the Treaty through the infringement procedure (Article 169, now Article 226 EEC) that allows the Commission to bring a state in front of the ECJ on charges of non-compliance. Member states can also bring cases against each other. The Court plays an adjudicating role, hearing the Commission's argument and determining if there has indeed been a violation. But the Court was only authorized to issue a declaration that a member state had failed to fulfil its obligations under European law. It could not order a remedy. Until recently, no fines could be attached. No sanctions or retaliatory actions could be authorized. Considering that the High Authority had the power to fine firms and states in the ECSC, the Community's monitoring and enforcement tools were actually weakened in the Treaty of Rome.[9] Indeed, if monitoring compliance had been such a high priority for member states, it might have served their interests better to have made ECJ decisions enforceable by granting the ECJ the authority to levy fines.[10] They might have made transfer payments from the EC contingent on compliance with Common Market rules, or given the Commission more monitoring resources. They could even have created a separate prosecuting agent independent from the Commission. This would have given member states the benefits of a court that could coerce compliance but would be less able to directly supplant national law and thus compromise national sovereignty.[11] That they did none of these things was no accident.

[8] The articles of the European Treaties were renumbered in the Treaty of Amsterdam. For most of the period of this study, the original numbering was in effect. I tend to include both the old and new numbering. I also do not change the numbering used by authors or judges when I quote them.

[9] In 1993 the ECJ was granted again the power to issue sanctions, but this mechanism is greatly restricted. The Commission can only pursue sanctions for the failure of a state to obey an ECJ decision, and the process is designed to facilitate negotiation rather than to sanction non-compliance. See note 13 for more. The ECJ has also developed its own doctrine about state liabilities, but this doctrine is also limited, and notably was not granted by member states.

[10] See n. 9 above.

[11] Thinking back to the national legal context in the 1960s as well, it is highly unlikely that states would welcome national court help. In most of the original member states, ordinary courts lacked the authority to invalidate national law for any reason. It is unlikely that politicians would give national courts a new power that could only be applied to European law simply to ensure better Treaty compliance, especially because in some countries it would mean that the European Treaty would be better protected than the national constitution from political transgression!

Original intent of the preliminary ruling system

The loophole through which the European legal system was transformed, and through which most European law cases still make it to the ECJ, has been the preliminary ruling mechanism (Article 177, now Article 234 EEC), which states:

The Court of Justice shall have jurisdiction to give preliminary rulings concerning:
  (a) the interpretation of this Treaty;
  (b) the validity and interpretation of acts of the institutions of the Community and of the European Central Bank;
  (c) the interpretation of the statutes of the bodies established by an act of the Council, where those statutes so provide.
Where such a question is raised before any Court or tribunal of a Member State, that Court or tribunal may, if it considers that a decision on the question is necessary to enable it to give judgment, request the Court of Justice to give a ruling thereon.

Where any such question is raised in a case pending before a Court or tribunal of a Member State, against whose decisions there is no judicial remedy under national law, that Court or tribunal shall bring the matter before the Court of Justice.

How did this mechanism fit into the ECJ's mandate?

Geoffrey Garrett and Barry Weingast have argued that the preliminary ruling system provides a decentralized mechanism to monitor member state compliance (Garrett and Weingast 1993: 198). The transformed preliminary ruling mechanism may fill this role today, but it was *not* designed to facilitate more monitoring of member states, or to help enforce the Treaty of Rome—that is what the Commission's infringement procedure was for.[12]

The preliminary ruling mechanism was created in the ECSC as part of the checking role of the Court. In the ECSC, individuals could challenge the validity of High Authority decisions in national courts and have these challenges referred directly to the ECJ. For the Treaty of Rome, European states expanded the preliminary ruling mechanism to include questions of interpretation, thus enhancing the Court's role of filling in incomplete contracts. The Common Market was to be built through regulations and directives

---

[12] The idea that national courts would be applying Community rules against or over national rules was never even discussed by the legal negotiators of the Treaty of Rome, let alone by the politicians. Negotiators of the Treaty confirm that only the Commission or member states was authorized to raise infringement charges. Interview with the Luxembourg negotiator of the Treaty of Rome (Luxembourg, 3 Nov. 1992), a Commissioner in the 1960s and 1970s (Paris, 9 June 1994), and a director of the Commission's legal services in the 1960s who also negotiated the Treaty for France (Paris, 7 July 1994).

specifying how European policies, such as the Common Agriculture Policy and the Common Customs Policy, would actually work. These programmes would be implemented largely by national administrations, and national courts would inevitably be called upon not only to assess the validity of these regulations and directives but also to interpret how these regulations were applied by national administrations and by the Commission.

Preliminary ruling questions were to pertain only to the interpretation or validity of *European* law. A private litigant who disagreed with how a national government was administering EC agricultural subsidies, for example, could raise a case in a national court asking the national judge to refer the issue to the European Court for clarification on how the *EC policy* should be interpreted and applied. The preliminary ruling mechanism did not authorize the ECJ to review the compatibility of national law with European law in these cases. In explaining how the preliminary ruling system is used today, ECJ Judge Mancini acknowledged the limitation on the Court's mandate:

It bears repeating that under Article 177 national judges can only request the Court of Justice to interpret *a Community measure*. The Court never told [national courts] they were entitled to overstep that bound: in fact, whenever they did so—for example, whenever they asked if national rule A is in violation of Community Regulation B or Directive C—, the Court answered that its only power is to explain what B or C actually mean.

But Mancini also admitted that the ECJ encouraged national courts to use the preliminary ruling mechanism to review the compatibility of national law with European law:

having paid this lip service to the language of the Treaty and having clarified the meaning of the relevant Community measure, the court usually went on to indicate to what extent a certain type of national legislation can be regarded as compatible with that measure. The national judge is thus led hand in hand as far as the door; crossing the threshold is his job, but now a job no harder than child's play. (Mancini 1989: 606)

Mancini subsequently abandoned the fiction that the ECJ was not reviewing the compatibility of national law to European law in preliminary ruling cases (Mancini and Keeling 1994: 185). But the pains taken by the ECJ for many years to try to defend its jurisdictional transgressions show that, by its own account, the ECJ lacked jurisdiction to review the compatibility of national law with European law in preliminary ruling cases.

Table 1.1 classifies the different Treaty articles defining the ECJ's jurisdictional mandate in the EU according to the functional roles of the ECJ. It shows that most of the Treaty articles pertaining to the ECJ are aimed at allowing the ECJ effectively to keep Community institutions in check, and to fill in contracts through dispute resolution. Least developed are the enforcement mechanisms of the European legal system. In 1987, 1993, and 1999 the ECJ's jurisdiction was extended significantly. But it is noteworthy that these expansions came mostly in the 'checking' and 'filling in contracts' role of the Court. The one exception is that the Commission's enforcement system was finally given sanctioning power in 1993.[13] The addition of sanctioning power came long after the transformation of the European legal system, and after scholars and politicians recognized the unusual effectiveness of the European legal system.

The ECJ's legal architecture absent the transformation of the European legal system: how effective was it?

The original European legal system was by all accounts ineffective at compelling compliance with European law. Despite the Court's compulsory jurisdiction, member states avoided raising infringement cases against each other, thus reducing the threat that a violation of European law would be challenged by another state.[14] The Commission was more likely to challenge a national policy, but it did not display any particular zeal in using the monitoring and enforcement resources it had in the early years of the European Union. Rasmussen noted that, especially in the 1960s and early 1970s, '[c]itizens of the several member states often in vain, drew the attention of the services of the Commission on flagrant breaches of Community obligations' (Rasmussen 1986: 238). Indeed in the first ten years of the Economic

---

[13] The Commission can now institute a process to get the ECJ to authorize fines against a member state that ignores an ECJ decision. The main incentive to add sanctioning power after 35 years was that law-abiding states felt that they were already being held accountable to European rules by their courts, while the worst cheaters still got away with their violations because of national judicial laxity and a lack of European sanction. In addition, by 1991 (when the Treaty on a European Union was negotiated) states feared that persistent non-compliance would undermine the creation of the internal market (Tallberg 1999: ch. 7). It took until 1997 for the Commission to actually request penalty payments under the new system. The Commission initiated the sanctioning process 16 times as of 2000, over half of which (11) have thus far been settled out of court and the rest of which are pending. In only one case so far has the Commission actually imposed fines (T. Jones, 'Greece counts the costs of defying the ECJ', *European Voice*, 6–12 July 2000, p. 4; the Court's press release is at: http://europa.eu.int/cj/en/cp/aff/cp0048en.htm). As far as I know, no money has actually been collected, however. The Commission posts this information on its web site: http://europa.eu.int/comm/secretariat_general/sgb/infringements/index_en.htm

[14] In the history of the Community, member states have only raised 4 cases against another member state. Data from ECJ.

Table 1.1. The European Court's Mandate[a]

Article 164 (now Article 220): The European Court shall ensure that in the interpretation and application of this Treaty the law is observed.

Checking the Commission and the Council	Filling in contracts	Monitoring defection
Articles 173, 174, 183, 184 (now Articles 230, 231, 240, 241): The Court can hear actions pertaining to infringement of the Treaty or any rule of law relating to its application or misuse of power. Member states, the Council, the Commission or individuals can bring suits challenging the legality of Community acts. The Court can declare void acts which it finds illegal.	Article 182 (now Article 239): The Court can hear disputes between member states regarding the substance of the Treaty if both parties agree.	Article 169 (now Article 226): The Commission can raise infringement suits against the member states.
		Article 170 (now Article 227): Member states can raise
Articles 175, 176 (now Articles 232, 233): Should the Council or the Commission fail to act, Member states and other Community institutions can bring an action to the ECJ to establish an infringement of duty. The ECJ's decision is binding on the EC institution.	**Article 177 (§ 1, 3) (now Article 234 (§ 1, 3)):** The Court can hear preliminary ruling references regarding the interpretation of the Treaty and statutes of the Council 'where those statutes so provide'.	infringement suits against other member states, but they must first bring alleged infringements to the Commission.
Articles 178, 179, 181 (now Articles 235, 236, 238): The Court can hear disputes regarding contractual liabilities between the Community and private bodies, and disputes between the Community and its employees.	*1999 amendment Article K.7 TA* (now Article 35 § 5 TEU): The Court has jurisdiction to interpret 'framework decisions', conventions and implementation of conventions	Article 180 (now Article 237): The Court can hear disputes about member state compliance with the statutes of the European Investment Bank.
Article 177 (§ 2) (now Article 234 (§ 2)): The Court can hear preliminary ruling references regarding the validity of acts of Community institutions.		*1993 amendment of Article 171 (now*

1987 amendment of what was Article 168a: Facilitated the creation of the Tribunal of First Instance, which increased the Court's resources to examine in detail Commission decisions regarding competition law, anti-dumping, and subsidy policy.

1993 amendment of what was Article 173 (now Article 230): The Parliament is given authority to challenge Commission and Council acts, and its own legally binding acts can now be challenged. The ECJ is also authorized to control the validity of actions taken by the European Central Bank.

1999 amendment Article K.7 TA (now Article 35 § 5 TEU): The Court has jurisdiction to review the validity of 'framework decisions', conventions and implementation of conventions adopted in the area of judicial cooperation in criminal matters. States can decide whether they accept preliminary ruling jurisdiction of the European Court in this area.

adopted in the area of judicial cooperation in criminal matters.[b] States were permitted to decide whether they accept preliminary ruling jurisdiction of the European Court in this area.

1999 amendment Article K.7 TA: (now Article 35 § 5 TEU): Court can rule on disputes between states in the area of judicial cooperation in criminal matters if the Council is unable to solve the issue within six months.

Article 228): The Commission can request a lump sum or penalty to be paid by a member state which fails to comply with an ECJ decision.

---

[a] This table paraphrases Treaty of Rome articles pertaining to the ECJ. Not included: Articles 165–8 (now 221–4) and 188 (now 245), which concern the composition of the Court, including judges, advocates-general, a registrar, and its rules of procedure. Articles 171 (now 228) and 185–8 (now 242–5) lay out the legal effect of ECJ decisions. All these articles come from the consolidated Treaty of Rome, unless otherwise noted. TA = Treaty of Amsterdam. TEU = Treaty on a European Union.

[b] These agreements do not create direct effects, and thus private litigants should not be able to use them to challenge national policies (Article K.6 TA, now Article 34 TEU).

Community, the Commission brought only twenty-seven cases against member states.[15]

The Commission's reluctance to pursue breaches was probably based on political concerns. In 1981 Stein argued that 'until quite recently the Commission obviously hesitated to aggravate its fragile relationships with member governments by bringing them into Court—and a decision by a member government to sue another posed political difficulties of a similar nature' (1981: 6). The Commission's highest priority was, and still is, to promote the integration goals of the Treaties by drafting legislation and persuading the Council to adopt that legislation. While the Commission was also responsible for monitoring compliance with the Treaty, rigid enforcement of European law may not have been the best way to promote further integration—especially given the unenforceability of ECJ decisions in infringement cases.

This is not to imply that the Commission did not contribute to the development of European law. The Commission plays a key role providing an independent source of factual information about the formation and implementation of European law within different member states (Helfer and Slaughter 1997: 303), and some have argued that it has served as a bell-wether for the Court in its decision-making, indicating where the greatest political controversy in a case lay and what concessions states might be willing to accept (Stein 1981: 24–6; Burley and Mattli 1993: 71). And the role of the Commission in pursuing national violations of European law has become more important over the years. As Table 1.2 shows, the number of Commission cases exploded in the 1980s.

Much of the increase in Commission action is due to the drive to complete the internal market. Between 1985 and 1993 69 per cent of Commission infringement cases concerned the non-implementation of Common Market directives, half of which were violations for not communicating with the Commission as to whether or not a directive was transcribed into national law.[16] The increase in number and the heightened importance of cases brought by the Commission came well after the transformation of the European legal system. Rather than more Commission cases leading to a greater effectiveness of the European legal system, it is more likely that the

---

[15] Data from the *Service Informatique Juridique* of the Court of Justice.

[16] Statistics on the content of infringement cases in the 1980s were compiled by the author from the 6th and the 11th *Annual Reports on the Control of the Application of Community Law* (tables 8 and 2.2 respectively).

Table 1.2. Cases brought by states, Commission, and national courts, 1960–1999

	1960–69	1970–79	1980–89	1990–99	1960–99
Infringement cases brought to the ECJ by member states	0	2	0	2	4
Infringement cases brought to the ECJ by Commission	27	70	646	861	1604
Preliminary ruling references from national courts to the ECJ	75	666	1255	2161	4157

Infringement statistics (1960–93) provided by the *Service Informatique*. Infringement statistics after 1993 from the Commission's *Annual Report Monitoring the Application of Community Law* (1999, p. 301). Preliminary ruling statistics from the Court's 1999 annual report.

more authoritative nature of ECJ decisions made using the infringement procedure a more successful strategy.[17]

European Court judges themselves and legal scholars see the transformation of the European legal system as the key to making the European legal system effective. Explaining the impetus for the European Court to issue its revolutionary rulings, European Court Judge Lecourt noted a recent failure of a state's administration to comply with an infringement ruling and said: 'The court could not but be struck by the extreme vulnerability of the Community's legal order if it could only rely on sanctioning through the censure of a long and insufficient infringement procedure' (Lecourt 1991: 360).[18] Judge Pescatore argued that ECJ judges simply presumed that the European legal system must be effective, and from this presumption came the doctrine of direct effects (Pescatore 1983a: 155). Writing on the impact of the European Court's direct effects and supremacy doctrines, ECJ Judge Federico Mancini wrote:

Without direct effect, we would have a very different Community today—a more obscure, more remote Community barely distinguishable from so many other international organizations whose existence passes unnoticed by ordinary citizens . . . The

[17] For a discussion of the use of the Article 169 procedure by the Commission, see Tallberg (1999).

[18] Robert Lecourt is the reputed author of the ECJ's famous *Van Gend en Loos* and *Costa v. ENEL* decisions through which the EC legal system was transformed. My translation.

effect of [the Doctrine of Direct Effect] was to take Community law out of the hands of politicians and bureaucrats and to give it to the people. (Mancini and Keeling 1994: 183)

And the eminent legal scholar Eric Stein wrote: 'It is safe to say, with the benefit of hindsight, that had the Court followed the Governments [and not established the direct effect and supremacy of European law], Community law would have remained an abstract skeleton, and a great variety and number of Treaty violations would have remained undisclosed and unredressed' (1981: 6).

As these quotes imply, in its original incarnation the Court was much like other international legal bodies—underused. Most disputes over the law never made it to the ECJ for interpretation. Without the ECJ to rule otherwise, national governments could offer their own interpretations of the law to justify their policies.

Member states intentionally created a very limited enforcement system. Why else would the European legal system's sanctioning powers present in the ECSC have been eliminated for the Common Market? Because of its limits the original 'toothless system'[19] was attractive. Most importantly, the original legal system protected national sovereignty. It relied largely on diplomacy and political will to realize the goals of the Treaty, but allowed a means through which disputes could be resolved through a relatively benign legal process. The European Court had the power to 'paint scarlet letters'[20] on member states which infringed on the Treaty, hopefully shaming them into compliance. Member states were willing to tolerate scarlet letters, which in contemporary times clearly carried less weight than in Hawthorne's famous tale. But they would not tolerate anything stronger. Member states placed very little emphasis on monitoring and enforcement because national politicians generally did not care to be monitored!

II. The transformation of the European legal system

The transformation of the preliminary ruling system was orchestrated by the ECJ through the creation of legal doctrines that granted access to private litigants to use the EC legal system to challenge national policies, and that

---

[19] This term comes from Mancini and Keeling (1994: 183).
[20] This terminology comes from Garrett and Weingast (1993: 198).

changed how ECJ decisions were enforced. The most important of the ECJ's legal doctrines were the Doctrine of Direct Effect and the Supremacy Doctrine (Weiler 1991; Stein 1981). The Doctrine of Direct Effect established that European law could, under certain conditions, create rights for individuals that could be invoked before national courts.[21] It was a well-accepted legal principle that by ratifying the Treaty of Rome previous national laws in areas covered by the Treaty were changed. But it was not clear what would happen if states passed new laws that violated European provisions. The Supremacy Doctrine made European law supreme even to subsequent changes of national law, so that states could not pass any law or make any new policy that contradicted European legal obligations. This transformation through judicial interpretation allowed the Court to use individuals and national courts to help monitor and enforce European law in the national realm, and to create a political and later a financial cost for governments violating European law. In the words of Weiler, it closed the possibility that member states could escape their obligations ('exiting' the Treaty) through non-compliance (Weiler 1991: 2412).

How could the ECJ just declare for itself these new powers? Surprisingly, it was asked to make these revolutionary pronouncements by national courts themselves. This was done not by entire national judiciaries, but by a few judges sending provocative references to the ECJ. The legal cases in which the new principles were declared were rather technical, and the material and political impact of the Court's decisions in these cases was not significant. But from a legal perspective, the decisions were revolutionary. They reversed fundamental presumptions about how treaties are interpreted, using activist techniques of legal interpretation.

The Doctrine of Direct Effect was declared in 1963 and based on a reference by a Dutch trade tribunal. Under Dutch law, international agreements such as the Treaty of Rome have precedence over national laws if the agreements are 'self-executing' in the national legal sphere. This provision of Dutch law led the trade tribunal to ask the ECJ a question that the Commission would never have asked, and that probably no court in another country would have framed in the same way. The Dutch court asked if the article of the Treaty of Rome in question could be seen as self-executing, that

---

[21] Not every European law or Treaty article can create direct effects. The Court has established rules and guidelines for when Treaty provisions and directives can create direct effects, depending among other things on the clarity of the text and the unconditionality of the obligation (Hartley 1988: ch. 7). The ECJ must decide on an issue-by-issue basis if direct effects are created.

is, if the Treaty created obligations for individuals enforceable without legislative implementation (Claes and De Witte 1998: 172–8).[22]

In the *Van Gend en Loos* decision, the European Court took the novel view that the Treaty could indeed create individual rights. To justify this claim it looked at the general 'scheme and spirit' of the Treaty, seeing where the rights and obligations of individuals were addressed. It noted that the Common Market was of direct concern to private actors in addition to states, that the preamble of the Treaty addressed the 'peoples' of Europe, and that the preliminary ruling mechanism was designed specifically for the use of private nationals. The Court went on to declare:

the Community constitutes a new legal order of international law for the benefit of which the states have limited their sovereign rights, albeit within limited fields, and the subject of which comprise not only Member States, but also their nationals. Independent of the legislation of Member States, Community law therefore not only imposes obligations on individuals but is also intended to confer upon them rights which become part of their legal heritage.[23]

The *Van Gend en Loos* decision meant, in essence, that private litigants have a right to have international treaties adhered to by their government, and to this end they can, in certain circumstances, have legal standing to demand government compliance. After the first case, national courts sent the ECJ a host of other references asking if different provisions of the Treaty created direct effects. Private litigants can always question the validity of European laws themselves, but only where European law creates direct effects can it be invoked to challenge national policy. The Court's doctrine allows it selectively to expand individual rights to different provisions of the Treaty on an article-by-article, directive-by-directive, legal provision-by-legal provision basis (Chalmers 1997; Craig 1992).

The Supremacy Doctrine followed logically from the *Van Gend en Loos* decision. European law must be supreme to national law if individual rights are to have any meaning, otherwise states could avoid their obligations simply by passing new national rules. This time the case came from an Italian

[22] The Dutch doctrine on this issue was not clear-cut. It was argued by some that since the Treaty of Rome in general, and the disputed article of the treaty in particular, was addressed to member states, under existing Dutch legal doctrine it should not have been considered to be 'self-executing', and thus it should not have created individual rights which the plaintiff could claim in court. For more on Dutch legal doctrine regarding the direct effect of Treaties, see Claes and De Witte (1998).

[23] *Van Gend en Loos v. Nederlandse Administratie Belastingen*, ECJ Case 26/62, [1963] ECR 1, [1963] CMLR 105. Quote from p. 12.

small claims court, raised by a lawyer who was trying to establish the supremacy of European law.[24] The case itself was absurd. Costa, in a dispute arising out his failure to pay an electricity bill of roughly $3, challenged in a small claims court the validity of the 1962 Italian nationalization of the electricity company ENEL. The Italian small claims court sent preliminary ruling references simultaneously both to the Italian Constitutional Court and to the ECJ.[25]

Of course the ECJ was not going to overturn the nationalization of the Italian energy industry on the basis of a $3 challenge in a small claims court. The ECJ had another problem as well: the Italian Constitutional Court ruled before it and declared that the case should never have been sent to the ECJ and that European law is not supreme to national law.[26] So before the decision was even issued, it was clear that the ECJ ruling would be ignored. Copying US constitutional history, the ECJ followed the strategy of Justice Marshall when he asserted the Supreme Court's power of judicial review in the landmark *Marbury v. Madison* case.[27] The ECJ ruled that European law was supreme to national law; thus if the Italian nationalization act had violated European law, it would be illegal. But it found that the Italian nationalization law did not, in fact, violate European law. Given that no change in policy was required, there was nothing for the Italian government to respond to. By simply doing nothing the Italian government seemingly accepted the decision. Nor was there any further case for the Italian Constitutional Court to consider. The ECJ precedent stood even though no one had really accepted its key tenet, and the Italian Constitutional Court had actually rejected the supremacy claim.

In addition to making European law hierarchically supreme to national law, the newly created Supremacy Doctrine carried with it an instruction to national courts to accord European law supremacy in their own application of law. The instruction was already present in the *Costa v. ENEL* decision (De Witte 1984), but was made even more explicit in the ECJ's *Simmenthal* decision of 1978. After restating the principle of European law supremacy, the Court said:

[24] *Costa v. Ente Nazionale per L'Energia Elettrica (ENEL)*, ECJ Case 6/64, [1964] ECR 585, [1964] CMLR 425.

[25] Italy has a similar preliminary ruling procedure in its constitution.

[26] *Costa v. ENEL & Soc. Edisonvolta*, Italian Constitutional Court Decision 14 of 7 Mar. 1964, [1964] CMLR 425, [1964] I Il Foro It. 87 I 465.

[27] Marshall also knew that his ruling would be ignored. He asserted the right of the Supreme Court to practise judicial review, but refrained from exercising this review in the case at hand. I am indebted to Anne-Marie Slaughter for this insight. On *Marbury v. Madison*, see Cox (1987).

It follows from the foregoing that every national court must, in a case within its jurisdiction, apply Community law in its entirety and protect rights of individuals and must accordingly set aside any provision of national law which may conflict with it, whether prior or subsequent to the Community rule.[28]

Thus the Supremacy Doctrine implied that European law was supreme to national law, and that national courts must, in their application of national law, grant primacy to European law.[29]

Revolutions are usually controversial, and the Court's decisions were no exception. The Court's jurisprudence challenged established practices for interpreting international law using suspect methods of legal interpretation to support its claims. Traditionally international treaties are interpreted narrowly, adhering closely to the wording of the text. But the ECJ interpreted lacunae in the Treaty as a licence to fill in gaps; although the Treaty did not say that European law created individual rights that could be claimed in national courts, the Court took strength from the fact that the Treaty did not say that the European law *did not* create such rights. Nor, as ECJ justices would later argue, did it say that European law *was not* supreme to national law.[30] The Court's approach has been called a 'teleological approach' to legal interpretation where, as ECJ Justice Robert Lecourt put it, 'Law [is] in the service of an objective. The goal is the motor of the law' (1976: 305). The ECJ's goal was to further European integration, and to increase the effectiveness of the European legal system (Wincott 1995; Craig 1992). At times this meant creative interpretation of the Treaty.

The legal basis of the ECJ's supremacy jurisprudence and the validity of a teleological approach to legal interpretation were not widely accepted in European legal communities in the 1960s. European judges are traditionally conservative in their interpretive approaches, adhering closely to the wording of legal texts and leaving it to political bodies to create significant innovations in the law. This is especially true where foreign policy is concerned, and

---

[28] *Amministrazione delle Finanze dello Stato v. Simmenthal SpA (II)*, ECJ Case 106/77, (1978) ECR 629; [1978] CMLR 263. Quote p. 283.

[29] For more on the Doctrine of Supremacy, see Bebr (1981), De Witte (1984), Docksey (1991), Hartley (1988), Stein (1981), Usher (1981), Weiler (1981, 1991).

[30] André Donner was a Dutch judge at the ECJ in the 1960s. He wrote about how the ECJ reversed the traditional presumptions of international law: 'A direct internal effect of treaty provisions is [usually] an exception that is not to be presumed, but that must at least be shown to be implicitly intended.' Donner argued that the ECJ turned this assumption on its head, asserting by implication 'that henceforth for the interpretation of the EEC Treaty . . . provisions reasonably capable of having such an effect are to be presumed to have it' (Donner 1968: 72). For more on how the ECJ went beyond the text of EC agreements, see Hartley (1996), Weiss (1979).

in the interpretation of international law (Benvenisti 1993). The ECJ tried to assert that the Treaty of Rome was not a typical international treaty, so that typical international law practices did not apply to European law. The Court pointed out a variety of supposedly original features of the Treaty to support its claim. But it is questionable how unusual these features are. And even if they are extraordinary, it would not mean that European law creates direct effects or is supreme to national law. Some legal scholars argued that the ECJ was putting too much weight on the preamble of the Treaty which mentioned the 'peoples of Europe', a preamble which according to lore was added at the end of the negotiations when each country was allowed to add one statement regarding its view of the Treaty's goal. Others questioned whether there was any sound legal basis for the ECJ's decisions. The German legal scholar Hans Heinrich Rupp called the ECJ's legal argumentation 'wishful thinking' (1970: 356), and in 1972 C. J. Mann wrote:

the Treaties themselves, viewed in their entirety, cannot be said to establish the supremacy of Community law over municipal law. The very absence of express agreement in the Treaties to that or equal effect speaks against such a revolutionary presumption. (Mann 1972: 26, n. 17)

Writing later in the 1970s and 1980s, observers continued to note national judicial reticence towards the Supremacy Doctrine despite the years of campaigning by the ECJ and its proponents (Jacqué 1981; Vedel 1987). As late as 1989 Ronny Abraham was still asking if 'in effect . . . the court has not exceeded its authority in pretending to dictate to national judiciaries the attitude to adopt in the case of a conflict between two norms' (1989: 184). And in 1996 Trevor Hartley found that the ECJ's rulings were 'outside of the text', with limited justification unless one accepted the argument of the most activist members of the European Court that the Communities Treaties were ' "genetically coded" to develop into the constitution of a fully-fledged federation' and thus that members of the court were 'doing no more than their duty in developing the law in the desired direction, even if some laggard member states are reluctant to accept such developments' (Hartley 1996: 107).

A new role for national courts—but do they want the job?

The ECJ's interest in transforming the European legal system is clear. Allowing private litigants to draw on European law in national courts to challenge national policy increased the number of cases heard by the European Court. Especially in the early years of the European legal system, national courts were the primary source of cases to the ECJ.[31] In addition to the larger number of cases, national courts asked questions which the Commission or a member state would never ask. Where state leaders did not go abroad to ask for a binding external opinion regarding what national policy should be, national judges have gone to the ECJ with such questions, allowing it to comment on national policy and to expand the reach and scope of European law. With national courts enforcing ECJ rulings, it was harder for national governments to ignore European law. The transformed system thus gave the ECJ more opportunities to influence national policy and the process of legal integration itself, and made ECJ decisions enforceable.

Less clear, however, is what the transformed preliminary ruling procedure brought to national judges or national governments. The ECJ was asking national judges to police government compliance with international obligations. Some national courts expressed concern that the ECJ was undermining national sovereignty and national legal protections, thus threatening the national legal system. Many feared legal anarchy, with different courts taking different positions on European legal issues and lower courts choosing whether to follow their own high court or the ECJ. Some national courts feared that the ECJ would contradict them, and claim for itself authority over whole areas of national law. In France, the *Commissaire du Gouvernement*— the *Conseil d'État's* internal lawyer who delivers a reasoned opinion for the *Conseil* to consider—stated: 'the argument (of European law supremacy) is enticing in order to encourage the development of a Community legal order; its evolution is more difficult to imagine if it withdraws from the action of the legislator whole sections of the life of the country because treaties have appeared in the area in question.'[32] A Tax Court judge in Rhineland-Palatinate likened the threat of widely interpreting the German constitution to accommodate European law to what happened in the Nazi era, arguing:

The undermining and destruction of the rule of law for a second time can be avoided only by the courts opposing every attempt to interpret another inadequately circumscribed constitutional provision so as to weaken . . . the Constitution's protection of the principle of separation of powers, and reduce the significance of the rule of law to a sham.[33]

[31] See Table 1.2 above.

[32] 'Semoules decision', Syndicat Général de Fabricants de Semoules de France, Conseil d'État decision of 1 Mar. 1968, [1968] Recueil Lebon 149, [1970] CMLR 395. Quote from CMLR, p. 405.

[33] *Re Tax on Malt Barley* (case III 77/63) FG Rhineland–Palatinate decision of 14 Nov. 1963, [1963] EuR 10 130, [1964] 10 CMLR 130. Quote from CMLR, p. 136.

A Frankfurt Administrative Court posed the question even more boldly: 'surely it is legitimate to question whether or not a decline in the national state institutions and rule of law must be paid as a price for the building of a politically united Europe.'[34] The German Constitutional Court and the Danish Supreme Court, which continue to fear that European integration may undermine basic rights protections and national democracy, have reiterated this latter concern, most recently in their Maastricht rulings.[35]

There was also the danger that such a bold step would provoke an unwelcomed political reaction against national judges, undermining their authority in the national political system. European judiciaries were traditionally deferential to political bodies (Stone 1990: 82). In 1968 ECJ Advocate-General Maurice Lagrange argued: 'the truth is that the judges do not dare to enter into open conflict with the parliament which is traditionally considered to be the only body qualified to sovereignly express the national will' (Lagrange 1968: 288). Certainly accepting European law supremacy would be going out on a political limb at a time when the EU project was in political crisis and politicians were divided regarding their enthusiasm for European integration.

As far as national judiciaries were concerned, the question of what to do in the event of a conflict of rules was an issue of national law—it was not for the ECJ to decide. Not willing to accept the ECJ's suspect assertion that ratifying the Treaty of Rome implicitly transformed national rules on the relationship of national law to the international treaty, national courts were in a difficult situation. For Dutch courts, the supremacy of European law was less of a problem once the issue of the direct effect of European law was resolved, because the Dutch constitution makes international law supreme to national law (Claes and De Witte 1998). But the other national legal systems did not allow for the supremacy of international law over national law. The practice in these systems was *lex posterior derogat legi apriori*—the last law passed

---

[34] *Internationale Handelsgesellschaft GmbH v. Einfuhr- und Vorratsstelle für Getreide und Futtermittel.* Reference to the ECJ by the VWG Frankfurt, 18 Mar. 1970, [1970] CMLR 294. Reference to the BVerfG by the VWG Frankfurt 14 July 1971, [1971] 11 AWD 541. Quote from AWD, p. 542. My translation.

[35] *Brunner and others v. The European Union Treaty, 'Maastricht* decision', BVerfG decision, 2 BvR 2134/92 and 2 BvR 2159/92 of 11 Jan. 1994, [1994] 1 EuR 95, [1994] CMLR 57 [hereinafter *German Maastricht* decision]. *Hanne Norup Carlsen and Others v. Prime Minister Poul Nyrup Rasmussen, 'Maastricht* decision' of 6 Apr. 1998, Ugeskrift for Retsvaesen H 800, [1999] 3 CMLR 854 [hereinafter *Danish Maastricht* decision].

trumps all previous laws.[36] If European law was the last law passed, then it clearly applied. But if there was a subsequent national law, national judges were to apply that law. To accept the Supremacy Doctrine, these national legal systems had to change existing legal practice from *lex posterior derogat legi apriori*. Making this step meant asserting that democratically elected national parliaments were constrained from passing laws that violated international obligations, and that national judges had powers of judicial review to control the compatibility of national law with international law.

It would be easy to conclude that, since national judges have relinquished their historical practices and seemingly overcome their fears, their concerns must not have been strongly felt or deeply rooted. Indeed, a reading of the EC law literature gives the impression that there was widespread consensus behind the supremacy of European law. Those academics who embraced European law supremacy were organized and highly visible. They published articles trumpeting the ECJ's jurisprudence and the very few national courts that applied European law 'correctly', giving full support to the validity of the ECJ's rulings.[37] But the academic European law enthusiasts remained only a very small minority of national legal communities—just as the World Federalists and the *Mouvement Européen* were. The silent majority of the national legal community was neither convinced nor supportive of European law supremacy. It was in no way pre-ordained that the legal ideas of what was seen as a group of ideologically committed 'United States of Europe' enthusiasts would succeed in permeating a larger legal and political audience. Indeed, as Chapters 3 and 4 will show, there were serious questions about the ECJ's supremacy doctrine within national legal systems, questions that persisted for many years.

The vast majority of the national legal community did not draw on European law in their legal practice—and not because of ignorance. Many lawyers and national judges who read the legal literature supporting the ECJ's legal arguments, and visited the European Court in Luxembourg, were

---

[36] The French case is somewhat confusing. According to the 1958 French constitution, international law is supreme over national law. But judges did not see themselves as authorized to apply this constitutional provision. The practice used instead was the 'Matter Doctrine'. Judges should assume that legislators did not intend to contravene international law, interpreting national laws as much as possible in ways consistent with international law, and reading treaties as the latest statement of the legislative will. But if a conflict between the treaty and a subsequent national act emerged, the judge was to follow French law. See further Ch. 4, Section II below.

[37] On the rather biased nature of European law scholarship, see Schepel and Wesseling (1997), Shaw (1994).

simply not convinced by the Court's controversial new legal doctrines. Writing in 1971, Stuart Scheingold noted:

The picture with respect to the recognition of the authority of the Court of Justice and the supremacy of Community law is a mixed one . . . in most matters there has been a real reluctance by national courts to use Article 177 [now Article 234] . . . only in Holland can the primacy of Community law be taken for granted. Elsewhere, the status of Community law and the willingness to use Article 177 remain in doubt, although national judges seem increasingly receptive on both counts. (Scheingold 1971: 34)[38]

This view was corroborated in my own research. The president of the *Association des Juristes Européens* in France, who is also a practising lawyer, noted that plaintiffs in the past and to a lesser extent today do not want French lawyers to raise European legal issues, fearing it may compromise their chances in the case or invite retaliation from an administration on which they are dependent.[39] Even among lawyers aware of European law, potential cases and potential European legal arguments are not pursued.

The national judicial concerns have also proved to be well founded. ECJ jurisprudence has indeed challenged cherished legal and political traditions, impinged on the exercise of parliamentary sovereignty, and led to the subjugation of some national high courts. European Court interpretations have become ever broader, so much that even law scholars inclined to support the ECJ are increasingly voicing concern over the lack of constraints on the broadening interpretations of the ECJ. And to make matters worse for national courts, government dissatisfaction with the European Court led to unwanted political scrutiny of national court actions.[40]

In the 1960s and 1970s, the perceived benefits for national courts in taking on a role enforcing European law in the national realm were few, and the

---

[38] Mann's analysis in 1972 came to a similar conclusion.

[39] Interview with a French lawyer (7 July 1994). Another French lawyer in an interview repeated this argument on 26 May 1994. Touffait also wrote of the reluctance of French lawyers and plaintiffs to draw on European law (Touffait 1975).

[40] In Germany, the Federal Tax Court was unhappily brought in to mediate between the Ministry of Finance and the ECJ in a case where the Federal Tax Court found the ECJ decision to be legally questionable. In Belgium, the legislature attempted to reverse the *Cour de Cassation*'s decision to accept European law supremacy. In France the National Assembly passed a measure sanctioning the *Cour de Cassation* for applying supreme European law over national law. The French legislature also removed the competences of the highest French judiciary court, the *Cour de Cassation*, over areas of indirect taxation, because it was unhappy with its jurisprudence applying European law. The French and German cases will be discussed in Chapters 3 and 4 below. On Belgium, see Bribosia (1995).

costs were many. Implementation of international treaties was, after all, the responsibility of political bodies, and the enforcement of the European treaties was the responsibility of the Commission. The fact that member states had failed to provide an effective enforcement mechanism for European law did not mean that national judges should shoulder the burden. And if judges were to step in wherever lacunae or political inaction existed, the nightmare of a government of judges would surely become a reality.

Nor did national governments welcome the transformation of the European legal system. It is often argued that if the member states created an international legal system for the EC and did not reverse the transformed ECJ's expansion of the system, then at some level they must be satisfied with how the European legal system is working. While member states sometimes disagree with ECJ decisions, most states do seem to be quite satisfied with how the ECJ helps keep European institutions in check, fills in incomplete contracts, and monitors compliance. But this does not mean that states wanted national courts to participate in enforcing European law against their governments. None of the functional roles of the ECJ required national courts to send challenges of national policy to the ECJ, or to enforce European law over conflicting national law.

There are also clear indications that legal integration proceeded despite the will of national governments. As Joseph Weiler has pointed out, the largest advances in European legal doctrine at both the national and the European level occurred at the same time as member states were scaling back the supranational aspirations of the Treaty of Rome and reasserting national prerogatives (Weiler 1981: 53). Indeed, when the issue of the national courts enforcing European law first emerged, representatives of the member states argued strongly against any interpretation which would allow national courts to evaluate the compatibility of European law with national law (Stein 1981). In the 1970s, while politicians were blocking attempts to create a common market, the ECJ's bold jurisprudence of European law supremacy was making significant advances within national legal systems. With politicians actively rejecting supranationalism, it is hard to argue that they actually endorsed an institutional transformation that empowered a supranational European institution at the expense of national sovereignty. And it is significant that member states have to this day refused to enshrine the transformation of the European legal system into the Treaties, refusing to insert a clause declaring the supremacy of European law over national law.

Today the supremacy of European law is largely an unquestioned truth. Each new member of the European Union knows that European law supremacy comes as part of the *acquis communautaire*, and law students are taught the Court's *Van Gend en Loos* and *Costa v. ENEL* decisions with few questions asked. While there may still be reasons to question the validity of the Court's supremacy claim, few dare to challenge such a bedrock and widely accepted principle.

How did what was clearly a minority view come to be thoroughly accepted within national legal communities, held by judges and legal scholars with no particular commitment to facilitating European integration and even endorsed by judges, lawyers and scholars who saw little legal basis to support the ECJ's *Van Gend en Loos* and *Costa v. ENEL* decisions? Why did national governments not reclaim their sovereign rights? This virtually wholesale transformation of the unbelieving and uncommitted, and the conversion of the losers in the process of legal integration, is precisely what needs to be explained.

III. Explaining the making of an international rule of law in Europe: the plan of the book

With the French *Conseil d'État* finally accepting a role enforcing European law supremacy in 1989, the last national judicial barrier to the ECJ's *Costa v. ENEL* doctrine disappeared. We can now say that European law is supreme to national law, and member states can be held accountable to their European legal obligations. Notwithstanding the isolated examples where European law is violated, there is a European rule of law where European law, as interpreted by the ECJ, is respected by national governments, and violations of European law are caught and rectified. This rule of law extends to the wider political process, with national governments avoiding policies in conflict with European law.

This book asks how and why a successful international rule of law emerged in the European Union. I break this issue down into three separate questions. Why did national courts accept a role enforcing European law supremacy (Chapters 2–4)? Why did national governments accept the ECJ's supremacy doctrine and national court enforcement of European law supremacy (Chapter 5)? How did the transformation of the European legal system contribute to the emergence of an international rule of law in Europe (Chapter 6)?

Chapter 2 explains the interests of national judges and the ECJ in working together to enforce European law supremacy. I argue that the central factor facilitating the expansion of European through judicial interpretation is the fact that the European Court sits as an institution outside the domestic realm which can be used by domestic actors (private litigants, interest groups, people with certain political beliefs, national governments, and national judges) and supranational actors (European institutions) to challenge national and European laws. The European legal system has become part of the policy-making process appealed to by those actors who lose during political negotiations over policy, and used by national judges to enhance their independence, influence and authority vis-à-vis other courts and political actors.[41]

Chapters 3 and 4 trace the process of national doctrinal change regarding European law supremacy in Germany and France, two original member states which entered the European Community under the initial bargain before European law was declared supreme to national law. I chose original member states because they joined the European Community before the extent of states' legal obligations to European law were clear. By the time the second, third, and fourth groups of states joined the Community, the ECJ's supremacy doctrine was considered to be part of the *acquis communautaire* that member states accept in full upon admission.[42] To select among original member states I used the standard practice of comparative political analysis; I looked for variation in the independent variables (King et al. 1994). Legal scholars identified two key institutional variables that probably influenced national reception of European law: whether a country had a monist or dualist legal system, and whether or not there was a tradition of judicial review in the country. Monist countries were expected to have an easier time accepting European supremacy because according to monist doctrine, international law is already part of the national legal system (and considered hierarchically supreme to national law). Dualist countries were expected to have a harder time accepting European supremacy because according to dualist doctrine the international system is not part of the national system, and international law only gains legal authority in the national system through direct incorporation into national law.

[41] Given that courts in Europe have not historically played such a central role in policy debates, the fact that the ECJ has become so central is quite remarkable. Indeed discussions of the ECJ have come to figure prominently in more general discussions about policy-making in Europe. See, for example: (Bulmer 1998; Pierson 1996; Pierson and Leibfried 1995).

[42] Indeed, British legal scholars debated the supremacy of European law during the accession debate in the UK. While the supremacy of European law may still have been a surprise to many British politicians, from a legal perspective it was part of what Britain accepted when it joined the Community.

The influence of a tradition of judicial review was less clear. Some legal scholars expected acceptance of European law supremacy to be easier in countries where courts were experienced in practising judicial review, while others saw the possibility of practising judicial review as an enticing reason for national judges to embrace European law supremacy. These institutional features did not prove as significant as I had expected.[43] A third independent variable was government positions on European integration. I wanted as much variation in judicial positions over time as possible, so that I could examine the influence of political factors on judicial decision-making.

France (a monist country with no tradition of judicial review) had the largest variation in national judicial positions, with the three highest courts taking divergent positions regarding whether or not they could enforce European law supremacy, and with these positions changing over time (allowing me to examine how political factors shaped judicial interpretation). French courts have a reputation for being unfriendly to European law; thus I chose Germany (a dualist country with a tradition of judicial review) as a balance. In 1992, when I selected my cases, Germany was considered strongly supportive of European law supremacy. The German Constitutional Court was the first national supreme court to endorse the supremacy of European law over national law, and the only court to create a sanction against national judges who refuse to refer cases to the European Court. In 1993, the German Constitutional Court issued its strongly worded Maastricht ruling.[44] The tone of this decision is very critical of the ECJ, and it may now seem that I indeed chose the hardest cases to examine. But in legal substance the German Constitutional Court's position is no different from that of the highest courts in Italy, France, and now Denmark.[45] Overall, I believe that Germany still

---

[43] The fact that the French constitution makes international law supreme over national law did not hinder French courts from refusing to accord European law supremacy over national law. The lack of a tradition of judicial review seemed to influence French judicial positions on the issue of EC law supremacy, but national judicial behaviour was not uniform. Appeals to a prohibition against judicial review were used to avoid applying European supremacy, but judges found other ways as well to avoid the supremacy issue. Some judges avoided the issue by focusing on which rule applied to the case at hand, European or national. Sometimes judges changed the classification of the national law in question, calling it a 'regulation' or a 'government ordinance', so that European law could be accorded supremacy, or a 'law', so that European law could not be accorded supremacy. And despite a prohibition against practising judicial review, the *Cour de Cassation* embraced judicial review in the first clear case that came its way. See Ch. 4 for more.

[44] *Supra, German Maastricht* decision, n. 35.

[45] Italy: *Frontini v. Ministero della Finanze*, Italian Constitutional Court Decision 183 of 27 Dec. 1973, [1974] Il Foro It. 314, [1974] 2 CMLR 372. *Fragd SpA v. Amministrazione delle Finanze*, Italian Constitutional Court Decision 232 of 21 Apr. 1989, [1989] 72 RDI. France: *Conseil*

can be seen as relatively receptive to the ECJ's supremacy doctrine, and these two cases are not particularly unusual.[46]

Chapter 5 explains why national governments accepted the transformation of the European legal system, and how national court enforcement of European law has compelled member states to play by the legal rules of the game when they disagree with the ECJ. The same factors that allowed the ECJ to transform the European legal system despite the intention of national governments continue to limit member states' ability to control how the ECJ interprets European law. I show how member states have learned from the transformation of the European legal system, and how they are seeking to better control legal integration in the drafting of new European rules and when new powers are given to the ECJ.

The conclusion of the book explains how the transformation of the preliminary ruling system contributed to the emergence of a rule of law in Europe where violations of the law are brought to court, legal decisions are respected, and the autonomous influence of law and legal rulings extends to the political process itself. It then shows how the transformation of the European legal system extended the influence of law and courts into the political process of European integration. Finally, it asks what the European experience reveals about how to make international legal systems more effective in other contexts, and what potential pitfalls such a change brings.

Ironically, just as the last national judicial barrier fell, new challenges to the ECJ's authority emerged, raising new questions about the absolute

Constitutionnel decision 91-294 DC of 25 July 1991, 'Schengen Decision', [1991] *Recueil des Décisions du Conseil Constitutionnel* 91, [1991] R. Fr. D. Admin. 173. *Conseil Constitutionnel* decision 92-308 DC of 9 Apr. 1992, '*Maastricht I*', [1992] *Recueil des Décisions du Conseil Constitutionnel* 55, [1992] RJC I-496, [1993] 3 CMLR 345. Denmark: above n. 35, *Danish Maastricht* decision.

[46] The cases not chosen were Italy, Belgium, the Netherlands, and Luxembourg. Italy also has a dualist system with a tradition of judicial review. The Italian Constitutional Court and German Constitutional Court differ in their tone and stridency, but there is really very little doctrinal difference between the two. Indeed, the Italian process of doctrinal change parallels the German experience (with the important distinction created by the fact that in Italy individuals cannot bring appeals directly to the Italian Constitutional Court as they can in Germany). I chose France over Belgium (the other monist system without a tradition of judicial review). The French *Conseil d'État* had finally relented in its opposition to enforcing European law supremacy (in 1989), and with three high French courts taking opposing positions the French case provided much variation to examine. An analysis of Belgium would, however, provide insight into my argument, because Belgium added a higher constitutional level court after the supremacy of European law was declared. I originally hoped to have Belgium as a third case, but time constraints prevented me from covering a third country. The only other monist system in the original six was the Netherlands (Luxembourg is too small). A limitation for me was that I do not speak Dutch. But specialists see this case as very unusual, and it probably fits least well the general account I give (Claes and De Witte 1998).

supremacy of European law within the national legal order. In the 1990s, constitutional courts in Germany, France, and Denmark boldly challenged the ECJ's authority to act as the supreme court of Europe, deciding where and when European authority supersedes state authority.[47] European populations are also increasingly questioning the democratic legitimacy of the European Union and the ECJ. These challenges are forcing scholars to reconceptualize what type of institution the EU is (MacCormick 1993; Bañkowski and Christodoulidis 1998; Bañkowski and Scott 1996; Eleftheriadis 1996).

Some see these challenges as a sign of the maturation of the European legal process. Now that the ECJ's authority is firmly established, it can be more openly questioned. The assumption is that the more powerful the legal and political institutions, the larger and louder the body of critics becomes. In this view, the challenges are a new phenomenon that is part of emerging checks and balances within the European polity.

Some see these challenges as a sign that the ECJ and the EU have entered a new, more polemical terrain as yet another phase of integration. The main areas of broad consensus have been resolved. The easier steps in integration have been accomplished. The next steps are far more contentious and involve relinquishing more sensitive areas of national control. In this view as well, the challenges are a new phenomenon that are part of emerging checks and balances within the European polity.

This study shows that tensions between national courts, national governments, and the ECJ were always part of European legal integration. The supremacy of European law became part of national systems by way of judicial negotiation. Conflicting legal interpretations were voiced by national courts, the ECJ, national governments, and the Commission, reflecting the different preferences and priorities of the actors involved. Some national high courts at first refused the supremacy of European law outright. The national positions were in effect ultimatums—declarations that national legal texts and constitutions trumped European legal texts and ECJ decisions, and that national high courts alone had the power to interpret these texts. These courts later softened their positions, but they refused to adopt the language or the reasoning of the ECJ. Indeed, they have for the most part refused to see the Treaty of Rome as anything other than an international treaty. National courts have taken this position to support the view that member states remain sovereign, and because they fear that adopting the ECJ's interpretation

---

[47] *German Maastricht* decision and decisions cited in n. 35 above.

would hand the ECJ a blank cheque which it could use to define where and when national prerogatives remain. Instead, national courts have created a legal barrier between national systems and European law so that they can police the boundary between national sovereignty and European authority, and so that they can create limits to European law's authority (and by extension the ECJ's authority) within the national realm.

This book reconstructs the negotiation process, looking anew at national court decisions on the issue of European law supremacy and embedding these decisions in their national legal and political context. It shows how national courts struggled amongst themselves and eventually accommodated the ECJ's supremacy claim, but then used national legal doctrine regarding European law supremacy to limit future encroachment of European law into the national realm. It explains why governments acquiesced in a judicial revolution that ceded significant national sovereignty. Finally, it shows how the interaction between private litigants raising cases, national courts referring cases and invoking ECJ jurisprudence, and the ECJ interpreting European law all contributed to the construction of an international rule of law in Europe.

2

National Judicial Interests and the Process of Legal Integration in Europe

The European Court of Justice played a decisive role in the transformation of the European legal system by declaring the direct effect and supremacy of European law. But the linchpins of the European legal system are the national courts of the member states. National court references provide the ECJ with opportunities to expand the reach and scope of EC law, opportunities that would not exist if the ECJ had to rely on member states or the Commission to raise infringement suits. In applying European law supremacy, national judges have made European law enforceable in the national realm.

Given the critical role played by national courts, the real question is not so much why the ECJ seized the opportunities presented to it to enlarge its jurisdictional authority and power, but rather why national courts have facilitated this expansion of power. This chapter provides a general explanation of judicial interests to help understand the role of national courts in European integration. Section I explains the different roles national courts play in implementing European law, identifying which aspects of national judicial behaviour are most puzzling. Section II examines how other scholars explain the puzzling aspects of national court behaviour in European integration. Section III provides an historical institutionalist explanation of judicial interests with respect to European law. Section IV explains how competitive struggles within the legal bureaucracy and between courts and political bodies led to a transformation of national doctrines regarding the compatibility of national law with international law. Finally, I explain how national courts are using their disagreements with the ECJ to increase their influence and create potential limits in the process of European integration (Section V).

I. Explaining change in national legal doctrines: the dependent variable

No one denies that national judges are key interlocutors in the European legal system. It is far less obvious, however, that there is something perplexing about national judicial willingness to play a role in the expansion and penetration of European law in the national realm. From a formal legal perspective, European law explains when national courts refer cases to the ECJ and apply European law supremacy. According to Article 234 (formerly Article 177) any national court may make a reference to the ECJ but courts of last instance are obliged to refer cases if there is a question about European law.[1] The ECJ's supremacy doctrine requires national courts to enforce European law over any conflicting national laws, including national constitutions. For national courts concerned that they lack the power to follow ECJ doctrine, the ECJ has implied that national courts are empowered by the autonomous nature of the EC legal order, by the direct applicability of EC law (Claes 1995: 125–7), and by Article 10 of the Treaty of Rome (formerly Article 5) that requires member states to take appropriate measures to ensure compliance with European law (Schockweiler 1991: 152).

But in practice, national judges often do not refer cases to the ECJ even when there is a question about European law. Indeed, by one calculation less than 25 per cent of cases involving EC law are actually referred to the ECJ.[2] The most visible sign that judges are exercising discretion is the varying reference rates of national judges to the ECJ (see Fig. 2.1). Most scholarship has focused on institutional characteristics of the national legal system— whether a national legal system was monist or dualist, whether there was a tradition of judicial review in the country and whether the country had a fed-

---

[1] There are a number of fairly ambiguous factors to take into account when determining whether a 'question' about European law exists. The ECJ has created guidelines for national judges: they should consider whether the ECJ has already ruled on the issue, whether an ECJ interpretation is necessary to rule on the issue, and whether the EC legal provision is subject to different interpretations by different courts and in different languages. For a very good legal analysis of the issue of when national judges should refer a case to the ECJ, see Barnard and Sharpston (1997).

[2] Damian Chalmers found that from 1972 to 1998 only 25% (269 out of 1,088) of the reported cases involving EC law in the UK were referred to the ECJ. This finding probably underrepresents the number of British cases that are not referred, since lower court decisions tend not to be reported and it is hard to know about cases where EC legal arguments were dismissed out of hand (Chalmers 2000a: 11). Jonathan Golub uses ECJ data regarding the total number of cases involving European law and finds that on average 22% of cases involving European law are referred to the ECJ (Golub 1996a: 14).

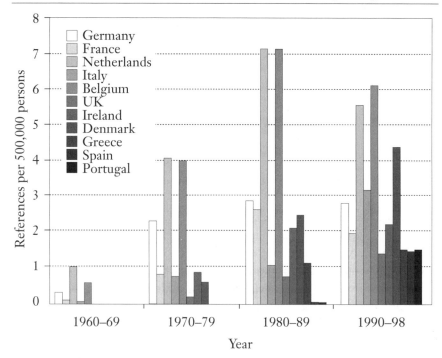

Fig. 2.1. Reference rates to the ECJ per 500,000 persons, broken down by country (excludes Luxembourg)

eralist or constitutional model—in an effort to explain the variation in reference rates. These approaches have failed because none of the institutional explanations hold across countries, nor do they account for significant variation in reference rates among courts within a single country (Alter 1998: 231–2; De Witte 1999: 179).

Recent political science analyses have explained this variation not by national characteristics, but rather by levels of trade flows. Jonathan Golub found that levels of trade flows (intra-EC imports, intra-EC exports, and total intra-EC trade) can explain virtually all (94–98 per cent) of the national variation in reference rates to the ECJ (Golub 1996a: 17). Alec Stone Sweet and Thomas Brunnel confirm this finding and offer a neo-functionalist account of the process of legal integration in Europe to explain the finding. They assume a demand for liberalization by importers and exporters, and argue that the more cross-national economic activity, the more conflicts between national and EC law will emerge. Stone Sweet and Brunnel essentially assume that national courts will play their part as conduits of private litigant challenges to the ECJ, dutifully referring cases when they arise. They use the correlation between reference rates and trade flows as the primary evidence that national judges are in fact playing this role (Stone Sweet and Brunnel 1998).

Correlation does not prove causation. But it is undeniable that more European laws, and more trade based on these laws, contribute to more legal cases about these laws. Because most European law is applied by national administrations, the designers of the EC legal system expected national courts to be involved in interpreting European rules. National judges are not trained to resolve complex questions about European law, which is why the drafters of the Treaty of Rome created the preliminary ruling system.[3] It is not surprising that national judges should refer technical questions about European law or challenges to Commission actions to the ECJ, or that reference rates should increase as more European law came into existence.

But cases involving the judicial review of national laws are different. As Chapter 1 explained, the European legal system was not designed to be used by private litigants to challenge national policy, and the ECJ lacks formal authority to respond to national court cases where the judicial review of national laws is at stake. Reference rates do not provide much insight into judicial behaviour in such cases, because most references do not involve judicial review of national laws.[4] Nor do reference rates provide insight into why national courts would embrace European law supremacy—a shift that was a prerequisite to using the European legal system for the judicial review of national laws.[5]

This study seeks to explain why national judiciaries accepted the supremacy of European law over national law. Accepting European law supremacy meant changing existing national legal interpretations and practices. National courts had three choices: (1) accept the ECJ's claim that the

[3] In the 1960s and 1970s few judges had any training in European law. Today it is more common for judges to be trained in European law, but still they are usually not specialists. See Ch. 1 above for more on the origins of the preliminary ruling mechanism.

[4] It is often hard to know if a question is about EC law per se, or about its relationship to national law. In reviews of cases referred to the ECJ, Jürgen Schwartz and Damian Chalmers find that roughly 40% of the national references in their sample are about the compatibility of EC law with national law, meaning that 60% are not about this question (Schwartz 1988: 15, 23; Chalmers 2000a: 34). Chalmers's findings also suggest that questions regarding European law and Commission decisions represent an even larger percentage (over 80%) of the cases heard by national courts that are not referred to the ECJ (Chalmers 2000a: 34).

[5] Golub came to a similar conclusion (1996a: 27), but Stone Sweet and Brunnel imply that their analysis covers, and indeed is mostly about, judicial review cases.

Treaty of Rome instituted a 'new legal order', and thus changed national legal obligations; (2) rely on the national precedent of *lex posterior derogat legi prior* and thus enforce the 'last law passed' by the parliament; or (3) change national doctrine so that it is no longer incompatible with European law supremacy, while still rejecting the notion that the Treaty of Rome creates a new type of legal obligation.

The interpretive choice mattered. It had broad political consequences within the domestic political and legal system, and for the process of European integration more generally. If the Treaty of Rome were to be seen as special, then the traditional limitations on international law would not apply to European law. This interpretation also would give the European Court the supreme authority to define the extent of member states' obligations under European law.[6] The second choice, the 'last law passed' doctrine, protects the sanctity of national legal authority, ensuring that only rules explicitly or tacitly endorsed by the parliament and the national government have legal effect at home. But this doctrine directly conflicts with the ECJ's supremacy claim, and in practice it allows governments to ignore their European legal obligations. National courts chose the third option of reinterpreting existing practices so that national doctrine was no longer incompatible with European law supremacy.

The ECJ, member states, and national courts had different interpretive preferences, because they had competing interests. The ECJ preferred its own interpretation because it had an interest in promoting European integration and facilitating the effectiveness of the legal process (Pescatore 1983a: 155; Lecourt 1965; Craig 1992), and in expanding the reach and scope of EU competences and its own powers (Burley and Mattli 1993: 58–60; Wincott 1995). National governments preferred the 'last law passed' interpretation because they had an interest in preserving national sovereignty, protecting existent national programmes, and avoiding financially and politically costly decisions.[7] National judges had interests of their own, which led them to prefer the third option. But within the third option there were also

---

[6] According to Eric Stein, the origin of this argument was a group of lawyers at the Commission's legal services, headed by its Director-General (Stein 1981: 24).

[7] National governments saw it as their role, not the role of national courts, to ensure respect for EC law. If they failed to comply, the appropriate remedy would be a Commission infringement suit, not a national legal case. This position was argued by national governments during the *Van Gend en Loos* and *Costa v. ENEL* cases, where the direct effect and supremacy of EC law was established. For a discussion of these positions, see Stein (1981). This position was also articulated through the efforts to sanction national courts for applying EC law supremacy in Belgium (see Bribosia 1998: 19) and France (see the discussion of the Aurillac amendment in Ch. 4 above).

contested interpretive choices to be made. Different national courts took opposing positions regarding the 'correct' interpretation of national and European legal provisions, and judges negotiated about interpretation across legal cases.

I call the process through which national courts and the ECJ develop doctrine on the supremacy of European law 'doctrinal negotiation', intentionally contrasting it to the term most commonly used in the legal literature, 'legal dialoguing'. A dialogue implies two or more actors talking to each other, using reason to reach a mutually accepted outcome. The notion of a dialogue implies that the outcome reached is the best reasoned outcome, the one that convinces all sides. A negotiation, on the other hand, implies competing interests where parties recognize that they may not be able to have it as they most like it. Negotiations usually lead to compromises that take into account the power of the negotiating parties, the conflicting interests of the different actors, and the intensity of those interests.

The best way to understand the current agreement between national courts, member states, and the ECJ regarding the doctrine of European law supremacy is as a negotiated compromise. The ECJ recognizes that it is in no position to impose its views on national courts. National governments, with their crude and limited tools of influence in the legal process, have been mostly unable to shape national doctrine regarding EC law supremacy. And because even high courts must seek support for their decisions by other national courts, the most sovereignty-jealous national judges were not able to impose their views on other national judges. Since the ECJ, national judges, and member states agree that a compromise is better than legal anarchy, each was willing to walk away from their most preferred positions. The ECJ ended up accepting that as far as national judges are concerned, there are limits to the supremacy of European law. National judges ended up changing existing doctrine, and ceding significant legal authority to the ECJ. And member states ended up accepting a significant compromise of national sovereignty.

What were the interests of national courts in negotiating with the ECJ over national doctrinal change? The next section examines how the scholarly literature has answered this question. I group the literature in categories, based on assumptions analysts share. While few scholars today accept purely legalist, neo-realist, or neo-functionalist explanations of legal integration, the different assumptions of these approaches concerning the primary motivation of judges, and the role of politics and political factors in shaping judicial behaviour, continue to animate scholarly debate.

II. Legalism, neo-realism and neo-functionalism: where are the politics?

As Chapter 1 showed, the supremacy doctrine was a legal creation of the ECJ, based on a broad and inventive reading of the spirit and structure of the Treaty of Rome. Nowhere does the Treaty actually state that European law creates direct effects and is supreme to national law. Most legal accounts of the transformation of the European legal system explain national judicial support for the ECJ's supremacy doctrine based on the legal logic and compelling legal reasoning of the ECJ's supremacy jurisprudence.[8] When national judges seemed to reject this reasoning, scholars discounted the conflicting national jurisprudence and implied it was based on ignorance or a misunderstanding of the ECJ's arguments. The assumption was that once national judges understood the ECJ's jurisprudence they would dutifully refer cases and apply European law as directed by the ECJ. While many legal scholars today have moved beyond formalist accounts, relying on legal logic alone, most European lawyers are still trained to examine European law from the legalist perspective. And legalism, with its assumption that legal reasoning is conclusive and that it alone shapes judicial behaviour, remains the dominant paradigm for analysing legal integration in Europe.

Martin Shapiro has characterized the legalist approach as 'constitutional law without politics' (1980: 538). Clearly law and legal reasoning shape judicial decision-making. But in most cases numerous legal interpretations are possible. And when the most obvious legal interpretation is extremely unappealing, judges have shown great ingenuity in finding ways within the text to reach counter-intuitive outcomes. Legal texts and legal methods alone can seldom resolve interpretative disagreements. Provided that judicial rulings are at least legally defensible, judges have significant discretion in their

---

[8] An example of such an argument is the claim made by Justice Federico Mancini (1989: 605–6): 'Knowing that the Court had almost no powers that were not traceable to its institutional standing and the persuasiveness of its judgements they made the most of these assets. Thus they developed a style that may be drab and repetitive, but explains as well as declares the law, and they showed unlimited patience vis-à-vis the national judges. . . . It was by following this courteously didactic method that the Luxembourg judges won the confidence of their colleagues from Palermo to Edinburgh and from Bordeaux to Berlin; and it was by winning their confidence that they were able to transform the procedure of Article 177 into a tool whereby private individuals may challenge their national legislation for incompatibility with Community law.' It is interesting that formalist accounts have been most strongly promoted by ECJ justices (see e.g. Pescatore (1983b; 1986; 1973)). But most legal accounts of European law supremacy still rely heavily on the Court's legal argumentation.

decision-making.[9] Certainly with respect to European law supremacy, there were a number of plausible legal interpretations.

In reaction to the early legalist approaches, political scientists developed accounts of judicial behaviour in European integration that explicitly brought political interests into the judicial calculus. The best known is the neo-realist analysis of Geoffrey Garrett and Barry Weingast, who assert that the ECJ is intentionally mirroring national-interest calculations in its decision-making, so that national government (and by implication national judicial) support will be forthcoming (Garrett 1992; Garrett and Weingast 1993; Garrett 1995). Mary Volcansek offered a different neo-realist argument, using national interest calculations to explain national judicial positions regarding the supremacy of European law. She correlated the timing of changes in high court jurisprudence with changes in the national government's enthusiasm for legal integration, implying that national courts changed their positions because their governments had altered their stance on European integration (Volcansek 1986). I consider these approaches to be neo-realist, and not simply neo-rationalist, because national interest is seen as the primary shaper of the political behaviour of judges and governments.

Volcansek's and Garrett's focus on political factors was an important corrective to the legalist accounts that had for so long denied politics entirely, but they misidentify how politics influences judicial decision-making, overstating the link between judges and national interests. One can come up with a *post hoc* definition of national interest to justify any legal decision. A reasonable strategy is to look at how governments themselves define their interests. If one examines the stated interests of governments, there is a preponderance of evidence that the ECJ and national courts regularly decide against national governments. There are also numerous cases where different courts in the same country (where the national interest should thus be the same) take opposing positions on the exact same ECJ legal doctrine.

For Garrett and Weingast, judges mirror national interests because they are concerned about non-compliance or a negative political response. The larger

---

[9] Walter Murphy (1964) has discussed the many techniques judges use to exercise discretion and pursue policy goals in legal decision-making. They stretch old decisions into new areas, 'explain' prior decisions, distinguish two factual situations, and misuse precedent. 'The Justices by applying most of these rules with discretion and considerable flexibility can take the cases they wish to decide, reject problems they prefer not to hear, and often decide litigation in the way that they want' (p. 30). There are of course limits. 'Justices are lawyers, trained to respect and work within these technical rules . . . were such bendings to become common-place or flagrant, the effect on the Court's prestige could well be disastrous' (pp. 30–1). Aharon Barak has written an entire book about techniques used by judges in exercising discretion (Barak 1989).

mistake in their approach is in overestimating the ability of these factors to shape judicial decision-making. To be sure, judges calculate whether politicians will respond to their decisions by attacking their independence, influence, and authority. But the institutional barriers to actually carrying out a threat to judicial autonomy and influence are so high, and the success of political actors in actually compromising judicial interests is so low, that in most cases judges have significant discretion in how they interpret law and decide cases. And the concern about non-compliance is greatly exaggerated. Governments *do* comply with decisions they did not want. Even if they choose not to comply, a few cases of non-compliance would hardly undermine the legitimacy of the judiciary. Chapter 5 will explain why the neo-realist assumptions are simply unsustainable. For now, what is important is that the interests of politicians do not decisively shape judicial behaviour at either the European or the national level. Indeed, eventually even Geoffrey Garrett has had to grant primacy to other factors in shaping judicial behaviour (Garrett et al. 1998), although his implausible assumption that courts mirror national interests from a fear of non-compliance remains stubbornly persistent.

Legalist and neo-realist accounts are clearly inadequate to explain why national judges accepted a role enforcing European law supremacy. Legalist accounts fail because they ignore politics, and neo-realist accounts fail because they misidentify how political factors shape judicial behaviour. Neo-functionalist accounts initially seemed more promising because they brought judicial self-interest into the equation.

In 1993 Anne-Marie Burley and Walter Mattli resurrected Ernst Haas's neo-functionalist theory, applying it to the European legal system (Burley and Mattli 1993). They claimed that the European legal system expanded and prospered by motivating actors within national legal systems to pursue their self interest and thereby promote legal integration:

The Court . . . created . . . opportunities, providing personal incentives for individual litigants, their lawyers, and lower national courts to participate in the construction of the community legal system. In the process, it enhanced its own power and the professional interests of all parties participating directly or indirectly in its business . . . The Court created a pro-community constituency of private individuals by giving them a direct stake in promulgation and implementation of community law. Further, the Court was careful to create a one-way ratchet by permitting individual [litigant] participation in the system only in a way that would advance community goals. (Burley and Mattli 1993: 60)

Of course European integration involves supra- and subnational actors. And who would claim that these actors are not following their interests? The key question is what defines judicial interests? Unfortunately, how the different actors—judges, litigants, and scholars—understand their interests was not well defined in the theory of Burley and Mattli. They rely on Joseph Weiler's assertion that national judges are enticed by the possibility of practising judicial review because it brings more interesting legal questions, gives national judges more power *vis-à-vis* politicians, and gives lower court judges the power to conduct the same type of review as higher court judges or constitutional court judges (Weiler 1991: 2426). Alec Stone Sweet and Thomas Brunnel (1998) claim support for this explanation through an analysis of national reference rates to the ECJ. They also add an efficiency claim: national courts want to dispose of their cases as rapidly as possible, 'to go home at the end of the day having disposed of more, rather than fewer, work-related problems' (p. 73).

European integration may empower some national judges some of the time. But neo-functionalist accounts are wrong when they say that legal integration is a win–win, mutually empowering prospect for all involved. European integration has encroached on the prerogatives of national actors, including domestic groups who enjoyed national privileges, national administrators who must now administer European rules, government officials who used to rule without interference from Brussels, and national judges. It is questionable whether European integration has offered these actors new powers to compensate for the loss of independence, influence, and authority that has come with the transfer of policy-making authority to the supranational level. Indeed, while one can find ways that the European legal system has increased the practice of judicial review in certain national legal systems (Claes 1995), it is not at all clear that national judges needed European law or the ECJ in order to practise judicial review.[10] The efficiency argument does not help. If national courts want to dispose of many cases rapidly, sending a reference to the ECJ is probably not the best strategy. The ECJ takes on average nearly two years to hear a preliminary ruling case, and then the case returns to the national court to be resolved. It would be more expedient for national courts to resolve the issue in the first hearing by interpreting European law on their own.

[10] In the British system, where courts previously lacked the authority to practise judicial review, Paul Craig finds a number of reasons having nothing to do with European law that can explain the increase in the practice of judicial review by British judges (Craig 1998: 216). There are also compelling accounts for the emergence of judicial review in France that do not portray European integration as playing a significant role (Stone 1992; Provine 1996). And in a number of EU member states—including Germany—national courts already had the power to conduct judicial review before European law came along.

Neo-functionalist theory ignores politics in other ways as well. Burley and Mattli claim that legal integration is a 'nominally apolitical' process with legal discourse masking the political issues at stake, and the force of law shielding judges from political pressures. Stone Sweet and Brunnel also minimize the political aspects by assuming that all actors want liberalization. There are costs associated with dismantling national barriers to trade. Indeed, many citizens, firms, and national officials *prefer* national rules and regulations, even if they create barriers to trade. Neo-functionalist accounts ignore the obvious point that there is a party that loses in every legal case where European law is applied instead of national law.

The process of European integration, like all political processes, involves struggles among competing interests. The actors involved know the stakes and they know how to fight for their preferred outcome. These struggles are the bread and butter of EU politics. Ignoring the importance of politics is where neo-functionalist theory originally went wrong (Caporaso and Keeler 1995: 35–6). While Burley and Mattli profess to take political factors into account, they, along with Stone Sweet and Brunnel repeat the original error of neo-functionalism by portraying legal integration as a largely apolitical and unidirectional project of ever-expanding European law—a 'one way ratchet' (Burley and Mattli 1993: 60), with European law triumphing over national law. As Slaughter and Mattli now acknowledge, neo-functionalist analysis cannot adequately capture the various motivations driving the participants in the legal process. Moreover, because actors are always presumed to follow their 'self-interest' (a concept which they admit is woefully underspecified), 'neofunctionalists cannot adequately specify the limits to integration. They have no tools to determine when self-interest will align with further integration . . . and when it will not . . . It was precisely this problem that ultimately led neofunctionalists, led by Haas himself, to abandon neofunctionalism' (Mattli and Slaughter 1998: 185).

EC legal scholarship in the late 1990s has gone beyond the early apolitical accounts. Contextual legal accounts, such as the studies in the edited volume *The European Courts and National Courts* (Slaughter *et al.* 1998) and Renaud Dehousse's book *The European Court of Justice* (1998), explicitly weave political factors into accounts of judicial behaviour. But politics is usually seen as a corrupting factor, allowing some self-interested or ideologically motivated actors to get in the way of common interests.

Contextual approaches are more sophisticated than the earlier legalist analyses, but at their core they share the assumptions of legalist approaches. Legal logic is seen as decisive in shaping judicial behaviour, with politics treated as a residual category, appealed to only when it is clear that legal logic cannot explain judicial behaviour. Such an approach refuses to acknowledge that there are often a number of plausibly 'correct' logically coherent legal answers, and that interpretive choices can create significant benefits for some, at the expense of others.

Karl-Heinz Ladeur's network theory of legal integration also underestimates the role of competing interests in shaping legal integration. Ladeur sees national systems with their internal hierarchies being replaced by 'heterarchical coordination and linkage between actors and institutions, [through] cooperative procedures which draw on the production of technical and scientific knowledge, and a process of political and economic experimental design' (Ladeur 1997: 46). He expects the transition from a national organization of the state to be achieved through cooperation among transnational networks, which create 'synergy effects' to overcome the 'unfruitful normative and analytical polarisation of national statehood and supranationality' (p. 48). This view assumes cooperation, in a context of rational and shared understandings of the need to move away from national systems, leading to consensus. It overestimates the erosion of national hierarchies, and the degree of consensus among the actors negotiating integration, while ignoring the fact that some actors win and some actors lose in the process.[11]

The legal process, and the process of expanding the reach and scope of European law in the national realm, is inherently political. In every case the ECJ hears there are adversaries vying for their preferred legal interpretation. Political decision-making—by which I mean actors with competing interests, values, and objectives trying to influence outcomes—is not corrupting the process; it *is* the process. The litigants are not the only actors with interests in the outcome. Judges and government actors also have interests.

Legal integration—by which I mean the expansion and penetration of European law into the national realm—is at its core a process of negotiation between legal and political actors at the national and supranational level.

---

[11] This error is not per se endemic to network theories or multi-level governance theories. While such theories tend to see common interest among actors facilitating (if not requiring) cooperation, Rainer Eising and Beate Kohler-Koch expect competition among national and EC actors to be a defining feature in the integration process. They note: 'EC societal and political actors come from very different national settings and traditions. Therefore European networks are characterised by an inbuilt rivalry over problem views and solutions which have to be accommodated . . . The negotiation of Community policies is always a competition about modes of governance' (Eising and Kohler-Koch 1999: 271). Gary Marks, Liesbet Hooghe, and Kermit Blank also expect the allocation of competences in the EU to be contested, and this contest fundamentally to shape the process of integration (Marks *et al.* 1996: 373).

These actors want to reach a cooperative solution to the conflicts between national law and European law, but they have their own self-interested, institutional and ideological preferences regarding the outcome. That outcome represents a compromise among these interests. The compromise is renegotiated over time in the different venues of the policy-making process—in the Council, Commission, and Parliament; during inter-governmental conferences; during the Commission's infringement procedure; and in subsequent legal disputes. The next section articulates an institutionalist explanation of judicial interests in the negotiation process.

III. A general theory of judicial interests[12]

Political interests are inherent in the legal process. As Martin Shapiro has argued, applying law means enforcing the interests of the central state over individual actors and subnational agencies and promoting a state-defined hierarchy of values—such as minimizing state intervention in the economy and in society, protecting private property, or promoting equality among groups in society (Shapiro 1981: 26–7). Prioritizing certain values over others necessarily means promoting the interests of some groups over others. Alec Stone Sweet puts it this way: 'the rules that underpin social settings appear as artefacts—they are revelatory—of power relations. Rarely "neutral", they serve the interests of some at the expense of others' (Stone Sweet 2000: 7).

Judges themselves also have specific institutional interests in the process of legal integration. As a group, judges share certain interests. *Judges are primarily interested in promoting their independence, influence, and authority.* By independence, I mean that courts want to protect their legal autonomy from political bodies. They want freedom to decide a case in the way they feel appropriate. By influence, I mean that courts want to promote their ability to make decisions that can influence the policy process and the judicial process. Some judges, although not all judges, want to influence policy and political debates. Other judges are less concerned with political debates, but are

---

[12] Kenneth Armstrong (1995; 1999a; 1999b) and Simon Bulmer (1998) have summarized the general characteristics of institutionalist explanations, showing how they may apply to the EC context. In what follows, I draw on general institutionalist literature and judicial politics literature to define the institutional incentives of courts, and to show how the institutional structure of the EC legal system shapes the politics of legal integration in Europe.

concerned about legal debates. They want to influence the development of legal doctrine and want their legal interpretations to be accepted by other courts and other legal and political actors. By authority, I mean that judges protect their legal turf (their jurisdiction) and the finality of their decisions. Courts act strategically *vis-à-vis* other courts, and *vis-à-vis* political bodies, calculating the political context in which they operate so as to avoid provoking a response which will close access, remove jurisdictional authority, or reverse their decisions.

Judges also have an interest in creating the appearance that their actions are shaped entirely by legal norms.[13] Judges appeal to legal norms to legitimize the legal process itself. As Martin Shapiro argues, all judges must ultimately rely on the consent of the parties to accept their decisions. To gain consent, judges try to appear as neutral arbiters of the dispute (Shapiro 1981: 17). By appearing neutral, by crafting compromise positions, and by appealing to norms that resonate in the general public (such as the liberal ethos of protecting individual rights), judges build legitimacy for the legal process and gain popular support for the idea that judges have a right to displace laws created by democratic means. Walter Murphy put it this way:

People, it would seem, are more ready to accept unpleasant decisions which appear to be the ineluctable result of rigorously logical deductions from 'the law,' than they are rulings which are frankly a medley of legal principle, personal preferences, and educated guesses as to what is best for society. (Murphy 1964: 17)

The appeal to legal norms is a way of promoting judges' institutional interests, but it is not all constraining. Where the influence of politics would be obvious, or where a legal outcome strays too far from the wording of the statute, legal norms may constrain judicial decision-making. But there are usually a number of possible legal interpretations, and clever judges can find a way to reach a desired outcome while staying within the legal rules of the game.[14]

Sharing these interests does not make judges as a group an 'epistemic community' as defined by Peter Haas (1992). Judges, and the legal profession more generally, do not share principled beliefs about the role of courts in the political process. They do not share causal beliefs about what type of legal

[13] I agree with Burley and Mattli that judges seek to stay within a legal discourse that looks apolitical, and that this discourse can create some constraints. Where we disagree is the extent to which this discourse acts as a meaningful mask and shield, keeping political actors from influencing the process.

[14] See n. 9 above.

decision-making contributes to democracy. They do not have a common policy enterprise that tells them how to decide a specific case. And while many
legal scholars would like to believe that law is a 'science', the legal method is
not so conclusive as to lead similar actors using the legal method to address
similar questions to a single conclusion.

The judiciary is not an epistemic community. It is a bureaucracy.[15] Within
the judicial bureaucracy, as in all bureaucracies, there are differences of opinion. There are also bureaucratic rivalries based on the institutional position
of the actors involved. Appeals to, and opposition to, European law can be a
tool wielded in bureaucratic politics. European law creates opportunities for
some courts to escape national hierarchies and thus to bolster their independence, influence, and authority *vis-à-vis* other courts and political bodies.
European law can also be a threat to the independence, influence, and
authority of a court because it disrupts national hierarchies and because it can
allow for different legal outcomes in a case. How national judges perceive
European law is filtered through the lens of how a judge understands his or
her role in the political process (Chalmers 1997). Judicial identity varies by
court, shaped by the statutes creating the court and the history of the court,
and reinforced through the appointment and training process of judges, and
through internal socialization within the court.[16] While judicial identities
can vary by court, and while the impact of EC law on a court's influence, independence, and authority can vary by legal issue, some general observations
can be offered.

The impact of European law on a given national court varies according to
the court's institutional position in the national legal hierarchy and to the

[15] Judiciaries fit the main definitions of bureaucracies of Downs (1967), Page (1985), and
Niskanen (1971). More directly, judges are civil servants working for the government. In the US,
one may become a judge at a later stage in one's career and judicial appointments are often political—made by the government or subject to a public election. In Europe, except for the very highest rung of constitutional court judges, the appointment process for judges is not political. Most
judges choose their vocation at the beginning of their career, qualify by passing exams or doing well
at university, and learn their trade through special training. The career trajectory of a judge is managed by the judicial bureaucracy, and judges enjoy all the employment and security benefits of
national civil servants.

[16] e.g. most labour and business courts are designed to act more as arbiters among disputants
than as courts applying state law. Penal courts are designed to ensure due process to the accused.
Administrative courts are usually designed to scrutinize government practices. First instance
courts need to weigh factual disagreements, whereas appeals courts are designed to review questions of law only. Ask a judge and she will tell you the history of her court, and what the court's role
is in the political process. The answer is usually consistent within a single court, but varies by
branch of the judiciary and level of the court.

extent to which a court's substantive jurisdiction is influenced by European law. High courts must worry about the stability of the national legal order as a whole. As protectors of the national legal order, last instance courts are especially sensitive to and concerned about disruptive influences of European law. Not infrequently, ECJ decisions have the effect of undermining legal certainty and disrupting the national legal system. As Renaud Dehousse argued:

From the standpoint of a national lawyer, European law is often a source of disruption. It injects into the national legal system rules which are alien to its traditions and which may affect its deeper structure, thereby threatening its coherence. It may also be a source of arbitrary distinctions between similar situations . . . What appears as integration at the European level is often perceived as disintegration from the perspective of national legal systems. (Dehousse 1998: 173)[17]

This is one reason why higher courts have objected to the ECJ's exercise of authority in the national realm.

The ECJ also is potentially a rival authority to high courts. Since lower courts can use references to the ECJ to challenge high court jurisprudence, the ECJ undermines the finality of supreme court decisions. The rivalry is especially acute with respect to the issue of European law supremacy. With European law supreme to national law, and the ECJ the highest legal authority regarding this law, the ECJ is de facto the highest court in the land whenever national policy is subject to European legislation. How could high courts not see this as a threat to their independence, authority, and influence?

High court behaviour *vis-à-vis* the ECJ reveals that high courts perceive this rivalry and threat. To avoid the expansion of ECJ authority in the national realm at their expense, supreme courts have withheld from the ECJ cases that involve far-reaching questions and cases that might allow the European Court to expand the reach of European law.[18] High courts have also in some cases tried to limit lower court references to the ECJ when these references would allow the ECJ to make a ruling with which the higher court disagreed.[19] High courts have protected their exclusive and supreme authority to evaluate the

---

[17]   Maher (1998), Joerges (2000: 124), and Chalmers (2000b: 26) make similar arguments.

[18]   Indeed, no constitutional court has made a reference to the ECJ. On withholding references, see Meier (1967a; 1967b), Buffet-Tchakaloff (1984: 95); Golub (1996b), Chalmers (2000b: 31-7).

[19]   e.g. the Italian Constitutional Court ruled a reference to the ECJ regarding the supremacy of European law to be invalid (*Costa v. ENEL & Soc. Edisonvolta*, Italian Constitutional Court Decision 14 of 7 Mar. 1964, [1964] CMLR 425, [1964] I Il Foro It. 87 I 465). The *Bundesfinanzhof* tried to limit the direct effect of EC law regarding turnover equalization taxes (see further Ch. 4 below). The *Bundesfinanzhof* and the *Conseil d'État* both overruled references to the ECJ based on

constitutionality of all laws applied in the national realm. And they have openly challenged the ECJ's declarations that it has the *Kompetenz-Kompetenz*, the authority to determine the confines of European powers, and thus its own powers.[20] At the same time, supreme courts do not want to become an appellate court to the ECJ. They do not themselves want to decide the many technical issues falling within the ECJ's jurisdiction, nor do they want to be called upon every time a litigant disagrees with the ECJ. Thus while they assert their right to review the constitutionality of EC laws, they do not make a constitutional appeal too easy or tempting for private litigants.

Lower court judges, with the luxury of focusing only on the case at hand, are usually less concerned with the coherence of the national legal system. In addition, the preliminary ruling mechanism allows lower courts to appeal to an authority outside the national legal system, securing an authoritative counter-precedent to the interpretations of national supreme courts. As long as a lower court agrees with ECJ interpretations, ECJ decisions actually lend legal credibility to a lower court decision and thus bolster the influence of the lower court within the national legal system. As such, references to the ECJ have become a convenient means to circumvent higher courts. The ECJ is like a second parent in a battle where parental permission wards off a potential sanction for misbehaviour—if the lower court does not like what they think one parent (the higher court) will say, they can ask the other parent (the ECJ) to see if they will get a more pleasing answer. Having the ECJ's approval increases the likelihood that the lower court actions will not be challenged. If the lower court does not think they will like what the ECJ will say, they simply do not ask. Lower courts can also in some cases play the ECJ and national high courts off against each other, appealing to national solutions to challenge EC law and EC law to challenge national law.

the direct effect of directives. '*Kloppenburg*', *Frau Kloppenburg v. Finanzamt Leer BFH*, decision II V R 123/84 of 25 Apr. 1985, [1989] 1 CMLR 873; *Minister of Interior v. Daniel Cohn-Bendit*, French *Conseil d'État*, 22 Dec. 1978 [1978] *Recueil Lebon* 524, [1980] 1 CMLR 545. This strategy is limited in that not all lower court decisions to make references are appealed to higher courts, so that references can and do slip through.

[20] Germany: *Brunner and others v. The European Union Treaty*, '*Maastricht* decision', 2 BvR 2134/92 and 2 BvR 2159/92, [1994] 1 EuR 95, [1994] CMLR 57. Italy: *Fragd SpA v. Amministrazione delle Finanze* (decision 232 of 21 Apr. 1989), (1989) 72 RDI. France: *Conseil Constitutionnel* decision 91-294 DC of 25 July 1991, 'Schengen Decision', [1991] *Recueil des Décisions du Conseil Constitutionnel* 91, [1991] R. Fr. D. Admin. 173. *Conseil Constitutionnel* decision 92-308 DC of 9 Apr. 1992, '*Maastricht I*', [1992] *Recueil des Décisions du Conseil Constitutionnel* 55, [1992] RJC I-496, [1993] 3 CMLR 345. Denmark: *Hanne Norup Carlsen and Others v. Prime Minister Poul Nyrup Rasmussen*, '*Maastricht* decision' of 6 Apr. 1998, Ugeskrift for Retsvaesen H 800, [1999] 3 CMLR 854.

I do not mean to imply that lower courts always support, and supreme courts oppose, ECJ authority. An ECJ decision can sometimes help bolster the influence, independence, and authority of national high courts *vis-à-vis* other legal and political actors.[21] Furthermore, judicial interests are not solely defined by the location of the court in the national hierarchy, and rivalries are not only manifest between lower courts and higher courts. As in most bureaucracies, rivalries also exist across branches of the judiciary. When courts' jurisdiction to decide legal issues overlaps, there is a potential for tension between the different courts interpreting the same rules. Because the subject matter of European law may create more jurisdictional overlap for some national courts compared to others, the intensity of bureaucratic rivalry between the ECJ and national courts varies. A court that virtually never hears European law cases might be happy to refer the odd case that comes up to the ECJ. The more central European law is to the court's daily practice, however, the more likely the court is to feel that its autonomy is compromised by the ECJ.[22] Similarly, a court might have no problem accepting aspects of ECJ jurisprudence which apply little to its daily practice, but find a problem once European law and the ECJ enter a legal area which is of importance to the court in question.[23]

[21] If a high court wants to challenge the validity of a European law, a favourable decision of the ECJ can bolster its position with respect to EC organs and national governments. If a high court wants to assert new powers within the national legal system, a statement by the ECJ that these new powers are consistent with European law can bolster the high court's position with respect to political bodies. A high court may use a reference to the ECJ in a controversial case to deflect criticism from itself (Maher 1994: 229). And if a high court does not want to be challenged by lower courts, a willingness to refer questions which clearly fall under the ECJ's jurisdictional authority can convince lower courts to rely on the court of last instance to refer relevant questions to the European Court, passing up opportunities to make a reference themselves. To bring back the analogy from above, such a tactic convinces the lower court that both parents will decide together so that there is no advantage to making the extra effort to appeal to the ECJ first.

[22] e.g. EC law covers much tax law, which is why the German Federal Tax Court has been more involved in EC law debates and more willing to challenge ECJ jurisprudence than other German Federal courts. And because the Federal Office of Nutrition and Forestry and the Federal Office for the Regulation of the Agricultural Market are located in Frankfurt, the Frankfurt administrative court hears nearly all challenges to the validity of EC agricultural policies (Voss 1987). Hearing more cases involving European law, it has been more affected by ECJ jurisprudence than most German administrative courts. The Frankfurt court, despite the fact that it is a low court, has been among the national courts most critical of ECJ jurisprudence and has been behind quite a few German challenges to ECJ authority.

[23] e.g. the German Federal Tax Court challenged most vehemently the ECJ's assertions that directives have direct effect in the national realm because EC tax law is adopted in the form of directives and the Federal Tax Court did not want the ECJ to gain direct authority over its jurisdictional realm. The German Constitutional Court did not, however, have a problem with the direct effect of directives. Its concerns were about the supremacy of European law over the German Constitution—its own jurisdictional domain. (See Ch. 3 below for a discussion of these cases.)

Procedural factors may also shape a court's ability to control its jurisdiction, and thus its position on EC legal issues. According to Bruno Genevois, the Secretary General of the *Conseil Constitutionnel*, because the French *Conseil Constitutionnel* must rule on the constitutionality of national laws before they are actually promulgated, the *Conseil Constitutionnel* prefers not to be involved in enforcing the supremacy of European law. The *Conseil Constitutionnel* fears that a national law that it found to be compatible with European law could subsequently be found to be incompatible by the ECJ, thus undermining the finality of its decision (1989: 827).

National judges may also simply disagree strongly with the ECJ's ruling, and be upset that it hinders their ability to decide differently. National courts have been known to baulk at ECJ interpretations which upset well-accepted national legal practices, or which create policy implications that will not sit well at home.[24]

It is worth restating that national courts do not *always* have strategic calculations in mind in deciding whether to refer a case or to apply ECJ jurisprudence. The majority of cases involving EC law are about the meaning and validity of EC law, or about keeping the EU's political institutions (especially the Commission) in check—not about national law per se. National courts seem to have no qualms about asking the ECJ how to calculate the social security benefits of migrant workers, or asking it to resolve litigant challenges to Commission decisions. Indeed, many prefer to refer these complex EC legal questions to the ECJ. Competing interests do arise, however, when there is significant disagreement about interpretations, and when there is a threat to a court's influence, independence, and authority.

The next sections animate this historical institutionalist account of judicial interests, providing a general account of how judicial rivalries have fundamentally shaped the way in which national legal systems incorporated the ECJ's supremacy doctrine, and continue to influence the evolution of the ECJ's doctrine. Chapters 3 and 4 apply this general framework to the specific developments in Germany and France, explaining how the different institutional

---

[24] e.g. the ECJ's decision that employers have to accept medical certificates from other member states, even when an Italian family of four working in Germany had for four years in a row all 'fallen ill' during their vacations in Italy, has been very controversial. This decision combined with some other ECJ rulings has led the German Federal Labour Court openly to criticize the ECJ and to assert that European law creates a danger for the consistency of codified law in Germany (Kokott 1998: 124). And the French *Conseil d'État*, never a fan of the ECJ's supremacy jurisprudence, was so incensed by the ECJ's 1974 *Charmasson* decision that it refused to make a reference to the ECJ for many years—even on technical questions of European law which were not about conflicts between European law and national law (Buffet-Tchakaloff 1984: 290).

interests of courts with respect to EC law supremacy contributed to the evolution of national legal doctrines.

IV. Integrating EC law supremacy into national legal systems: an (historical) institutionalist account

Few consider the negotiated compromise regarding European law supremacy to be the best-reasoned, most logically coherent outcome. Indeed, the negotiated outcome creates a constant tension in the European legal process, a tension that could one day lead to open rupture. Private litigants, national political bodies, and member states readily exploit the difference of legal opinions regarding European law supremacy to challenge European rules and national rules with which they disagree. And the inherent logical tensions in national legal doctrine and ECJ doctrine are a source of constant critique by legal scholars.

How did the negotiated compromise regarding European law supremacy emerge? The central factor facilitating the expansion of EC law through judicial interpretation is the fact that the European Court sits as an institution outside the domestic realm which can be used by domestic actors (private litigants, interest groups, people with certain political beliefs, national governments, and national judges) and supranational actors (EU institutions) to challenge national and European laws. The European legal system has become part of the policy-making process appealed to by those actors who lose during political negotiations over policy.[25] Domestic actors use European law and the ECJ to achieve outcomes that they are institutionally and politically unable to achieve through the domestic legal or political process alone. Member states, the Commission, the Council, and the Parliament use the European legal system to challenge deals that they are unable to sway in the political process. Litigants will often appeal to the transnational dimensions of the case, linking the law in question with one of the four freedoms (free movement of goods, people, capital, or services). Given the content of European law and the predilections of the ECJ, this is a sound strategy. But one cannot infer from this strategy, however, that liti-

---

[25] Given that courts in Europe have not historically played such a central role in policy debates, the fact that the ECJ has become so central is quite remarkable. Indeed, discussions of the ECJ have come to figure prominently in more general discussions about policy-making in Europe (Bulmer 1998; Pierson 1996; Pierson and Liebfried 1995).

gants are motivated by transnational interests, or by the desire to increase transnational trade. It is more likely the case that they are motivated by the possibility of challenging European and national rules they do not like, regardless of whether these rules are limiting free movement in the Common Market.[26]

The European Court is not a neutral arbiter in this process. It has a bias in favour of European integration—after all, its mandate is to see that in implementing the Common Market the law is observed (Article 220, formerly Article 164). It also has a policy bias in favour of dismantling national barriers to trade—after all, the objective of the Treaty of Rome is the creation of a Common Market (Weiler 1999; Shapiro 1999: 333–40; Ball 1996). The strengthening of the EC legal system tends to advantage those who profit by dismantling national barriers, or by following European rules instead of national rules. The losers tend to be those who benefit from or prefer national rules.

Those who dislike European policies, however, can also seek satisfaction by using the European legal process to challenge and limit advances in European integration. While the European Court seems to favour European authority over national authority,[27] litigants can still win when they use the European legal system to challenge European policy. Furthermore, litigants can exploit differences between national courts and the ECJ in their challenges, using the national system to challenge European rules or decisions they do not like.

In either case—challenging EC or national law—and regardless of the outcome of the specific case, raising such cases influences the process of legal integration in Europe. In invoking EC law in legal disputes and in referring cases to the ECJ, national courts and private litigants create opportunities for the ECJ to expand the reach of EC law into the national domain, and to refine its jurisprudence to cultivate support for its doctrine in national legal communities. As the ECJ expanded the number and type of European legal provisions that created direct effects (rights that litigants could claim in national courts), it increased the ways national actors can draw on European law to

---

[26] For more on the motivations of litigants in European cases, see Alter (2000), Alter and Vargas (2000), Harlow and Rawlings (1992), Rawlings (1993), Harding (1992).

[27] This is as yet an unproven fact, but the ECJ's case law has created this opinion; e.g. the ECJ's doctrine of preemption, which precludes member states from enacting legislation in areas where the Community has policy-making competence, is perceived as a clear example of a pro-EC bias. For an analysis of why the ECJ is perceived as biased in favour of the EC, see Abraham (1989: 173–85).

challenge national policy. Indeed, it was largely through national court references that the ECJ turned the Treaty of Rome into a sort of constitution of Europe (Stein 1981; Mancini 1989; Weiler 1991).

The trajectory is not, however, unidirectional. The very same cases that have advanced European integration have contributed to perceptions that European integration, and the European Court, unduly compromise national sovereignty and threaten the national constitutional order. As it expanded the reach of European law, the ECJ also increased the number of national actors on which it and European authority encroached. And the success of the European Court in creating influence for itself in national and European policy debates has led it to become a target of Euro-sceptics and sovereignty-jealous actors,[28] and of national supreme courts.[29] The European Court is of course not exclusively responsible for the expansion of European law or for fomenting political backlash. National governments, after all, agreed to and even demanded the laws that so encroach on national actors.[30] And the lack of democratic legitimacy in the European Union has far more to do with the choices of member states than with anything the ECJ has done. But the ECJ contributes to generating political backlash because it contributes to the expansion and penetration of European law at the national level, and to the specificity of European law that so constrains national actors. It is also responsible for finding national policies in violation of European law. It was the ECJ that invalidated Germany's beer purity law, and upheld European rules affecting the hunting season in France. Rightly or wrongly, those concerned about European integration infringing on national prerogatives see the European Court as a threat to national sovereignty.

If they could have controlled the process, national supreme courts and national governments probably would not have referred such far-reaching legal questions to the European Court. No constitutional court has referred a case to the ECJ, and many supreme national courts are clearly reticent

---

[28] The ECJ was a target of James Goldsmith's Referendum Party, and of the British Euro-sceptics (Smith 1990). It has been a target of French Gaullists (see further Ch. 5 below). And ECJ Judge Mancini noted that 'for some time now the Court has been the object of ferocious attacks articulated on the front pages of newspapers and echoed, especially in Germany, in the speeches of politicians, even at the most senior levels' (Mancini and Keeling 1994: 185–6).

[29] N. 20 above, *Brunner and others v. The European Union Treaty*, '*Maastricht* decision'. N. 20 above, Danish Supreme Court's *Maastricht* decision.

[30] Indeed, the Council's use of Article 308 (formerly Article 235 EEC) to pass legislation in areas outside EC authority was criticized by the German Constitutional Court in its Maastricht ruling, and was the main plank used by the Danish challengers in their case against the Maastricht Treaty. N. 20 above, *German* and *Danish Maastricht* decisions. On the Danish decision, see Høegh (1999).

about sending anything but technical cases to the ECJ (Bebr 1983; Buffet-Tchakaloff 1984: 300–15). National high courts did in some cases try to limit European law from encroaching on the national domain by contesting EC legal doctrines and limiting national court references to the ECJ. In Britain, the Court of Appeal and the House of Lords developed narrow guidelines about when a lower court referral to the ECJ was justified,[31] guidelines that probably contributed to low reference rates by British courts to the ECJ (Golub 1996b). In Italy, the Constitutional Court declared that all issues of the validity of European law and national law were constitutional issues, so that only it could decide if European law was supreme to subsequent national law.[32] In other cases, high courts issued their own narrow interpretations of European law to limit its applicability in the national realm and ward off referrals to the ECJ.[33] Sometimes high courts even quashed lower court decisions to refer a case to the ECJ, or directly challenged ECJ jurisprudence to discourage courts below it from accepting ECJ doctrine.[34]

But the courts wanting to limit or hinder European law from entering the national realm cannot really keep it from doing so. Each judge can decide for him or herself whether or not to make a reference to the ECJ. In the few cases where high courts were able to quash a referral to the ECJ, it was because the decision to refer had been appealed to them. But usually the decision to refer a case to the ECJ is not appealed. And some national courts are willing to make referrals simply to provoke the ECJ to contradict other national courts.[35]

---

[31] Bermann *et al.* (1993: 261–6), *H. P. Bulmer Ltd. v. J. Bollinger S.A.*, English Court of Appeal decision of 22 May 1974, Common Market Law Review, 1974 (2), p. 91.

[32] *Soc. Industrie Chimiche Italia Centrale v. Ministero Commercio con l'Estero*, Italian Constitutional Court Decision 232 of 30 Oct. 1975, [1976] Il Foro It. 542. *Ministero Finanze and Ditta Fratelli Grassi v. Greco*, Italian Constitutional Court Decision 205 of 28 July 1976, [1976] Il Foro It. 2299. Soc. Unil-it (Avv. U. Ferrari), *Soc. Ariete (Avv. N. Catalano) v. Min. Finanze (Avv. dello Stato Zagari)*, Decision of 29 Dec. 1977, no. 163, [1978] Il Foro It. 288.

[33] e.g. in the Turnover Tax Struggle, the Federal Tax Court used narrow legal interpretations to stop lower courts from sending references to the ECJ or interpreting the compatibility of national turnover equalization taxes with EC law. ('Lutticke', Firma Alfons Lütticke GmbH, Köln-Deutz. VII B 106/67 BFH decision of 19 Oct. 1968. *Firma Molkerei-Zentrale Westfalen/Lippe GmbH v. Hauptzollamt Paderborn*, BFH decision of 11 July 1968, [1968] 4 EuR 394, [1968] 8 CMLR 300.) See the discussion of the Lütticke case in Ch. 4 below. Another example of this is the attempts of the Employment Appeals Tribunal to keep European law from influencing British equality law (Alter and Vargas 2000: 461–2).

[34] See e.g. n. 19 above, '*Cohn-Bendit*' and '*Kloppenburg.*'

[35] The ECJ's *Simmenthal* ruling that national judges can ignore constitutional provisions that undermine their ability to apply European law supremacy contradicted the Italian Constitutional Court on this issue (Claes 1995: 123); *Amministrazione delle Finanze dello Stato v. Simmenthal SpA (II)*, ECJ Case 106/77, [1978] ECR 629, [1978] CMLR 263.

Those courts fighting the encroachment of European law also faced a legal context shifting from under them. As lower courts sent references to the ECJ, and more courts applied ECJ jurisprudence, EC law entered the national system. Thus more and more areas of national law became interpreted through the lens of European law. Britain's Lord Denning referred to this phenomenon as the 'incoming tide' of European law. At first he welcomed this tide, but later he grew to dislike it, arguing:

> Our sovereignty has been taken away by the European Court of Justice . . . It has put on the Treaty an interpretation according to their own views of policy—which is to make all laws of the European community the same—or in their own words to 'harmonise' them . . . Our courts must no longer enforce our national laws. They must enforce Community law . . . No longer is European law an incoming tide flowing up the estuaries of England. It is now like a tidal wave bringing down our sea walls and flowing inland over our fields and houses—to the dismay of all. (Denning 1990: 7–8)

And as European integration progressed, more and more national law was of European origin. According to a report by the French *Conseil d'État*, by 1992 European law included 22,445 European regulations, 1,675 directives, 1,198 agreements and protocols, 185 recommendations of the Commission or the Council, 291 Council resolutions, and 678 communications, and the European Union had become the largest source of new law, with 54 per cent of all new French laws originating in Brussels.[36] Even France's *Conseil d'État*, which had resisted a role enforcing European law supremacy for twenty-four years, had to acknowledge this fact. In the famous *Nicolo* case, *Commissaire du Gouvernement* Frydman noted that increasingly national law had a clear European imprint:

> It cannot be repeated often enough that the era of the unconditional supremacy of internal law is now over. International rules of law, particularly those of Europe, have gradually conquered our legal universe, without hesitating furthermore to encroach on the competence of Parliament . . . In this way certain entire fields of our law such as those of the economy, employment or protection of human rights, now very largely originate genuinely from international legislation.[37]

The fact that international legal bodies (including but not limited to the ECJ) were reviewing the compatibility of national laws with international rules also spurred national courts to claim a similar power for themselves. In the *Nicolo* ruling, *Commissaire du Gouvernement* Frydman concluded that if the

[36] *Conseil d'État* (1992: 16–17).
[37] 'Nicolo', Raoul Georges Nicolo & Another. *Conseil d'État* decision of 20 Oct. 1989, [1989] Recueil Lebon 190, [1990] 1 CMLR 173.

Conseil d'État did not accept a role enforcing European law supremacy, it would not be able to influence this growing body of national law. He urged: 'At a time when the European Commission and the European Court of Human Rights are for their part beginning occasionally to examine the compatibility of French laws, with the 1950 convention . . . you should yourselves assume this function and break their monopoly.'[38]

Recalcitrant national courts faced other pressures as well. Because even supreme courts have divergent preferences regarding European law, there is no united opposition to European law supremacy among the highest national courts. Indeed, in some countries a lateral pressure emerged, with different high courts within the national system pressuring each other to change their jurisprudence so as to eliminate inconsistencies in the national system that upset their sense of logic and which they feared would undermine public faith in the legal process. For example, one challenge raised against the French *Conseil d'État*'s supremacy doctrine was that it created an illogical and increasingly intolerable divergence in how French courts resolved EC law cases (Abraham 1989: 120). This concern was noted by the *Commissaire du Gouvernement* in the case in which the *Conseil d'État* ultimately accepted a role enforcing EC law supremacy.[39]

Obstructionist national judges also faced a critical academic press. In continental Europe legal scholars play a larger role in the legal process than in the United States because most national decisions are not published. This forces the Bar to rely on professional journals that reprint and report on important legal decisions.[40] Scholars of European law tend to be sympathetic to the

---

[38] Ibid. 189. See Ch. 4 below for more on the *Conseil d'État*'s *Nicolo* decision. A similar motivation is attributed to the Danish Supreme Court's *Maastricht* ruling. Hjalte Rasmussen argued: 'It seems safe to assume that the [Danish Supreme Court] president's prophesy [that Danish judges would be more involved in creating law] was based on another "international" premise as well, this one inarticulate. That is that the Strasbourg [European Court of Human Rights] has within the lapse of the last decennium declared a handful of politically important Danish acts of parliament to be in violation of the European Convention on Human Rights. This must have impacted on the president of a court which has systematically refused to come to the rescue of Danish citizens and companies . . . In comparison, the ECHR showed more diligence in this regard' (Rasmussen 1998: 81).

[39] N. 37 above, 'Nicolo' M. Frydman notes that the 'legal inconsistencies arising from the [*Conseil d'État*'s 1968 Semoules judgment rejecting a role enforcing EC law supremacy] are as serious as they are numerous . . . [leading to] absurd practical consequences'. Cited from CMLR pp. 182–3. See further Ch. 4 below.

[40] Each important decision is accompanied by a discursive note that analyses the decision and puts it in legal and political context. According to Glendon *et al.*, '"the doctrine" is everywhere taken into account by legislators and judges when they frame, interpret or apply law . . . A critical case note by a leading author, is, in effect, like an important dissenting opinion, indicating where controversy exists and the possible future direction of the law' (1985: 162–3).

larger project of integration, often uncritically supportive of the ECJ's efforts to build integration through law. Indeed, one could say that EC legal scholars have acted as a sort of legal lobby in support of ECJ jurisprudence and ECJ authority. According to Hjalte Rasmussen, European law journals have functioned 'as a sort of bastion for the European federalist legal thinkers for more than three decades' (1986: 267).[41] Scholars writing on EC legal issues are organized in academic societies, and in the 1950s–1970s these societies coordinated a strategy to further integration by disseminating and explaining the jurisprudence of the ECJ and publishing criticisms of national judicial decisions that contradicted ECJ jurisprudence.[42] Also building support for the ECJ are the contributions to legal scholarship by members of EU institutions, which account for nearly 25 per cent of the contributions to the leading European law journals (Schepel 1997: 172). According to Harm Schepel and Rein Wesseling (1997), the net effect of the legal scholarship is a rationalizing and homogenizing pressure to accept a viewpoint on European law drafted and orchestrated by the ECJ itself. (Although it must be said that many national court judges have dismissed the EC legal scholarship as too one-sided, and have thus not been so convinced by it.)

Supreme courts clearly want to avoid a direct conflict with the European Court, conflict that could cause significant damage to the process of European integration and set the precedent that it is legal to ignore international courts if their decisions conflict with national law. As mentioned, supreme courts also do not want to become appeals courts for ECJ decisions. They have accepted key elements of ECJ doctrine. But their *obiter dictum* contains criticisms and refutations of ECJ doctrine and legal

---

[41] This has changed somewhat in the last 10 years as the number of European law experts with different viewpoints has grown (Weiler 1994; Shaw 1994).

[42] e.g. the German *Wissenschaftliche Gesellschaft für Europarecht* (Scientific Society for European Law, *WGE*) engaged in efforts to promote legal integration in Germany by launching a quarterly series of articles in the mainstream legal journal (the *Neue Juristische Wochenzeitschrift*), by introducing European law topics into other professional legal contexts in Germany, by working to include European law in conferences on other general areas of law, by founding a specialized journal (*Europarecht*), and by launching publishing campaigns in all the major German legal journals against national legal judgements unfavourable to European law. According to participants in the *WGE* in the 1960s, these strategies were coordinated informally within the small group of like-minded scholars and even included telephoning judges to tell them that their decision was not consistent with European law. As membership grew, it became harder to coordinate policy, and internal disagreements also emerged. (Based on interviews with two founding members of the *WGE*, 26 Jan. 1994, Hamburg, and 11 Jan. 1994, Brussels, as well as an examination of the Trier archives and conference proceedings of the association.) See also Ipsen (1990). All member states have similar organizations, though not all have been as active as the *WGE*.

reasoning.[43] And they have provided clear signals that they may well challenge future expansions of EC authority.

Unable to actually stop legal integration from progressing, seeking to avoid direct conflict, and facing significant pressures created by the actions of national lower courts, national high courts were compelled to accept a significant compromise regarding the issue of EC law supremacy. They accepted the principle of EC law supremacy, ceding to the ECJ significant influence over national law and policy. Interpretation of national law now takes place among a larger group of actors, including lower level courts and the ECJ. National governments, national parliaments, national administrations, and national high courts that had decisively influenced and even controlled the national policy-making process have had to give up autonomy and control, and thus real power.

But national supreme courts have not capitulated entirely. They rejected the ECJ's argument that European law created a new legal order. Instead they found that, since European law gains its authority by virtue of the national constitution, the EU's and ECJ's authority is limited by the national constitution.[44] While accepting a role enforcing European law supremacy, national high courts have declared that in the future any European law or ECJ interpretation which crosses over what national courts believe their state agreed to, or what their governments were constitutionally allowed to agree to, will not be valid in the national realm.[45] Some have also asserted the right to control the validity of European rules, determining whether or not EC law conforms with what member states agreed to, or with the national constitution.[46] In taking this step, national courts are explicitly and intentionally challenging the ECJ's exclusive jurisdictional authority regarding issues of EC law. They are doing this to be able better to influence the ECJ as it interprets European law, and to give the ECJ a compelling reason to take national judicial concerns into account as it develops its jurisprudence. Thus while accepting the

[43] e.g. they disagree with the ECJ's reasoning, but find another reason why its decision is valid. Or they accept the reasoning only for the case at hand, and signal that it may not apply to other cases. Another strategy has been to let cases languish on their docket, in the hope that the political process will create a solution that can avoid a damaging ruling.

[44] See n. 20 above for the relevant decisions.

[45] Germany: n. 20 above, *Maastricht* decision. France: n. 20 above, *Schengen* decision and *Maastricht I* (see further Ch. 4 below). *Frontini v. Ministero della Finanze*, Italian Constitutional Court Decision 183 of 27 Dec. 1973, [1974] Il Foro It. 314, [1974] 2 CMLR 372. Denmark: n. 20 above, 'Maastricht' decision.

[46] The German and Italian Constitutional Courts have taken this step, as has the Danish supreme court: n. 20 above, *German* and *Danish Maastricht* decisions; Fragd.

ECJ's authority to rule on national policy, national courts also positioned themselves to have more influence over the ECJ, European law, and European policy.

Unlike neo-functionalist analysis, this account does not imply that a harmony of interests propels European integration forward, or that the actors gaining power or wealth through European integration determine when and how European law expands and replaces national law. Indeed, it argues that battles between actors with competing interests fundamentally shape the process of European integration. The European legal system is an arena for these battles, sitting outside national legal and political systems yet able decisively to influence national and European political debates. While many of the ECJ's expansive interpretations have been accepted, including the idea that European law is supreme to subsequent national law, those opposed to ceding national powers and national sovereignty have won key victories. As the next section will show, the constraints created by national courts seek to ensure that European integration does not create a 'one-way ratchet' whereby national sovereignty is ceded to the EU piecemeal.

V. National judicial constraints on European legal integration

National judges protesting the ECJ's expansion of authority through its supremacy doctrine endured significant criticism. They fought against this criticism, often against the prodding of other courts in their legal system, because they knew that the legal basis on which European law gained supremacy in the national realm would affect national sovereignty, and their own ability to influence the legal and political process. What do the disagreements between the ECJ and national courts mean for the supremacy of European law in the national realm, and for the future ability of the ECJ to expand EC authority through legal interpretation?

The ECJ needs to be invited to issue an interpretation of European law. National courts decide which cases to send to the ECJ in the first place, how European law applies to a given national policy, and whether or not they are going to accept the ECJ's interpretation of European rules. While the competitive dynamic between courts creates a pressure within national legal systems to accept ECJ jurisprudence, the ECJ's dependence on national courts creates significant limits for it. If there is agreement among national courts about where European law should not reach or how European law should be interpreted, references can be avoided and the penetration of ECJ jurisprudence thwarted. For example, according to Jonathan Golub British judges decided that the ECJ would always interpret environmental directives more broadly than necessary. Exercising their discretion to interpret 'clear' European law on their own, British judges have withheld references from the Court which might have become ammunition for additional adverse rulings (Golub 1996b).

The prospect of unified opposition by national courts has led the ECJ to practise judicial restraint. For example, vocal national court challenges to the ECJ's claim that directives could create direct effects encouraged the ECJ to limit its doctrine. Legal logic would imply that if directives can be drawn on by private litigants to challenge government policy, private litigants should also be able to use directives to challenge the policies of firms. But national judicial dissent encouraged the ECJ not to expand the direct effect of directives to include challenges to the actions of private actors (Chalmers 1997; Morris and David 1987).

National court challenges have also motivated the ECJ to reverse itself. ECJ Justice Mancini acknowledged the influence of high courts over the ECJ with respect to human rights:

The [European] Court's discovery that European citizens have fundamental rights was provoked by a well-founded fear that in Germany and Italy the constitutional courts would assume power to test Community laws for compliance with fundamental rights enshrined in their own Constitutions. (Mancini and Keeling 1994: 26).

The ECJ now takes greater pains to ensure that European laws do not violate basic rights. Constitutional concerns go beyond human rights issues. National constitutions contain rules about the separation of powers between the federal and state governments, and between legislative bodies. National high courts have made it clear that these rules can be used to challenge European laws agreed to by the executive branch, opening up a whole new avenue through which to challenge the authority of European law even when the ECJ has upheld the validity of the law.[47]

National courts are fair-weather supporters of the ECJ. They use references to the ECJ to challenge national laws and jurisprudence with which they disagree. But, as Chapters 3 and 4 will show, national courts also use domestic legal avenues to challenge ECJ jurisprudence with which they

---

[47] Indeed, this approach was used in the broadcasting directive dispute (see below, Ch. 3, Section II, Round 5, for a discussion of this dispute).

disagree. The disagreements between the ECJ and national courts matter. Differences in interpretation are often signals to the ECJ that national courts are unhappy with aspects of ECJ jurisprudence. Divergences in legal interpretations create room for a rupture between the ECJ and national courts, room that can be used by clever litigants and by national judges to influence European policy. By disagreeing with the ECJ about the supremacy of European law in the national realm, national courts have in essence inserted themselves into both the legal and political process of European integration. They have inserted themselves into the policy-making process not so much to advance the process of European integration as to create limits on the transfer of national powers to the European level. Their ability to play an influential role in this process depends in large part on the organization of the national legal system, and specifically on rules of access to constitutional courts, and the willingness of litigants to use the legal system to challenge EC laws. As Chapter 4 will show, the German Constitutional Court is much better positioned than the French *Conseil Constitutionnel* to influence the policy process, allowing German litigants a greater opportunity to influence German and European policy when compared to French litigants.

National courts are certainly not the only barriers to expanding European authority. National governments can also constrain legal integration in the drafting of laws and in arguments before the ECJ. National governments have also had some success in pressuring the ECJ to change its jurisprudence, though far less success than neo-realists expected. The complex relationship between national governments and the ECJ will be examined in Chapter 5.

Left out entirely of this analysis is the relationship between national governments, national courts, EU institutions, and the broader public. We know there is a democratic deficit in the European Union, and that the ECJ lacks legitimacy among the broader public (Caldeira and Gibson 1995; 1997). But it is unclear how popular concerns, and concerns about democratic legitimacy, are affecting the legal process regarding European integration. This book offers a historical study of the integration of the ECJ's doctrine of European law supremacy into national political and legal systems. Since most of the past debate over European law supremacy has taken place while there was little public scrutiny of the ECJ or of the process of European integration more generally, examining the past does not offer much guidance for understanding this important issue. The EU can no longer avoid public scrutiny, and the role of the public needs to be brought more directly into future analyses of judicial politics in the EU.

The ECJ remains an international court. But it is different from most international courts in the opportunities and constraints it faces. International courts worry primarily about states accepting their decisions. National judicial support gives the ECJ greater autonomy from states compared to most international legal bodies, because if the ECJ can carry the support of national courts, it can be confident that its decisions will be accepted by national governments. But the support of national courts cannot be assumed, and maintaining this support is not easy. In the final analysis national courts are still loyal to their constitutions and to domestic political concerns.

While the ECJ can be less concerned about responses by national government than many international courts, it also has a larger and more diverse constituency to please. National court constraints are multiplied many times because each country has its own constitution and its own domestic political concerns. And even within national systems different courts can have different concerns. In some cases, it may well be impossible to please all national courts and national governments. The ECJ may thus need to withdraw from such heated issues so as to avoid a rupture with national courts.[48] Thus its source of strength is also a source of weakness, forcing it in some cases to constrain rather than expand its authority.

---

[48] It can do this by a number of judicial techniques, e.g. limiting its jurisdiction, finding technical ways to avoid speaking on an issue, or finding reasons not to apply existing jurisprudence to a specific case.

3

German Judicial Acceptance of European Law Supremacy

German courts have been both strong supporters and harsh critics of the ECJ. They send by far the most preliminary ruling references to the ECJ, and in 1971 the German Constitutional Court was the first supreme national court to uphold the supremacy of European law in Germany. As integration progressed, however, German courts became more critical of the ECJ and more willing to limit the supremacy of European law. In 1974 the German Constitutional Court (*Bundesverfassungsgericht* or BVerfG) reversed one of its earlier rulings and challenged the ECJ's exclusive authority to assess the validity of European law. The *Solange I* decision established the authority of the BVerfG to assess the constitutionality of European rules, and thus the validity of European law in Germany. There was a warming trend from 1979 to 1987, when the BVerfG implied that it would no longer review the constitutionality of European rules and created a sanction for German courts that refused the authority of the ECJ. This trend was reversed in 1993, however, when the BVerfG issued its most critical ruling, reasserting its willingness to review the constitutionality of European laws and asserting its power to determine the limits of EC authority in Germany. While the supremacy of European law over German law is not in question, the 1993 *Maastricht* decision established the BVerfG's ultimate authority to decide where European law does and does not apply in Germany.

This outcome of fluctuating national judicial positions and reservations that increase over time is the opposite of what scholars had predicted. European Community legal scholars expected support for European law to grow as the older generation of judges was replaced by younger, more 'Europe'-oriented judges. Neo-functionalist theory anticipated that the more contact national officials had with the European Community, the more support they would have.[1] Instead, it seems that the more contact German courts have with the EC, the less comfortable they are delegating authority to European institutions. Indeed, German courts with the most contact and experience are actually the most critical of the ECJ.

One cannot plausibly argue that the German courts were following political cues in their opposition to ECJ doctrine. German judicial positions changed at a time when the German government was strongly supportive of European integration and sought to build a federal 'United States of Europe'. Indeed, the Federal Government was often forced to defend the EC before German courts. Later, when the German public became increasingly concerned about the lack of democracy in the EC, German courts portrayed themselves as protectors of democracy. But this change in public sentiment came well after the German judicial positions were established, and thus cannot account for the sceptical actions of the national courts.

The German case provides a clear example of how judicial rivalries and divergent judicial preferences regarding European legal issues shaped the process of doctrinal change. Divergent preferences created a dynamic of legal integration that both propelled the expansion of European law into the national sphere and created limits to its reach in the national sphere. In Germany, a reference to the ECJ provided a means for lower courts to escape the national legal hierarchy and to challenge or tie the hands of courts higher up in the legal system. German courts can also refer constitutional issues to the BVerfG, and lower German courts have used references to the BVerfG to question ECJ jurisprudence. The result has been numerous references to ECJ and the BVerfG, providing the latter with numerous opportunities to intervene and influence European legal debates. The many steps in legal process, between referrals to the ECJ, the appeals process, and referrals to the BVerfG, provided time and a means for courts to negotiate over doctrinal and legal outcomes. While full doctrinal agreement was not achieved, German courts and the political actors have thus far found ways to accept the legal substance of ECJ decisions and thus keep legal tensions from rupturing and undermining the authority of European law and the ECJ.

This chapter traces the negotiation process in Germany. Section I identifies the main judicial actors in Germany and their preferences in European legal issues. Section II explains the evolution of the German doctrinal debate

---

[1] While Haas later recanted much of his theory (Haas 1975: 52), more recent neo-functionalist theory has been revived along with the assumption that judicial support should grow in tandem with the rising number of legal suits brought (Burley and Mattli 1993; Stone Sweet and Brunnel 1998).

over time, divided into rounds in which the debate developed. Section III explains how the German experience contributed to European integration.

I. The main judicial actors in the legal debate

Most of the pressure for doctrinal change in Germany came from lower courts. These courts used the ECJ to challenge national jurisprudence and the national system to challenge ECJ jurisprudence. They were able to play the ECJ and BVerfG off against each other because of the organization of the German legal system. The German legal system is divided into five separate legal branches according to legal substance (see Fig. 3.1). Each substantive area of law has its own hierarchy, with a federal-level court that is the highest court on substantive legal questions within each branch. The BVerfG is the highest court on all constitutional issues and all German courts are under the its constitutional authority. Lower courts and appeals courts are able to interrupt their proceedings to send a constitutional question to the BVerfG without waiting for the question to be appealed up the legal hierarchy. This provides one means for lower courts to circumvent or challenge the jurisprudence of Federal supreme courts. The BVerfG considers only constitutional issues and will not entertain questions of legal substance. But it will allow decisions of German courts to be appealed on constitutional grounds (through an individual constitutional complaint). The possibility that a court's decision might be appealed to the BVerfG helps keep ordinary German courts respectful of BVerfG jurisprudence. The strong hierarchical nature of the German legal system creates a largely uniform and coherent national legal doctrine, especially regarding constitutional issues.

In Germany, European law gains its supreme authority by virtue of the German constitution. This means the issue of European law supremacy falls within the BVerfG's supreme jurisdiction. Unlike France, where no supreme constitutional body can decide on disagreements over legal doctrine,[2] divergences in national doctrine regarding European law supremacy cannot endure in Germany. The BVerfG resolves disagreements to create a single doctrinal position for Germany on issues related to European law supremacy. Also in contrast to the French system, where rivalries exist across branches of

---

[2] A special *Tribunal de Conflits* is supposed to resolve conflicts between the administrative and ordinary court branches, but it has not been used to resolve disputes over European law that have persisted between these branches. For more on the role of the Tribunal de Conflit in France see: Dadomo and Farran (1996: 107–11).

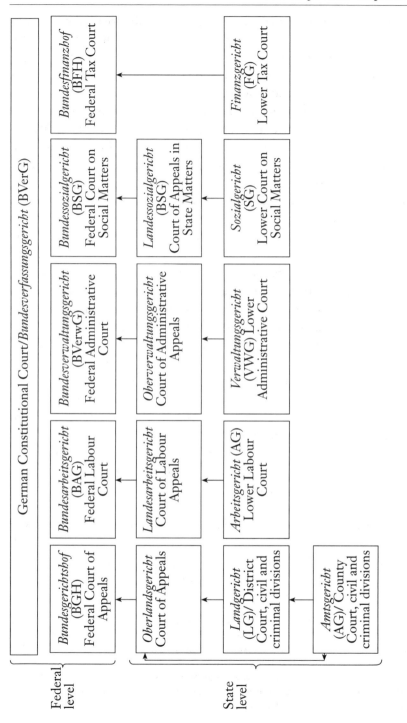

Fig. 3.1. Organization of the German judiciary

This figure is modified from a chart in Horn *et al.* (1982), repr. in Glendon *et al.* (1985: 111).

the judiciary, the clear separation of branches by legal substance in Germany means that there is no real threat that jurisdictional authority might be transferred from one German branch to another. Instead of competitive tensions across branches, rivalries among German courts tend to arise within branches, between lower and higher courts.

As a whole, German courts have sent more references to the ECJ than any other national judiciary, and they have been very active in negotiating key ECJ doctrines. But not all German courts participate in European legal debates. Table 3.1 shows the distribution of references to the ECJ across branches and levels of the judiciary.

When one breaks down the reference statistics by individual courts, the pronounced role of certain courts becomes even more apparent. The tax branch is the smallest branch of the German judiciary, with fewer than 3 per cent of all judges, yet it alone accounts for 49 per cent of all references to the European Court (and nearly 60 per cent of all references in the 1960s and 1970s). The top two sources of references are the Federal Tax Court and the Tax Court in Hamburg. The administrative court in Frankfurt is the third largest source of references. Together these three courts sent 35 per cent of all German references to the ECJ between 1960 and 1994.[3] Jurisdiction and subject matter can explain in part the clumping of cases in certain courts.[4] But this explanation is only partial. German tax courts in the 1960s and 1970s referred more cases than the entire judiciaries of Belgium, France, the Netherlands, and Italy. Given the significant number of references to the ECJ by German tax courts and by the Frankfurt administrative court, it is not so surprising that these courts have been at the heart of the development of the supremacy doctrine in Germany. These courts have also been behind the movement to create limits to the reach of European law in the national realm.

Focusing on reference rates can be misleading. Not all German references question the compatibility of national law to European law. According to one study, only 37 per cent of German references from 1961 to 1985 involved questions about the compatibility of national law with European law (Schwartz 1988: 15, 23). The Federal Tax Court which is itself responsible for

---

[3] Indeed, just 11 individual courts account for 65% of all references.

[4] Because customs regulations of the EC were the first to be harmonized (in the 1960s) and because tax law is one of the most harmonized areas of EC law, tax courts have been more involved in legal integration from an early period compared to penal courts, which deal almost exclusively with national law. Because the Federal Office of Nutrition and Forestry and the Federal Office for the Regulation of the Agricultural Market are located in Frankfurt, the Frankfurt administrative court hears nearly all challenges to the validity of EC agricultural policies (Seidel 1987).

Table 3.1. Preliminary ruling references of German courts, 1960–1994[a]

	Civil and Penal courts			Labour courts			Administrative courts			Social courts			Tax courts			Totals		
		No.	%[b]		No.	%		No.	%		No.	%		No.	%		No.	%
	Federal Court of Appeals	27	3	Federal Labour Court	10	1	Federal Administrative Court	37	4	Federal Social Court	43	5	Federal Tax Court	140	16	All federal courts	257	29
	Court of Appeals	27	3	Court of Labour Appeals	2	*[c]	Court of Administrative Appeals	10	1	Social Court of Appeals	27	3				All appeal courts	66	7
	District and County Courts	58	6	Lower Labour Courts	38	4	Lower Administrative Courts	148	16	Lower Social Courts	31	3	Lower Tax Courts	303	33	All lower courts	578	64
Total by branch		112	12		50	5		195	22		101	11		443	49		901	100

[a] The figures in this chart are based on data provided by the research and documentation division of the Court of Justice. Included are references for opinions even if the opinion did not result in an ECJ decision; thus the total number of references varies slightly from the number reported by the ECJ's annual report.
[b] Percentage of total references by German courts.
[c] * = <1%.

140, or 16 per cent, of all German references—probably more references than any other national court—is known for referring picky, technical questions about the meaning of European laws.[5]

Courts can also influence ECJ and national doctrine without making references. None of the major French cases involving EC law supremacy was referred to the ECJ. And the BVerfG has significant influence over national doctrine and ECJ doctrine even though it never refers cases. The German Constitutional Court's rules of access allow it to be drawn into political debates by a variety of different actors—private litigants, national courts, *Land* governments, members of parliament—ensuring it an important voice in doctrinal debates. There are four separate ways in which the BVerfG can be brought into European legal issues.

(1) *'Concrete judicial review': references from a national court.* When a legal case raises a constitutional question which must be answered in order for the national court to render a decision, the national court can stop the case and refer the question to the Constitutional Court for resolution. This mechanism allows lower German courts to pull the BVerfG into debates over European law supremacy.

(2) *Individual constitutional complaints.* Individuals can file charges of a constitutional violation of their rights by any public entity including national courts. This mode of access allows private litigants to challenge national court decisions, and thus indirectly ECJ decisions, and government decisions in issues of European integration.

(3) *'Federal–state disputes': references by state governments. Land* governments can refer challenges to Federal laws that encroach on their jurisdictional authority. This mode of access could be very important as the debate over European Union, Federal government, and *Land* legislative authority develops.

(4) *'Abstract review' of German laws.* At the request of the Federal government, a state government, or one third of the members of the *Bundestag,* the Constitutional Court can be called upon to review the compatibility of a German law with the Basic Law. This mode of access has thus far not been used, as German political parties have been united in the goal of European integration. Should German parties start to disagree on

---

[5] It has sent a large number of questions about the classification of goods under EC customs codes, wanting to know how to classify e.g. turkey tails and jeans with button flaps (Zuleeg 1993: 117–18). It tends to resolve important questions of legal principle on its own, without a reference to the ECJ (Behr 1983: 456–7).

European issues, minority parties who disagree with the government's European policy could challenge it before the German Constitutional Court.

Few national courts, constitutional or otherwise, have as many means of being brought into legal debates. The French *Conseil Constitutionnel* only has the authority to conduct abstract review. The Italian Constitutional Court lacks the authority to entertain individual constitutional complaints. The UK has no constitution and no court with powers of abstract or concrete judicial review.[6] The wide rules of access are one reason why the BVerfG is more actively involved in European constitutional debates than other national supreme courts. As we shall see, the wide access rules give the BVerfG significant influence in European integration, more influence than courts in other countries.

The German Constitutional Court has de facto *certiorari* powers with respect to individual constitutional complaints. But it must issue a decision in response to national court references, Federal/state disputes or requests for abstract review. While the BVerfG must rule, it can still extricate itself from disputes if it so wishes. By deciding that certain issues are not germane, the BVerfG can avoid addressing politically tricky questions. With constitutional complaints and national court references, it can choose to leave issues pending for a number of years, watching to see what evolves. These techniques allow the German Constitutional Court in practice to pick how and when it wants to intervene in European legal and political debates. Because the BVerfG insists that questions involving European law be sent to the ECJ first, and that other domestic remedies be exhausted in individual complaints, it also gets to have the final word in individual disputes.

The next section shows how the interests of national courts vis-à-vis European law evolved over time, and how the interactions of German courts influenced the debate over European law supremacy, contributing to a change in German judicial doctrine.

II. Negotiating doctrinal change regarding European law supremacy

When Germany joined the European Union, it had a traditional dualist interpretation of the relationship of treaty law to national law. International

---

[6] The formal incorporation of the European Convention on Human Rights in Oct. 2000 could well change this.

law was considered an entirely separate realm of law, which operated on a different plane from that of national law. Treaty law entered the German legal realm through its formal incorporation by parliament, and was thus subject to the same constitutional constraints as national law and could be superseded by a subsequent act of parliament. This meant that the German government could legally circumvent or ignore its European legal obligations simply by passing a new national law. In order for national courts to be able to apply European law over subsequent and conflicting national law, a national legal basis for the supremacy of European law had to be created.

The German constitution was quite amenable to such an interpretive evolution. Article 25 of the German constitution makes international law 'an integral part of federal law'. It also states that the general rules of public international law 'shall take precedence over the laws and shall directly create rights and duties for the inhabitants of the federal territory'. Article 24 allowed the German government 'by legislation to transfer sovereign powers to intergovernmental institutions'. But despite the seemingly 'friendly' nature of these constitutional provisions, they did not in fact change the traditional dualist doctrine of *lex posterior derogat legi prior*.

Article 25, which refers to 'the general rules of public international law', was intended to apply to customary international law and not to Treaty law (Henkin et al. 1993: 154), and it is still not seen as being applicable to the EC context.[7] Article 24 was created for collective security organizations and was originally seen as not applicable to economic organizations such as the EC (Menzel and Tomuschat 1981; Menzel 1981). To allow German courts to enforce European law over subsequent national law, the BVerfG expanded its understanding of Article 24 to included economic and other types of international organizations. Because European law gained supreme authority by virtue of a constitutional interpretation of Article 24, however, constitutional interpretation could also be used to find limits to the Article 24 authority of European law in Germany.

At first the BVerfG implied that German sovereignty had been completely transferred to the European institutions in certain areas of authority. Later the Constitutional Court decided that the German government could not transfer authority it did not have. This meant that European institutions did not have authority to pass laws that contravened German basic rights and protections. Nor could any law or treaty amendment agreed to by the

---

[7] In contrast, the French constitution specifies that international treaties are superior to national law, which is why France has typically been seen as having a monist legal system where international law is part of the national legal order and of a higher order than national law.

German government be valid in Germany if it violated the separation of powers between the federal and state governments, or if it compromised certain unalterable provisions of the German constitution. According to the BVerfG, because Article 24 was the only basis for European law supremacy in Germany, and only German courts could interpret this provision, ECJ decisions about European law supremacy based on European Treaty provisions are not necessarily valid in Germany.

This interpretive evolution emerged over thirty-three years. I divide this period into five separate 'rounds' during which key issues of German doctrine were debated and resolved. Round 1 (1963–7) considered whether it was constitutional for Germany to be in the European Community and established that Article 24 provided a constitutional means for German membership. It also established that directly applicable European regulations were binding in Germany and that German courts lacked the authority to assess the validity of acts of European institutions. In Round 2, the 'turnover tax struggle' (1965–71), the BVerfG found that Article 24 implied the supremacy of European law over subsequent national law and created an obligation for national courts to accord European law supremacy. In the first two rounds German doctrine was seemingly consistent with the ECJ's supremacy doctrine. In Round 3, the *Solange I* and *Solange II* debates (1971–85), limits to the Article 24 transfer of sovereignty were found. In Round 4 (1981–7), there was a warming trend towards the ECJ. The German Constitutional Court declared that the ECJ was the *gesetzlicher Richter* (legal judge) in European legal matters, creating a constitutional obligation for German courts to send cases to the ECJ and to respect ECJ rulings. Round 5, the *Maastricht* era (1993–2000), marked a return to the BVerfG's confrontational position, and then an easing of tension. This round created limits to what the German government could agree to at the European level, provided new avenues for private litigants to challenge the validity of European laws, opened the door for *Länder* to challenge European acts that encroach on their authority, and asserted that the BVerfG has the final authority to determine the limits of European authority in the national realm. These positions were upheld in the BVerfG's *Banana* ruling, though the BVerfG signalled that it would use these powers sparingly, intervening only when the protections offered to German citizens under European law sank below a certain level.

While legal interpretations regarding European law supremacy became more restrictive through the years, there remained an rigid commitment to the principle that European legal obligations are binding. Because these ideas were not qualified, the institutional underpinnings of European law supremacy were ultimately strengthened at the same time that limitations on European law supremacy were created.

Round 1. EC membership does not violate the constitution: establishing the possibility of European law supremacy, 1960–1967

The German legal community has never accepted the 'special' nature of the EC treaty or that European law is in some fundamental way different from international law. But the ability of European institutions to pass regulations which are 'directly applicable' in the national setting (formerly Article 189 EEC, now Article 249) created a new legal situation in which the traditional dualist notion of international law becoming part of national law through parliamentary ratification clearly did not apply. The European Court and pro-integration legal scholars drew from the legislative capacity of the EC that European law constituted a 'new legal order' of international law, not bound by traditional international public law doctrines.[8] In Germany, a number of constitutional law scholars drew from the unusual legislative capacity of the EC that the Treaty of Rome was quite possibly unconstitutional.

What started as an academic debate became a judicial debate in 1963 when a tax court in Rhineland-Palatinate challenged the constitutionality of the ratification act of the Treaty of Rome. The court also questioned whether Article 24 of the German constitution could be used to justify a transfer of legislative authority to the European Community. The tax court was being asked to review the validity of a European regulation. Rather than sending the question to the ECJ, it took the provocative position that the regulation was not valid because Article 189 of the EEC Treaty was unconstitutional.

The tax court voiced the fear that allowing the European Council to pass directly applicable regulations would undermine judicial protections in the German constitution. Its concern was that the EC violated the German separation of powers. The court acknowledged that at present such a violation was not a serious threat to the rule of law in Germany. But interpreting Article 24 to allow for transfers violating the separation of powers opened the possibility that constitutionally protected democratic controls could be circumvented through international endeavours. The Rhineland-Palatinate judge criticized legal scholars who were embracing legal integration uncritically, likening them to the academics who embraced Nazi doctrine uncritically. It argued:

[8] *Van Gend en Loos v. Nederlandse Administratie Belastingen*, ECJ 26/62, (1963) ECR 1, [1963] CMLR 105. Quote from ECR 12.

The transfer of sovereignty to an international institution must not become a means of upsetting, from outside, the balance of power carefully worked out and protected by the Constitution for setting up a free society . . .

The most important aim of the Constitution is to avoid a repetition of the developments which, in the Weimar Republic, led to the abolition of the separation of powers, and thus to the collapse of the rule of law. The path to the complete surrender of the doctrine of the separation of powers through the Special Powers Act of 24 March 1933 took its first open form in the excessively wide interpretation of Art. 48 (2) of the Weimar Constitution in favour of the executive. As early as this, the thinking of leading academic lawyers had reached the highly dangerous stage, in which an inadequately circumscribed clause in the Constitution had itself become a gap in the Constitution. The undermining and destruction of the rule of law for a second time can be avoided only by the courts opposing every attempt to interpret another inadequately circumscribed constitutional provision [meaning Article 24] so as to weaken Article 79 (3) of the Constitution's protection of the principle of separation of powers, and reduce the significance of the rule of law to a sham.[9]

The Rhineland-Palatinate judge stopped the legal proceedings and referred the question to the Constitutional Court.

The Constitutional Court did not immediately respond to the tax court's challenge. According to Mann, the Constitutional court was 'biding its time for [a] decision until the issue had been thoroughly discussed in the literature and legal opinion had tended to consolidate' (Mann 1972: 420). Mann found this festering period to be useful, because it forced other national courts to take positions on the issue. But staying silent on the issue did nothing to bolster the new European legal order.

Before the tax court's decision, scholars openly questioned the constitutionality of the EC. But the academic response to the Rhineland-Palatinate decision was overwhelmingly critical (Mann 1972: 69). The decision implied that Germany could not be a member in the EC. Clearly Germany was going to be a member, and in light of this membership, and of the ECJ's new *Van Gend en Loos* and *Costa* jurisprudence, German legal thought started to shift. According to Mann, 'in stark contrast to a similar conference five years earlier', in the 1964 meeting of the Assembly of Constitutional Law Scholars 'there was . . . general agreement that Community law should be granted a position independent of member state constitutions and must be understood in terms of its own needs and conceptions' (p. 420). The German Bundestag also weighed in to counter the Rhineland-Palatinate decision, passing a resolution stating that the

---

[9] *Re Tax on Malt Barley* (case III 77/63), FG Rhineland-Palatinate decision of 14 Nov. 1963, [1963] EuR 10 130, [1964] 10 CMLR 130. Quote from CMLR, p. 36.

ratification law on the EEC was constitutional (Deutscher Bundestag, Sitzungberichte 6501 B. 132 Sitzung: 4 Wahlperiode, 1964).

The Rhineland-Palatinate tax court remained defiant. Faced with the application of the same EEC regulation a year later (1965), it refused to revise its earlier opinion, and argued strongly against its critics. It referred to the debate its decision had provoked, and criticized the arguments levied against its ruling. For example, it argued:

the views expressed by Ipsen and Scheuner cannot wholly conceal the fact that the legislative functions bestowed on the Council by Article 189 of the EEC Treaty appear to be repugnant to the principles of the Federal Constitution. Ipsen finally said that the member states had accepted the terms of the treaties and could not now resile from them: but that is a weak argument, and underlines the absence of any other arguments of law to support that position . . .[10]

According to the tax court, 'the main task of all the lawyers and politicians involved must be to find ways of removing these [unconstitutional] discrepancies . . . not just by refined legal arguments, but by reorganizing the European Communities'.[11]

The tax court's argumentation makes it clear that it was not interested in foiling the German role in European integration, but rather in provoking the Constitutional Court to become involved and to push for a reorganization of the European Community along more democratic institutional lines. But given the turmoil in the European Community at that time, including de Gaulle's empty-chair policy and the crisis that led to the Luxembourg compromise, any renegotiation of the EC's legislative capacity would probably have undermined the goal of European unification and the nascent European legal order.

With the BVerfG silent on the issue, German courts took contradictory positions on the status of European law in Germany.[12] On 12 December 1966 the administrative court in Frankfurt refused to apply a European regulation, declaring it invalid and therefore challenging the interpretive authority of the European Court.[13] The Turnover Tax Struggle, which will be discussed next, was also beginning to heat up at this time, leading to a huge number of cases involving European law, with the German government attempting to stymie compliance with a recent European Court decision.

---

[10]   *Re Excess Profits Levy* (Case III 47/65), FG Rhineland-Palatinate decision of 25 Mar. 1965, [1966] 18 CMLR 67. Quote p. 71.

[11]   Ibid. quote p. 72.

[12]   See discussion of divergent legal positions of German courts in Torrelli (1968).

[13]   VWG Frankfurt decision of 12 Dec. 1966, [1967] AWD 67.

Faced with a growing body of cases and no indication that the Constitutional Court was going to enter into the debate, the Federal Tax Court decided to go forward on its own. On 25 April 1967 it rejected the Rhineland-Palatinate court's arguments, taking into account the German government's political goal of European unification and the difficult political context within Europe.[14] The Federal Tax Court argued:

> The political unification of Europe, to which the Basic Law is committed, can be realized only step-by-step under the [prevailing political] circumstances. The EEC represents a significant step in this direction . . . Article 24 of the Basic Law, therefore, should be interpreted to mean that the transfer of sovereign powers to the EEC cannot be measured by the strict standards which apply to the exercise of these sovereign powers by the constitutional authorities within the State itself.[15]

Thus, the Federal Tax Court was asking for less stringent constitutional constraints in the interpretation of Article 24 compared to other constitutional clauses.

Nearly four years after the original reference was filed, the second senate of the Constitutional Court (BVerfG) finally issued a decision on the Rhineland-Palatinate case, but its decision did not answer any of the legal questions at hand.[16] The second senate did declare that the unconstitutionality of a single provision would not render the entire Treaty unconstitutional, but it left the question of the constitutionality of European regulations conspicuously open.[17] The fact that the decision was split (four judges to three), and that the largest issue at stake was left unanswered, revealed the lack of consensus in the Constitutional Court itself. While deciding the case on a technicality 'permitted the Constitutional Court to sidestep a potentially embarrassing constitutional conflict with the Treaty' (Mann 1972: 422), the decision left open the possibility that all European regulations would be invalid in Germany.

This unresolved outcome was unsatisfactory, especially because German courts were increasingly being called upon to interpret European regulations.

---

[14] *Firma Max Neumann v. Hauptzollamt Hof/Saalen*, BFH decision of 25 Apr. 1967, [1967] 6 AWD 227, [1967] EuR 239.

[15] BFH Decision VII 198/63 of 18 Apr. 1967 [1967] 3 EuR 239. Quote in 3 EuR 244. Cited in Mann (1972: 421). Even though the Federal Tax Court is the appeals court and a higher court than the Rhineland-Palatinate court, its decision was not binding on the latter. Since what was at stake was a constitutional question, only the Constitutional Court could resolve the issue decisively.

[16] *Re Tax on Malt Barley* (case III 77/63), BVerfG decision of 5 July 1967, BVerfG 2 BvL 29/63, [1967] 2 EuR 351, [1967] 27 CMLR 302.

[17] The Constitutional Court found the reference from the tax court to be inadmissible because the constitutionality of the Treaty was not relevant to the case before it.

Three months later the first senate of the Constitutional Court took the opportunity offered by an individual appeal to clarify the constitutional position of Article 189 EEC. This was the only European-related decision the first senate has made; the second senate has decided all subsequent EC matters.[18] In the case under consideration, some trading companies were arguing that a European regulation violated their basic rights. While the BVerfG found the constitutional complaint itself lacking foundation, it used the case as an opportunity to speak to the constitutionality of Article 189 of the European Treaty, and to give the European Treaty a firm grounding in German constitutional law. The first senate affirmed the independent nature of the EC, and the EC's right to issue regulations binding inside of Germany. The language the first senate used lent credence to the developing legal opinion that Article 24 allowed Germany to transfer sovereignty to the EC. It also seemed to support the European Court's jurisprudence on the 'special' nature of the EC Treaty. The first senate said:

The institutions of the EEC exercise sovereign rights of which the member states have divested themselves in favour of the Community set up by them. The Community itself is neither a state nor a federal state. It is a gradually integrating Community of a special nature, an 'interstate institution' in the sense of Article 24 §1 of the Basic Law to which the Federal Republic of Germany—like many other member states—has 'transferred' certain sovereign rights. A new public authority was thus created which is autonomous and independent with regard to the state authority of the separate member states. Consequently its acts have neither to be approved ('ratified') by the member states nor can they be annulled by them. The EEC Treaty is as it were the constitution of this Community.[19]

The 1967 decision closed off an important legal avenue through which private litigants had been attempting to challenge Commission regulatory policies and regulations passed in the Council. Sending a message to other litigants who might want to appeal ECJ decisions to the BVerfG, the first senate declared that since European regulations are not acts of German authorities, it lacked the jurisdiction to assess the validity of them.

---

[18] The first senate is responsible for cases involving substantive law. The second senate is responsible for political disputes between branches and levels of governments, elections, questions pertaining to the legality of political parties, impeachment proceedings, constitutional complaints, and concrete review cases dealing with civil and criminal procedure (Kommers 1989: 19–21). This division does not mean that the first senate cannot hear European law cases, but an agreement seems to have been reached so that, in practice, the second senate now hears all European legal issues.

[19] BVerfG decision, 1 BvR 248/63, 1 BvR 216/67 of 18 Oct. 1967, [1968] 1 EuR 134, [1967] 12 AWD 477. My translation from EuR, pp. 135–6.

In 1967, the German Constitutional Court had gone further than any other national high court in affirming the European Court's *Van Gend en Loos* jurisprudence. The debate over the constitutionality of European Community membership has become a footnote in Germany's European law jurisprudence, having been overtaken by subsequent rulings. But it revealed deep concern about the legal consequences of EC membership, a concern shared by German legal scholars and jurists alike. The strength of this concern was apparent in the German Constitutional Court's refusal to close the issue when it was first asked by the Rhineland-Palatinate court to do so in 1963, and in the first split decision from the BVerfG's second senate, which handles most cases involving highly political issues.[20] Analysing the debate shortly after it occurred, however, Mann found that the tax court's opinion in many respects 'voice[d] the doubts of German jurists in previous years' (1972: 422). As time wore on, the argument that the EC was 'special'—seemingly accepted in the 1967 decision—came to change, and the arguments used by the Rhineland-Palatinate judge to question the constitutionality of EEC membership resurfaced.

What was driving national judicial behaviour in this debate? There was certainly a genuine concern for how EEC membership would affect the safeguards of the Constitution. Specifically, the Rhineland-Palatinate judge wanted European law to be subject to national constitutional review. The BVerfG's second senate was too ambivalent to endorse the ECJ's doctrine on the new and special legal order, and not bold enough to create a constitutional review for European law. Its ambivalence is understandable if one remembers the context of the time. The EC was politically paralysed, and thus it was perhaps not the best moment to challenge European integration. At the same time the corpus of European legislation, and thus the body of law over which the ECJ presided, was so limited that it was hard to imagine that the EC could some day seriously undermine the German constitutional order. The first senate was more willing to endorse the ECJ's fragile supremacy jurisprudence to stop national courts from refusing the validity of European laws and to endorse the nascent European legal system. It also clearly did not want to be an appeals court for anyone unhappy with European law or a Commission decision. But by denying any authority to assess the validity of European laws, the BVerfG was denying itself future influence in the process of legal and political integration. The argument used to get out of this situation—that the Constitutional Court was not competent

---

[20] N. 18 above, *Re: Malt Barley*.

to assess the validity of acts of non-German institutions—conceded too much, and much acrobatics were needed in future decisions to reclaim its right to assess the validity of laws emanating from European institutions. But that is exactly what happened.

Round 2. The 'turnover tax struggle' and the acceptance of European law supremacy, 1965–1971

The first senate's decision regarding the constitutionality of Article 189 EEC did not establish the supremacy of European law in Germany. When the BVerfG did declare the supremacy of European law over 'simple' German law, its ruling was anticlimactic, in part because it was so anticipated and in part because the supremacy of European law over subsequent national law was the least controversial aspect of the case. The supremacy of European law in Germany was affirmed in a 1971 decision upholding the Federal Tax Court's ruling regarding German turnover taxes. The BVerfG's decision was the final chapter in heated judicial-political fight, but by the time the ruling came the litigants had already resolved the main dispute.

The 'turnover tax struggle' began in 1965 when a German lawyer challenged a German turnover equalization tax in a lower tax court in Saarland, and the tax court sent the case to the ECJ. 'Turnover equalization taxes' were taxes on imports designed to equalize the level of taxes paid on domestic products. Because turnover taxes were levied at each stage of the production process, it was very difficult to know how much tax had been paid during the domestic production process. Importers tried to get the European Commission to crack down on what they claimed was an abusive practice of using 'equalization taxes' as hidden tariffs. The Commission's meagre efforts did not satisfy the importers, who then tried to get the European Court to create a legal basis for them to challenge German turnover taxes in national courts by declaring that Article 95 of the EC Treaty which prohibits discriminatory taxation on imports creates direct effects—individual rights that can be drawn on in national courts to challenge national laws. A test case was carefully selected to present a clear German violation of the EC Treaty; the legal dispute involved an 'equalization' tax levied on milk-powder imports when German milk-powder was explicitly tax exempt. The violation of European law was clear, and the lower tax court referred the case to the ECJ asking if Article 95 creates direct effects.

In the Saarland case the German government argued that national courts were not an appropriate venue for enforcing European law. It noted that the

Commission was responsible for policing the enforcement of European law, and asserted that only the Commission could raise a case involving a turnover tax violation. This position reflected the general understanding of member states at the time the Treaty was negotiated.[21] The Commission had reviewed German taxes on milk-powder in 1965, and found the taxes to be too high, at which point the Parliament had lowered the tax rate from 4 per cent to 3 per cent. Given that German milk-powder was tax-exempt, this deal looked more like a political compromise than enforcement of European law. The German government argued, however, that since the Commission did not raise another case, the new tax rate must be in conformity with European law. The German government also wanted to minimize its obligations to remove national barriers to trade before the common market was achieved. Turnover taxes were slated to be harmonized, but until the time that common European legislation emerged, it wanted to preserve its own arguably protectionist system.[22]

The ECJ rejected the German government's arguments. The ability of the Commission to raise cases did not mean that national courts could avoid enforcing European law. It found that Article 95 of the Treaty created direct effects, and thus could be used by litigants in national courts. The ruling also implied that the German milk-powder tax was illegal.[23] Since the German parliament had changed this in 1965 after the Commission's case, the issue of the supremacy of European law over subsequent legislation was also at stake. The decision also implied that a member state had an obligation proactively to change all national legislation that conflicted with the EC Treaty, even in the absence of commonly adopted European tax rules (Waelbroeck 1967).

The *Lütticke* ruling raised the prospect that all sorts of German turnover equalization taxes could violate European law. Lawyers and the German Association of Exporters (*deutschen Verbände der Außenwirtschaft*) solicited copycat cases, sending letters advertising the possibility of a tax refund to

---

[21] This understanding is clearly stated in the ratification debates for the Treaty of Rome. See Document 5266, annexe to the verbal procedures of 26 Mar. 1957 of the debates of the French National Assembly, prepared by the Commission of the Foreign Ministry; 'Entwurf eines Gesetzes zu den Verträgen vom 25 März 1957 zur Gründung der Europäischen Wirtschaftsgemeinschaft und der Europäischen Atomgemeinschaft', Anlage C; Report of representative Dr Mommer from the Bundestag debates of Friday 5 March 1957, p. 13391; Atti Parlamentari, Senato della Repubblica; Legislatura II 1953–1957, disegni di legge e relazioni, document 2107-A, Camera dei deputati, document 2814, seduta del 26 marzo 1957.

[22] Arguments raised by the German government during the *Lütticke* proceedings. See *Lütticke (Alfons) GmbH v. Hauptzollamt Saarlouis*, ECJ Case 57/65, [1966] ECR 205.

[23] Ibid.

their clients and publishing complaint forms in trade journals. This led to a flood of legal challenges to potentially 'illegal' taxes. Faced with a staggering number of claims, the German government tried to make the problem disappear. The Ministry of Finance issued a decree: 'We hold the decision of the European Court as invalid. It conflicts with well reasoned arguments of the Federal government, and with the opinion of the affected member states of the EC.' The decree instructed customs officials to ignore the ECJ ruling and to reject all legal claims based upon the decision.[24]

The government's actions angered lower tax courts, which saw the decree as an attempt to intimidate plaintiffs, stifle legitimate legal debate, and exclude involvement in an important European legal issue. They refused to follow the Minister's decree, and proceeded to consider the legal claims (Wendt 1967a; 1967b). Pressure on the government from lawyers and from the Association of Exporters mounted to the point that representatives in the *Bundestag* questioned the Ministry of Finance as to whether its edicts were consistent with the principle of a *Rechtstaat*, a state ruled by law.[25] With lower tax courts sending more cases to the ECJ, it was clear the government could not make the problem disappear by decree. A solution that addressed the legal issues had to be found.

The German government adopted a test case strategy, participating in one of the pending disputes and asking the Federal Tax Court to refer a case to allow the ECJ to re-evaluate its earlier decision.[26] In its reference to the ECJ, the Federal Tax Court voiced its disagreement with the ECJ's *Lütticke* jurisprudence, and the ECJ's doctrine of European law supremacy.[27] The Federal Tax Court noted that there were 200,000 complaints and 15,000 legal cases pending in an already overburdened tax court system and that 'the ECJ's jurisprudence . . . had led to a troubling condition of legal uncertainty'.[28] It argued that it was not a legitimate task of German tax courts to be required to review thousands of single decisions taken in application of material tax law. The Community had its own means of enforcing the Treaty (infringement suits raised by the Commission), and the Federal Tax Court agreed with the German government that this was the appropriate mechanism through which the Treaty should be enforced. Taking direct aim at the

---

[24] 7 July 1966 (IIIB.4-V 8534-1/66), republished in AWD (1966), p. 327.

[25] (Meier 1994; 1967b).

[26] Interview with a German lawyer involved in the turnover tax struggle, 8 Nov. 1993, Cologne.

[27] Firma Molkerei-Zentrale Westfalen-Lippe GmbH, Trockenmilchwerk in Lippstadt. BFH reference to the ECJ of 18 July 1967, Case VII 156/65, [1967] 4 EuR 360.

[28] Ibid. 363.

ECJ's *Van Gend en Loos* decision, the Federal Tax Court argued that the ECJ's Doctrine of Direct Effect was 'in essence of a political nature', implying that it was not legally valid.[29] It pointed out that in Germany there was no legal directive that gave national courts the responsibility or authority to control of implementation of Community law. The Federal Tax Court asked the ECJ to reconsider its *Lütticke* decision and to find that European law did not create direct effects with respect to turnover taxes.

The Federal Tax Court wanted the ECJ to reverse itself, but it also offered another legal exit. The original *Lütticke* case centred on the question of whether a tax levied on imports that was not also levied on domestic products was a disguised tariff, and thus it centred on Article 95 EEC. In the test case, debate shifted to the question of whether states were allowed discretion in devising average tax rates, thus whether or not Article 97 EEC, which concerned average tax rates, created direct effects. The German government suggested that it was all a legal misunderstanding. In focusing on Article 95, the lower tax court had erred and had asked the ECJ the wrong question. The government worked within the legal debate to shift the focus to Article 97, publishing legalistic articles supporting their new position (Everling 1967; Stöcker 1967).[30] The Ministry of Finance issued a new decree:

> The German turnover equalization taxes are average tax rates in the sense of Article 97 EEC. In the system of cumulative multi-phase taxes, it is not possible to make an exact comparison between every exact or similar internal product. The German turnover equalization taxes can therefore only on average equalize the tax charges. The aforementioned average tax rates are not based in Art. 95 EEC, and by Art 97 §2, only the Commission has the authority to raise cases against specific guidelines or the effected country. The aforementioned ECJ decision therefore did not open any means for the German turnover tax to be challenged before tax courts.[31]

This argument was also attractive to the Federal Tax Court because it meant that lower courts would lose their authority to evaluate the compatibility of German equalization taxes with the EC Treaty.

The BFH's (Federal Tax Court's) antagonistic tone, and the legal trick employed, were apparent to actors directly involved. Lower German tax courts saw the Federal Tax Court's reference as an attempt to stifle debate and to exclude them from examining issues of Treaty compliance. They felt that

[29] Ibid. 364.

[30] Interestingly, Ulrich Everling, the government's European law lawyer at the Ministry of Economics, devised this strategy. He later was appointed as a judge on the ECJ.

[31] [1996] AWD 449.

the Federal Tax Court was too willing to trust the tax administration (Meier 1994). Countering the political-legal strategy, lower court judges sent references to the European Court arguing that Article 95 also applied to the issue. They tried to develop legal rules to evaluate whether tax rates were average tax rates, to create for themselves the jurisdictional authority to decide if a German tax fell under Article 95 or 97 EEC.[32]

The ECJ allowed the Germans their legal exit to relieve the pressure of so many legal claims. It refused to reverse its position regarding the direct effect of Article 95, but it did agree that Article 97 could not create direct effects. It turned over to the national courts the issue of whether a German turnover equalization tax was an average tax rate (and thus fell under Article 97) or a specific tax (and thus fell under Article 95).[33] The ECJ also answered the pending lower court references one by one,[34] addressing in detail the legal issues raised by the lower courts and thus allowing them to participate in the legal debate from which the Federal Tax Court had tried to exclude them.

The Federal Tax Court overruled the Saar court's decision in the original *Lütticke* case, interpreting the milk-powder case so narrowly as to make the case virtually ungeneralizable, and minimizing the tax refund awarded to the plaintiff so as to discourage others from raising cases.[35] For the test

---

[32] *Firma Kurt A. Becher v. Hauptzollamt München-Landsbergerstraße*, FG München, decision FG III 245/66 Z4. Reference to the ECJ 26 Apr. 1967, [1967] EuR 249, [1967] RIW 236. *Firma Gebrüder Lück v. Hauptzollamt Köln-Rheinau* FG Düsseldorf decision IV 1961/66 UA. Reference to the ECJ (IV 1961/66 UA) 6 Sept. 1967, [1967] RIW 444. *Firma Kunstmühle Tivoli v. Hauptzollamt Würzburg, FG München*, reference to the ECJ decision FG III 419/66-Z 1 and 2 of 17 May 1967, [1967] RIW 278. *Firma August Stier v. Hauptzollamt Hamburg-Ericus* FG Hamburg decision (IVA322/66 H (IVB)). Reference to the ECJ 11 Aug. 1967, [1967] EuR 364, [1967] RIW 404. *Firma Fink-Frucht GmbH v. Hauptzollamt München-Landsbergerstraße*, reference to the ECJ 12 July 67 FG München (III347/66—Z 1) [1967] RIW 368. *Firma Milch-, Fett- und Eierkontor GmbH v. Hauptzollamt Saarbrücken FG Saarland*, reference 2238/67 to the ECJ, 19 June 1967, [1967] RIW 366. There were also attempts made by lower tax courts to determine if a tax was genuinely an 'average tax' as stated in Article 97 EEC. These attempts appeared in references to the ECJ by the lower tax courts in Munich and Hamburg. The ECJ decisions in these cases are cited above.

[33] *Firma Molkerei-Zentrale Westfalen-Lippe GmbH, Trockenmilchwerk in Lippstadt*, ECJ Case 28/67, [1968] ECR 143.

[34] *Firma Gebrüder Lück v. Hauptzollamt Köln-Rheinau*, ECJ case 34/67, [1968] ECR 245. *Firma Kurt A. Becher v. Hauptzollamt München-Landsbergerstraße*, ECJ Case 13/67, [1968] ECR 187. *Firma August Stier v. Hauptzollamt Hamburg-Ericus*, ECJ Case 31/67, [1968] ECR 235. *Firma Kunstmühle Tivoli v. Hauptzollamt Würzburg*, ECJ Case 20/67, [1968] ECR 199. *Firma Milch-, Fett- und Eierkontor GmbH v. Hauptzollamt Saarbrücken*, ECJ Case 25/67, [1968] ECR 207. *Firma Fink-Frucht GmbH v. Hauptzollamt München-Landsbergerstraße*, ECJ Case 27/67, [1968] ECR 223.

[35] 'Lütticke', *Firma Alfons Lütticke GmbH, Köln-Deutz*, BFH decision VII B 106/67 of 29 Oct. 1968, [1969] NJW 1135, [1969] RIW 37.

case, the Federal Tax Court created a broad definition of what constituted an 'average tax rate' so that only a narrow category of importers were entitled to a small refund, and all the other plaintiffs lost their standing to raise suit.[36] This solution made the pending cases disappear, although it included important concessions to ECJ doctrine.

The plaintiff appealed the Federal Tax Court's decision in the original *Lütticke* case to the BVerfG. He argued that in reversing a national court decision that implemented an ECJ decision, without having made a new reference to the ECJ, the Federal Tax Court had denied the plaintiff his constitutional right to a legal judge. The German Constitutional Court upheld the Federal Tax Court's decision, but it criticized arguments the Federal Tax Court had raised in its test case reference to the ECJ. The BVerfG argued:

> Article 24 Paragraph 1 of the Basic Law implies . . . not only that the transfer of sovereignty to interstate organs is valid, but also that decisions of the ECJ . . . are to be recognized. The conclusion from this legal situation must mean that . . . German courts must also apply these legal rules, including laws which come from autonomous sovereign authorities but through the ECJ become directly effective within the national sphere . . . for only this way can the citizens of the Common Market claim their given rights.[37]

Thus in 1971 the German Constitutional Court became one of the first European supreme courts to change its national legal doctrine, to accord European law supremacy over subsequent national law, and to declare a role for national courts in enforcing European law. Its decision was clearly supportive of the EC legal order and the ECJ's jurisprudence.

The turnover tax struggle is revealing of the differing incentives motivating lower and higher courts. These institutional incentives, in turn, created a dynamic for legal integration. The Federal Tax Court wanted to make the overwhelming legal backlog disappear because it was concerned for the smooth functioning of the legal system. It also clearly wanted to minimize the tax authority's costs in the case. In addition, it had an incentive to find that Article 95 and 97 EEC did not create direct effects, so that it could control the interpretation of the German tax code with respect to customs issues. Lower tax courts were unconcerned about the logistical difficulties created by their

---

[36] *Molkerei-Zentrale Westfalen/Lippe GmbH v Hauptzollamt Paderborn*, BFH decision of 11 July 1968, [1968] EuR 52. [1968] 8 CMLR 300.

[37] *Firma Alfons Lütticke GmbH, Köln-Deutz*, BVerfG 2 BvR 225/69, [1972] 1 EuR 51, [1971] NJW 2122, [1971] RIW 418. My translation from NJW, p. 2124.

actions, and wanted to be able to review what they considered to be legally valid complaints. Their desire to influence legal doctrine and circumvent restrictive Federal Tax Court rulings further motivated the lower courts to send references to the ECJ. Interjudicial dynamics overtook the Federal Tax Court's and German government's management of the issue. Lower court judges worked to influence doctrinal development through references to the ECJ, and these references in themselves meant that neither a Federal Tax Court judicial fiat nor a government fiat could make the issue simply disappear.

A lasting legacy of the 'turnover tax struggle' was a distinct cooling of the Federal Tax Court's relationship with the ECJ, and a clear willingness of lower tax courts to refer broad legal questions to the European Court and to challenge Federal Tax Court jurisprudence on European law. In 1967 the Federal Tax Court had come out in support of the constitutionality of EC membership and had advocated a broad interpretation of transfer of sovereignty to the EC level. In part because of the harsh attacks on its turnover tax jurisprudence in the legal literature, and in part because of the increasing encroachments of European law into its domain,[38] the Federal Tax Court increasingly decided cases on its own, often reaching conclusions opposite to those of the ECJ (Meier 1970). Whereas lower tax courts had originally displayed willingness if not a preference to let the Federal Tax Court send important legal issues to the ECJ,[39] after learning that the Federal Tax Court would not send important questions of European law to the ECJ, they became more willing to refer such issues on their own.[40]

The passivity of the Constitutional Court during the turnover tax struggle is not surprising when one considers that it had no jurisdictional issue at stake. Not competent to decide substantive questions of law, it had no interest in wading into the minutiae of whether Article 97 or 95 EEC applied to the case. Its 1971 judgment resolved the issue of the supremacy of European law over subsequent national law, and of the supremacy of ECJ interpretations in substantive legal matters. But, as some scholars noted, the decision

[38] Based on interviews with German lawyers and a retired tax court judge who served as a clerk at the BFH in the late 1960s (Nov. 1993 and Feb. 1994).

[39] In 1963, a Nuremberg tax court 'ruled out submission to the European Court at this stage, not least, because this is a test case of fundamental importance, at the beginning of a line of tax court decisions on the EEC excess profits levy, and it would be better if they went to the European Court at the last instance'. *Re Potato Flour Tax*, FG Nuremburg decision of 9 Oct. 1963, Case K II 9/10/63 Z [1964] 9 CMLR 96. Quote from p. 106.

[40] Based on interviews with lower tax court judges in Munich and Hamburg, 26 Jan. 1994 (Hamburg), 22 Feb. 1994 (Fussen), and 21 Feb. 1994 (Munich).

left open the question of whether or not European law was supreme over the German constitution, its own area of jurisdictional authority.

This case also shows the political limits of controlling the judicial process, and how the short-term focus of political actors on the material aspects of a case facilitates the building of legal doctrine. The government's first attempt to order customs officials to ignore the ECJ failed because it interfered too directly in the legal process, and thus was ignored by lower tax courts. The second strategy of using a test case was still irksome to lower tax courts, but because it was within legal parameters, it was harder for them to counter. The success of the German government in shifting the legal debate shows that political pressure can influence judicial decision-making. But the government's prioritization of eliminating the legal claims led it to concede many issues of principle. It conceded that national courts can play a role enforcing the European Treaty—a point it had argued against in the original *Lütticke* case. It implicitly conceded the supremacy and direct effect of European law, the authority of the ECJ to use the preliminary ruling procedure to indirectly strike down national laws, and the direct effect of Article 95 EEC. It also conceded that the German government is obliged to change national tax schemes even when there is no European-level legislation to replace the national legislation—a strongly liberalizing position. The ECJ gave in to the German government's material concerns, accepting that protectionist measures would remain in place. But it stood firm on the legal principles, which mattered more to the ECJ. In the longer run, these principles proved more important in constructing an effective legal edifice for Europe.

Round 3. Finding limits to the supremacy of European law, 1971–1985

By 1971 the German legal community had fully embraced the constitutionality of EC membership and the supremacy of European law over simple German law. The Constitutional Court's 1967 and 1971 decisions lent legitimacy to European legal integration and the ECJ's early *Van Gend en Loos* and *Costa v. ENEL* decisions. But the issue of whether there were constitutional limits to the supremacy of European law remained unresolved. A significant part of the German legal and political community was uneasy about the lack of basic rights protection and the lack of democracy in the EC. Pro-integration legal scholars tried to minimize the importance of these nagging concerns. They argued that it was inconceivable or at least extremely improbable that European law could violate the Basic Law, and that national limitations on the supremacy of European law would undermine uniform legal interpretation within the EC. The ECJ had been somewhat dismissive of basic rights concerns raised in legal cases in the 1950s,[41] but in light of the German legal community's unease, the European Court had made overtures to its critics. In 1969 ECJ Judge Pescatore wrote a treatise on human rights and European integration (Pescatore 1969), and the ECJ started to take basic rights issues more seriously in its jurisprudence.

The ECJ's overtures did not appease its critics. In January of 1970 German law professor Hans-Heinrich Rupp made a fiery speech at the German Academy of Judges (*Deutsche Richterakademie*). He highlighted the danger of the EC's running amok without proper democratic (meaning judicial) safeguards, and called the EC a *Herrschaft ohne Herrn* (a government without a sovereign) and a *Herrschaft ohne Grundrechte* (a government without basic rights). Rupp argued that the ECJ did not have the competence to resolve the issue. The Constitutional Court should be the final arbiter of collisions between European law and basic rights issues in Germany. The provocative speech was published shortly thereafter as the lead article in the widely read legal trade journal, *Neue juristische Wochenzeitschrift* (Rupp 1970). It is hard to gauge the impact of Rupp's speech and article, but only a few weeks after publication of his article the administrative court (*Verwaltungsgerichthof* or VWG) in Frankfurt sent a reference to the ECJ asking the ECJ to find a European regulation in violation of the litigant's basic rights.[42] This reference became the basis for the ECJ's well-known *Internationale Handelsgesellschaft* ruling, where it asserted the supremacy of European law over national constitutions.

The administrative court's reference transformed the debate over the constitutional limits of European law from the theoretical to the practical realm. The legal case involved a European regulation requiring deposits for firms wanting import licences. The import licences were free, but the deposits were forfeited if the firm failed to import the goods. In its past jurisprudence, the administrative court had refused the validity of the deposit forfeiture because of its conflict with German basic rights protections (Zuleeg 1971: 448). Perhaps because of Rupp's article it decided to send to the ECJ this case in which an importer had lost his deposit for reasons which, while not beyond the importer's control, were at least defensible.[43] From the text of the

[41] See the discussion regarding basic rights in Möhring (1965).

[42] *Internationale Handelsgesellschaft mbH v. Einfuhr- und Vorratsstelle für Getreide und Futtermittel*, reference to the ECJ by the VWG Frankfurt, 18 Mar. 1970, [1970] 44 CMLR 294.

[43] When the VWG received an ECJ response it did not like, it referred the issue to the BVerfG. In its reference, it cited Rupp's argument in support of its case.

reference it is clear that the Frankfurt court expected the ECJ to agree that European law could not violate German Basic Law protections, and that thus the licence forfeiture scheme was invalid. The administrative court was, however, mistaken.

The European Court's 1970 *Internationale Handelsgesellschaft* decision asserted the supremacy of European law even over national constitutions. While the ECJ agreed that 'respect for fundamental rights forms an integral part of the general principles of law protected by the Court of Justice',[44] after an analysis of the administrative court's arguments regarding the deposit scheme, it found that the European regulation was not in violation of any basic rights. The assertion that European law was supreme even to the German constitution lent credence to the argument that EC membership could undermine democratic and basic rights protections in Germany.

The Frankfurt *Verwaltungsgerichthof* refused to accept the ECJ's decision in the *Internationale Handelsgesellschaft* case, saying it was unconstitutional and therefore not binding. Hoping that the BVerfG would restore its right to review the constitutionality of European law, the Frankfurt Court referred to the Constitutional Court the same questions it had sent the ECJ. In its reference it argued that 'that the primacy of European law must yield before the principles of the German Basic Law'.[45] It asked whether national courts could review European law that the ECJ had already reviewed, and how far European law could be reviewed with respect to constitutional principles. It wrote its reference for maximum effect within the Constitutional Court, criticizing those who would defend the supremacy of European law over the constitution as trying to facilitate European integration at the expense of basic rights protection. The administrative court argued: 'Surely it is legitimate to question whether or not a decline in the national state institutions and rule of law must be paid as a price for the building of a political united Europe.'[46] It then appealed to the Constitutional Court's own interests and mission:

If one exempts the EC legal order from all the obligations envisioned in Art. 19 §2 and Art. 79 §3 of the Basic Law, that would create a constitutional and juridical vacuum. In effect, constitutional law would be eliminated as a means to control supreme

---

[44] *Internationale Handelsgesellschaft mbH v. Einfuhr- und Vorratsstelle für Getreide und Futtermittel*, ECJ Case 11/70, [1970] ECR 1125. Quote from p. 1134.

[45] *Internationale Handelsgesellschaft mbH v. Einfuhr- und Vorratsstelle für Getreide und Futtermittel*, reference to the BVerfG by the VWG Frankfurt 14 July 1971, [1971] 11 AWD 541. My translation from AWD, p. 542.

[46] Ibid. 542.

national bodies, in exchange for an ever-expanding EEC legislation without equivalent guarantees of basic rights.[47]

The administrative court exhorted the Constitutional Court to find that ECJ decisions are only binding in their interpretations of European law, and that the ECJ cannot decide on the compatibility of European law with national law.

The BVerfG could have relied on its 1967 jurisprudence, reasserting its incompetence to assess the validity of acts not emanating from German authorities and by extension asserting the administrative court's incompetence (Ehlermann 1975; Riegel 1974).[48] But the majority of the second senate wanted to enter the debate. It used the administrative court of Frankfurt's reference as an opportunity to assert its own authority to find European law and ECJ decisions inapplicable in Germany. The BVerfG's *Solange I* decision was very controversial, and three judges wrote a highly critical dissenting opinion in the case.[49]

While the BVerfG maintained that it was not reversing its previous jurisprudence, for all practical purposes the majority repudiated the first senate's 1967 decision. In 1967 the BVerfG had argued that being 'autonomous and independent', EC acts 'neither [have] to be approved ('ratified') by the member states nor can they be annulled by them'. At the time, it refused the idea that European regulations could be seen as acts of German authorities, arguing:

if one wanted to see as an act of German public authorities every type of supranational or international public authority which . . . involved the Federal Republic of Germany, then the current decision's decisive difference between 'German' and 'non-German' public authorities would be lost . . . for no supra or international authority can take any action without some involvement of the German state's power.[50]

In 1974, the BVerfG argued: 'if a Community regulation is implemented by an administrative authority of the Federal Republic of Germany or dealt with by a court in the Federal Republic of Germany, then this is an exercise of

    [47] Ibid. 543.
    [48] BVerfG decision 1 BvR 248/63 of 18 Oct. 1967, [1968] 1 EuR 134, [1967] 12 AWD 477.
    [49] *Internationale HandelsgesellschaftmbH v. Einfuhr- und Vorratsstelle für Getreide und Futtermittel, 'Solange I'*, BVerfG decision 2 BvL 52/71of 29 May 1976, 37 BVerfGE 271, [1974] 2 CMLR 540.
    [50] BVerfG decision of 18 Oct. 1967, First Senate, [1967] 12 AWD 477, [1968] 1 EuR 134. My translation from EuR, p. 136.

German state power.'[51] By this logic virtually any European act could be seen as act of German authority.

The BVerfG admitted that the ECJ was the sole court with the authority to find a European law to be 'invalid', but gave itself the authority to find a European act 'inapplicable' in Germany.[52] German legal scholar Reinhard Riegel argued that this distinction between 'invalidating' law and finding it 'inapplicable' was a mere euphemism (Riegel 1976: 360). The dissenting judges also found the distinction dubious, arguing that:

this distinction between invalidity and inapplicability of a norm exhausts itself in the use of different words. If a court declares a legal norm generally inapplicable because of a violation of superior law, it is thereby stating, on a commonsense view, that the norm does not apply, that is, that it is invalid.[53]

The minority of the BVerfG, and for a number of scholars, the *Solange I* decision was mainly a power grab by the BVerfG. In the dissenting opinion, the BVerfG judges argued:

The Bundesverfassungsgericht possesses no jurisdiction to examine rules of Community law against the criteria of the Constitution . . . The fact that the majority of the Court nonetheless claims this power is an inadmissible trespass on the jurisdiction reserved to the European Court . . .[54]

French legal scholars Jean Darras and Olivier Pirotte reached a similar conclusion. They argued that the decision had 'as [its] underlying motivation a defensive reflex against a power which pretends to exclude [its] control and which puts in check the hierarchy of internal rules for which [the German Court is] the supreme guardian' (Darras and Pirotte 1976: 420).

The ECJ's *Internationale Handelsgesellschaft* had gone too far when it asserted the supremacy of European law over national constitutions. This decision stepped onto the Constitutional Court's own jurisdictional turf. *Solange I* was designed to let the ECJ know that the BVerfG would not see its authority subjugated. The BVerfG stated this point clearly:

Only the Bundesverfassungsgericht is entitled, within the framework of the powers granted to it in the Constitution, to protect fundamental rights guaranteed in the Constitution. No other court can deprive it of this duty imposed by constitutional law.[55]

---

[51] *Internationale Handelsgesellschaft mbH v. Einfuhr- und Vorratsstelle für Getreide und Futtermittel*, '*Solange I*' BVerfG decision 2 BvL 52/71of 29 May 1976, 37 BverfGE 271, [1974] 2 CMLR 540. Quote from p. 552

[52] Ibid. *Solange I* decision (1974). Quote from p. 552.

[53] Ibid. 565.

[54] Ibid. 564–5, and 567.

[55] Ibid. 552.

The silver lining in the *Solange I* decision was that basic rights challenges to European law had to first be sent to the ECJ before being appealed to the BVerfG. This gave the ECJ an opportunity to try to avoid a conflict. It also lessened the likelihood that plaintiffs would be able to use the EC legal system to circumvent BVerfG jurisprudence since the BVerfG got the last word.

The legal press was overwhelmingly critical of the *Solange I* decision, finding significant flaws in its legal reasoning and seeing the BVerfG's assertion of an authority to review European law as an explicit threat to the EC legal system (Cohen-Jonathan 1975; Hilf 1975; Ipsen 1975; Soulas de Russel and Engels 1975). The European Commission also took this view, arguing the decision 'sets the founding principle of the treaty in play . . . Through it, a legal fragmenting in the Community could be introduced. The decision of the Second Senate represents an invalid intrusion into the European Court's exclusively reserved competences.'[56]

The most contested part of the decision—and the clause that gave the decision its well-known name—was the statement that the Constitutional Court would exercise its authority to review the 'applicability' of European law only:

As long as [*Solange*] the integration process has not progressed so far that Community law also receives a catalogue of fundamental rights decided on by a parliament of settled validity, which is adequate in comparison to the catalogue of fundamental rights contained in the Constitution.[57]

Critics used this 'as long as' statement to argue that the Court's goals were not the noble protection of basic rights. If the BVerfG cared only about violations of basic rights, why should the Constitutional Court only want to consider such violations in 'the current stage' of EC development? They argued that it is not necessary to have a catalogue of rights that resembles the German one to have basic rights protection, and that having such a catalogue and having the catalogue decided on by a democratically elected and politically powerful parliament in no way ensures the greater respect of basic rights (Cohen-Jonathan 1975: 205; Zuleeg 1975: 46). They found the BVerfG's criteria for ensuring basic rights onerous and, given the political climate, unfeasible, and they questioned whether the BVerfG had set the conditions high so as to make them unachievable.

---

[56] The Commission articulated this view in a letter to German Foreign Minister Hans Dietrich Genscher. Discussed in: Die Kommission kritisiert das Bundesverfassungsgericht FAZ 21 December 1974. My translation.

[57] '*Solange I*' BVerfG decision 2 BvR 52/71of 29 May 1976, 37 BVerfGE 271, [1974] 2 CMLR 540. Dissenting Opinion, [1974] 2 CMLR 569. Quote from p. 551.

Many legal articles openly called for a reversal of the decision, either by a plenary session of the BVerfG's two senates or by a decision of the first senate. A pro-integration lawyer even created a case that he submitted to the first senate in hopes it would enter into the debate (Meier 1975: 168). There were also political attacks against the decision. The European Parliament condemned the ruling. The Commission attacked the decision in a press conference and threatened to bring Article 169 infringement proceedings against the German government.[58] In exchange for dropping the Article 169 case, the German government promised to work to ensure that the BVerfG did not carry out its threat to find a European law 'invalid' in Germany.[59] The German Minister of Justice conveyed to the President of the Constitutional Court that the BVerfG's jurisprudence was undermining German participation in the EC by calling into question whether or not Germany would follow through in applying European law. The Ministry of Economics monitored the issue of European law and basic rights, participating more actively in basic rights cases in front of the ECJ and following cases involving basic rights within the German legal system. It went so far as to buy off a plaintiff in a case to ensure that the BVerfG did not find a European law inapplicable.[60] But the Constitutional Court did not back down, at least not immediately.

Pro-integration advocates had been concerned that the Frankfurt Administrative court's refusal of an ECJ decision would set a bad precedent. They had argued:

If this practice became a model, it could take away all practical significance of European Court preliminary ruling decisions. Such a practice would ineluctably degrade a preliminary ruling decision of the Court of Justice to a mere consultative opinion that the national judge could if it wanted not respect. (Bebr 1973: 99)[61]

The *Solange I* decision opened up the possibility that ECJ decisions could be inapplicable if they were unconstitutional. Some lower German courts worked with the ECJ to develop its basic rights jurisprudence further in order to promote legal integration, and the ECJ embraced the issue of basic rights with new enthusiasm. A few German courts, however, continued to try to

---

[58] Brüssel kritisiert Verfassungsgericht. Handelsblatt, 23 Dec. 1974. Brüssel pocht auf Vorrang für EG-Recht, *Die Welt*, 23 Dec. 1974. Die Kommission kritisiert das Bundesverfassungsgericht. *Frankfurter Allgemeine Zeitung*, 21 Dec. 1974.

[59] Based on interviews with current and former officials at the German Ministry of Justice and the German Ministry of Economics, Bonn, 11 May 1993, 6 Dec. 1993, and 17 Feb. 1994.

[60] Ibid.

[61] This view was also voiced in a memo prepared by the Legal Services of the Council, JUR/3095/71-F, 9 Dec. 1971.

provoke the BVerfG to undermine ECJ rulings, essentially playing the BVerfG and the ECJ off against each other, in order to get the courts to contradict each other and say what they wanted to hear.[62]

Overall, however, the constitutional challenges to European law which continued in the late 1970s and early 1980s were not as numerous as one might have expected, nor were they the type of case which would allow the BVerfG to influence important policy or constitutional issues in European integration. The *Solange I* decision had accomplished the BVerfG's goals. It had reasserted the BVerfG's ultimate authority and extended its influence in the process of European integration. It had catalysed politicians and the ECJ to take basic rights more seriously and pushed the German government to advocate harder for a democratically elected parliament. Combing through European policy and finding specific regulations to be unconstitutional would not influence policy-making more broadly.

In 1977 the administrative court in Frankfurt sent another reference to the BVerfG challenging the validity of an ECJ decision.[63] The Constitutional Court refused the admissibility of this case for a procedural reason, but it used the opportunity to signal its willingness to revise the most controversial aspects of its earlier *Solange I* jurisprudence.[64] It suggested that 'in view of political and legal developments in the European sphere occurring in the meantime', its *Solange* decision might no longer apply to regulations and directives. The friendlier stance taken by the BVerfG in this decision led academic commentators to call it the '*Vielleicht*' ('Perhaps') decision. The softening of the BVerfG's *Solange* position was further evidenced in the *Eurocontrol* decision where the BVerfG implied that a catalogue of basic rights

---

[62] e.g. in 1979 an administrative court in Neustadt challenged the constitutional validity of an European regulation. The case involved a plaintiff who was refused a licence to grow grapes and thereby did not qualify for subsidies. The administrative court first referred the issue to the ECJ, but the VWG made it clear that the reference was only made as a necessary step in bringing the case to the BVerfG. The case went to the BVerfG on 31 Jan. 1980, and languished on the BVerfG's docket until June 1982, at which point the plaintiff received the subsidies from the Land government and dropped the case. (Based on interviews with German government officials, Bonn, 11 May and 6 Dec. 1993, 17 Feb. 1994.) *Hauer (Liselotte) v. Land Rheinland-Pfalz* (GR79-II.0749 SV79-621 FI79-621), ECJ Case 44/79, [1979] ECR 3727. VW Neustadt/Weinstraße K 205/76 decision of 31 Jan. 1980, [1980] 4 EuR 360.

[63] The VWG was challenging an ECJ decision that found Article 92 EEC not to create direct effects, so that the administrative court could not hear challenges to national law based on that Treaty article. VW Frankfurt decision I/1-E 331/74 of 28 July 1977, [1977] RIW 715.

[64] It dismissed the claim by arguing that the VWG Frankfurt was challenging an ECJ interpretation of 'primary' European law (Treaty law) but not challenging the constitutionality of the EC Treaty. *Steinike und Weinling v. Bundesamt für Ernährung und Forstwirtschaft 'Vielleicht'* decision. BVerfG decision 2 BvL 6/77 of 25 July 1979, [1980] 2 CMLR 531.

and a democratic parliament may no longer be necessary, as long as there is an adequate system in place to protect basic rights.[65] The *Eurocontrol* case did not deal with any aspect of European law, but it implied that European legal protections might be sufficient to relieve the BVerfG's constitutional concerns over basic rights protections.

Meanwhile more German courts were challenging the validity of ECJ jurisprudence and trying to find new constitutional limits to ECJ jurisprudence (these challenges will be dealt with in the discussion of 'Round 4'). The Constitutional Court had little institutional interest in hearing these complaints regarding substantive questions about European rules, nor did it have an interest in encouraging judicial mutiny to ECJ authority. The Constitutional Court took advantage of a provocative and annoying constitutional complaint to discourage national courts and individuals from using the German constitutional system to attack unwanted ECJ jurisprudence.

The plaintiff in what came to be known as the *Solange II* case was challenging a Commission decision regarding the saturation of the EC preserved-mushroom market. The ECJ sided with the Commission, as did the administrative court of Frankfurt and the Federal Administrative Court. The plaintiff appealed these decisions to the BVerfG, asking it to order a new reference to the ECJ and to find the ECJ decision to be unconstitutional, because 'incorrect' or 'unclear' ECJ rulings cannot be binding.

The plaintiff's case was extremely weak, and was exactly the type of case that the Constitutional Court wished to avoid. The dispute came down to a factual disagreement between the Commission and an importer. The Federal government, the Federal Supreme Court, and the Federal Social Court all submitted arguments for the BVerfG to consider. The Federal government, now watchful of BVerfG cases involving basic rights, argued against the factual merits of the case. The Federal Social Court and the Federal Supreme Court were most concerned that the case might establish a precedent of individuals using constitutional complaints to reopen factual interpretations of the ECJ and, by extension, their own factual interpretations and their own application of ECJ decisions.

It was not in the interest of the BVerfG to open up factual disputes or to make itself available as an appeals tribunal for Commission and ECJ decisions. The Federal Constitutional Court also did not like the plaintiff's claim that if one deemed an ECJ decision 'incorrect', the decision was not binding.

---

[65] '*Eurocontrol*' *Internationale Zustundigkeit der belgischen Gerichte fur Gebuhrenforderungen von Eurocontrol*, BVerfG decision 2 BvR 1107, 112/77 and 195/79 of 23 July 1981, 58 BVerfGE 1.

Such a principle is not in the interest of any judicial body because it legit-
imizes the idea that one can second-guess and even ignore a court's decisions.
In *Solange II*, it qualified its demands for a catalogue of human rights adopted
by a democratic parliament with real powers while sending a message to
plaintiffs to stop using the German constitutional system to challenge
European laws and ECJ interpretations. The Constitutional Court declared:

> In view of [the democratic and basic rights developments in the EC] it must be held
> that, so long as the European Communities generally ensure an effective protection
> of fundamental rights . . . the Federal Constitutional Court will no longer exercise its
> jurisdiction to decide on the applicability of secondary Community legislation . . . and
> it will no longer review such legislation by the standard of the fundamental rights con-
> tained in the Constitution; references to the Court under Article 100 (1) for that pur-
> pose are therefore inadmissible.[66]

This statement was seen as ending the conflict between the ECJ and the
Constitutional Court regarding the issue of basic rights protection in the
ECJ.

Most observers interpreted the *Solange II* judgment as a victory for the ECJ
because the Constitutional Court acknowledged the ECJ's efforts to protect
basic rights and said it would no longer review the compatibility of European
law with the German constitution. But I would argue that the entire *Solange
I–Solange II* interaction was a victory for the Constitutional Court. The
Solange II decision left the new powers asserted by the Constitutional Court
in the *Solange I* decision fully intact. Furthermore, in the *Solange II* decision,
the BVerfG abandoned all pretence that the EC was a 'special' international
institution, and that the special nature of the Treaty of Rome established the
supremacy of European law in the national legal order. The decision made it
clear that European law only gained internal validity and internal primacy
because of Article 24 of the German constitution that reinforced the
BVerfG's claim that the constitution was supreme to European law and thus
reinforced its own authority to review the compatibility of European law
with the German constitution.[67] And the BVerfG's substantively meaningless
distinction between finding a European law 'inapplicable' and finding a
European law to be 'invalid' became accepted. In other words, the
Constitutional Court prevailed it its attempt to create a legal-institutional
basis for it to influence the development of European law.

---

[66] *Solange II* decision: *Wünsche Handelsgesellschaft*, BVerfG decision of 22 Oct. 1986, 2 BvR
197/83, [1987] 3 CMLR 225. Quote from p. 265.
[67] Ibid. 256–7.

The *Solange I* debate marked the beginning of a more confrontational relationship between national courts and the ECJ. Many aspects of ECJ jurisprudence were controversial in the 1960s and 1970s, but before the *Solange I* decision the ECJ and national courts had taken pains to avoid open confrontation and contradiction. To challenge ECJ jurisprudence, it was felt, would undermine the fragile authority of the ECJ and detract from the goal of creating a uniform interpretation of European law. It would create a war of courts, which would undermine faith in the legal process. *Solange I* broke the taboo against openly challenging ECJ jurisprudence and legitimated lower court challenges to ECJ authority. It also showed that by disagreeing with the ECJ, national courts could influence its jurisprudence. Whereas in the 1970s it was feared that disagreement between national courts and the ECJ could have 'disastrous effects', by the 1980s there was a perception that a little disagreement between national courts and the ECJ was healthy, part of a maturing legal process where national courts and the ECJ were relative equals.

Solange I had provided a carrot along with the stick. The stick was the refusal to accept the supremacy of European law over the constitution and the threat to find European law inapplicable in Germany. The carrot was that the German Constitutional Court might relinquish its threat if the ECJ showed that it respected basic rights, and if the EC made general progress towards greater democracy. The *Solange II* decision rewarded the EC and the ECJ with the carrot it had promised. But as the next round shows, other German courts were less encouraging of the ECJ, and learned from the BVerfG's strategy that a stick was an appropriate tool to use if they disagreed and wanted to influence the ECJ.

In the end, the Constitutional Court's provocation in the *Solange I* decision contributed significantly to legal integration both in Germany and at the EC level. In requiring national courts to first send challenges to the validity of European law to the ECJ, the Constitutional Court stopped the earlier practice of the administrative court of Frankfurt of ruling autonomously on the validity of European law. While few admitted it at the time, since many German scholars felt that the ECJ's supremacy doctrine and basic rights jurisprudence rested on weak foundations, respect for European law was actually strengthened by having the BVerfG assert the final authority in assuring a constitutionally correct application of European law.[68] The

---

[68] Two German scholars envisioned that the BVerfG's decision would have salutary effects (Rupp 1974; Scheuner 1975), but they were in the minority.

Solange I decision motivated the German government and EC institutions to work harder to ensure the protection of basic rights at the EC level,[69] and made it acceptable for the ECJ further to 'constitutionalize' the EC Treaty by developing for it a bill of rights (Mancini and Keeling 1992). The ECJ's basic rights jurisprudence is now offered as evidence that the ECJ is the supreme *constitutional* court of the EC.

Round 4. The warming trend continues: creating a constitutional sanction for national courts which refuse ECJ authority, 1981–1987

As the BVerfG was resolving its *Solange* dispute with the ECJ, other German (and French) courts were openly challenging aspects of ECJ jurisprudence with which they disagreed. To quell these challenges, the BVerfG created a constitutional sanction for national courts that disobey an ECJ decision. The BVerfG's *Kloppenberg* decision made the German system the only system constitutionally to oblige national courts to respect the ECJ, and for this reason the exchange over the direct effect of directives is seen as part of the larger warming trend in the BVerfG's European law jurisprudence. But while the decision was more generous towards the ECJ than most national high courts were willing to be, the BVerfG was careful not to hand the ECJ a blank cheque.

The substance of the dispute concerned the ECJ's declaration in its 1974 *Van Duyn* decision that directives can, in certain limited circumstances, create direct effects.[70] The Treaty of Rome clearly states that regulations are 'directly applicable', while directives are 'binding in their end to be achieved' and thus have to be transposed by national parliaments into national law to gain legal effect. The less binding nature of directives was intended to give national authorities discretion in how they achieved the goals of a directive, ensuring significant national control in policy areas regulated by directives. Critics of the *Van Duyn* jurisprudence argued that it turned a directive into a regulation, encroaching on member states' authority to decide how the goals

---

[69] In light of the German Constitutional Court's decision, the European Parliament passed a resolution that reaffirmed the supremacy of Community law and the protection of basic rights (OJ No C 159/13).

[70] Directives only create direct effects after the specified period for their formal adoption had expired, after which it had to be determined case by case based on the clearness of the directive, if a given provision of a directive created direct effects. The first decision on this issue was based on a reference by a German tax court. *Grad v. Finanzamt Traustein*, ECJ Case 9/70, [1970] ECR 838. The jurisprudence was expanded and better justified in *Van Duyn v. Home Office*, Case 41/74, [1974] ECR 1337.

of the directive are achieved. Among the critics were administrative agencies and parliamentary bodies who were also upset that directives had become increasingly specific, leaving them little discretion. The executive branch did not support this grumbling. Indeed, it was the executive branch that had negotiated the detailed directives in the first place, seeking to limit the possibility of member states cheating on their obligations.

The European Court's jurisprudence on the direct effect of directives also affected national court authority. If directives gained legal force by virtue of their implementation by national parliaments, directives were national law, and thus part of the exclusive interpretive domain of national courts. If directives created direct effects, however, the ECJ would be the supreme authority in interpreting areas of European law governed by directives. This was a special concern for the fifth senate of the Federal Tax Court, which feared it would lose its independence and authority regarding value added taxes (VAT).

The French *Conseil d'État* was the first court openly to defy the ECJ's doctrine on the direct effect of directives (see Chapter 4 for more on the *Cohn-Bendit* decision).[71] In 1981 the Federal Tax Court followed suit, quashing a reference made by a lower tax court to the ECJ because directives could not be used to challenge national policy. It noted its agreement with the *Conseil d'État*'s *Cohn-Bendit* decision and declared that the ECJ's *Van Duyn* jurisprudence was not binding on member states or national courts.[72]

The Federal Tax Court was able to quash the lower court's reference because the decision to refer the case to the ECJ had been appealed by the tax authorities to the Federal Tax Court. But a similar case from the tax court in Munich had already been sent to the ECJ (*Becker*) because the decision to refer the case was not appealed.[73] Certainly, the Federal Tax Court knew of this case and was trying to influence the ECJ's jurisprudence in *Becker* through its 1981 decision (Stein 1986: 729). Undeterred by the *Conseil d'État*'s or the Federal Tax Court's defiance, the ECJ granted direct effects to the directive in the *Becker* case, creating a counter-precedent in Germany to that of the Federal Tax Court.

Thus lower tax courts had a choice. They could either follow the Federal Tax Court's jurisprudence and rely only on German law in tax disputes, or

---

[71] '*Cohn-Bendit*', *Minister of Interior v. Daniel Cohn-Bendit. Conseil d'État* decision of 22 Dec. 1978, [1978] Recueil Lebon 524, [1980] 1 CMLR 545. See further Ch. 4 below.

[72] *Re: Value Added Tax Directives* BFH decision (Case V B 51/80) of 16 July 1981, [1982] I CMLR 527.

[73] *Becker v. Finanzamt Münster-Innenstadt*, ECJ 8/81, [1982] ECR 53.

they could follow the ECJ's jurisprudence and rely on the EC directive. Most lower tax courts followed the ECJ's jurisprudence. Furthermore, lower tax courts deliberately sent the ECJ cases dealing with directives to allow the ECJ to develop its jurisprudence on the issue further.[74] The Federal Administrative Court also disagreed with the Federal Tax Court, for reasons of legal argumentation. It sent a reference involving the direct effect of directives to the ECJ, making an argument in the reference that clearly ran counter to that of the Federal Tax Court.[75]

The Federal Administrative Court's reference to the ECJ was pending when in 1985 the Federal Tax Court got another opportunity to review a case where a plaintiff was basing its claim on an EC directive. This time, the Federal Tax Court was not reviewing the decision to make a reference to the ECJ, but rather was reviewing a lower court ruling applying an ECJ preliminary ruling judgment. In the *Kloppenburg* proceedings, the plaintiff argued that in anticipation of the timely adoption of the EC directive, she had not passed on value-added tax to her customers and therefore should not be liable for the tax. The government argued that the plaintiff had not been following the EC directive and had in fact collected the VAT, which the government was now demanding. The Federal Tax Court could have used the government's argument as a basis to overturn the lower court's decision, without raising the issue of the direct effect of the directives. But instead, the fifth senate of the Federal Tax Court took the opportunity presented by the case to reassert and better support its earlier jurisprudence refusing the direct effect of directives.

The Federal Tax Court's decision was the first national court ruling directly and openly to reject an ECJ decision in the very case it was reviewing.[76] It intentionally relied on national law and national legal texts only, so that it was not obliged to make a reference to the ECJ and so that the ECJ's legal decision in the case, and its general jurisprudence, would not apply.

The Federal Tax Court argued that there was no German statute giving directives direct effects so that 'the individual has no claims against the State if it has not fulfilled' its obligations under the directive. According to the

---

[74] In interviews, lower tax court judges acknowledged that they looked for cases to send to the ECJ in order to challenge the BFH jurisprudence with which they disagreed (27 Jan. 1994, 22 Feb 1994). Examples of references regarding the direct effect of directives included: FG Munster decision of 24 May 1984, [1985] EFG 310. FG Niedersachsen decision of 9 Feb. 1984. [1984] EFG 527.

[75] BVerwG decision to make a reference for a preliminary ruling, 24 May 1984, [1985] 31 AWD (2) 143.

[76] 'Kloppenburg', *Frau Kloppenburg v. Finanzamt Leer* BFH decision II V R 123/84 of 25 Apr. 1985, [1989] 1 CMLR 873.

Federal Tax Court the ECJ's decision was not binding because preliminary ruling decisions can only interpret community law. The ECJ did not have the jurisdictional authority 'to create rules having force within the national sphere'; instead the national court 'has to decide in the context of interpreting the [national] EEC membership act whether the legal instruments of institutions of the European Community take effect within the national jurisdiction'.[77] Focusing on the text of the German Ratification Act, the Federal Tax Court conducted its own interpretive review of the meaning of Article 189 EEC. It examined how the article had been discussed in the German parliamentary ratification debates and concluded that directives did not create direct effects, and that agreeing to use directives in the area of turnover taxes was not intended to mean that member states were transferring the national legislative jurisdiction to the EC level.

The Federal Tax Court's legal approach was radical and potentially very powerful. The Federal Tax Court was claiming for itself the so-called *Kompetenz-Kompetenz*, the power to determine the limits of the Community's jurisdiction. It wanted to exercise this power by relying on the original intent of the founding member states. If national courts could interpret the EC Treaties themselves (based on the ratification texts), and directives did not create direct effects, the ECJ would really only have supreme authority over European regulations. In addition, using the Federal Tax Court's method of analysis could well lead to the conclusion that much of the ECJ's jurisprudence, including its jurisprudence on the direct effect and supremacy of European law, was not applicable in the national sphere! In 1967 the Federal Tax Court had argued that the transfer of powers to the EEC via Article 24 should not be subject to the same 'strict standards' that traditionally apply to German institutions (Betten and van Thiel 1986: 25). Why was the Federal Tax Court now advocating a very narrow and strict interpretation of the Article 24 transfer of sovereignty in this case?

Some have explained the Federal Tax Court's strong reaction by saying that the legal foundations of the ECJ's doctrine on direct effects were especially weak (Friedrich 1985; Hilf 1988; Stein 1986). But the ECJ's *Van Duyn* doctrine is no more of an interpretive leap than many other ECJ doctrinal developments, and it is far less bold than the ECJ's assertion of European law supremacy. The main reason this doctrine became legally controversial was because national courts had actually taken a stand against the ECJ's judge-made law.

---

[77] '*Kloppenburg*', *Frau Kloppenburg v. Finanzamt Leer*, BFH decision II V R 123/84 of 25 Apr. 1985, [1989] 1 CMLR 878. Quote p. 879.

Most of the interaction between the ECJ and the Federal Tax Court had been with the seventh senate of the Federal Tax Court, which was in charge of customs issues. The fifth senate had seen the seventh senate's authority diminished and feared that its own supreme authority over Value Added Tax (VAT) issues was going to be undermined next. Since all tax-related European legislation has to be adopted in the form of directives, the Federal Tax Court focused primarily on ruling that directives could not create direct effects in any circumstance. The fifth senate's interest in this outcome was clear. If individuals could draw directly on tax directives, then the European Court would become the highest court on issues of VAT. As lower court tax judge Voss observed:

The logical continuation of [the ECJ's] case law will have the result that in the field of harmonized taxes the Court of Justice will have to take over the role of the national tax courts. Considering the advanced level of harmonization of the value added tax, this might have the consequence for the Federal Republic of Germany that the Chamber of the Bundesfinanzhof, that is the five judges who are in charge of VAT jurisdiction, would hardly be needed any more. (Voss 1987: 65)

It is one thing to criticize the legal reasoning of the ECJ's jurisprudence, but quite another to reject an ECJ decision. In overturning a lower court ruling based directly on an ECJ decision, the Federal Tax Court crossed the limits of acceptability. It went where the BVerfG only threatened to go. The Commission considered the Federal Tax Court's action to be very serious, and it contemplated bringing an infringement suit against the German government. But since the plaintiff had appealed the decision to the German Constitutional Court, the Commission decided to wait. While the case was pending in front of the Constitutional Court, the Federal Administrative Court issued its decision based on the reference it had made to the ECJ in 1984. Not sharing the Federal Tax Court's concern about directives (since it usually dealt with European regulations), the Federal Administrative Court agreed with the ECJ's jurisprudence on the direct effect of directives. It argued that to apply national legislation in the face of a clear European legal obligation violated the principle of 'good faith'.[78]

The Constitutional Court's decision, issued just six months after the *Solange II* decision, strongly rebuked the Federal Tax Court for challenging the authority of the ECJ.[79] It declared that the ECJ had the power of final

[78] *Denkavit Futtermittel GmbH gegen Land Nordrhein-Westfalen*, BVerwG decision BVerwG 3 C 12.82 of 5 June 1986, [1986] 4 EuR 372.

[79] *Kloppenburg* decision, BVerfG decision, 2 BvR 687/85 of 8 Apr. 1987, BVerfGE 75, [1988] 3 CMLR 1.

decision with respect to secondary Community law. The most the national court could do was make a second reference to the ECJ if it disagreed with the ECJ's ruling in the case. The BVerfG found that by refusing to follow the ECJ's decision in the preliminary ruling, and refusing to make a new reference to the ECJ, the Federal Tax Court had acted arbitrarily and denied the plaintiff her constitutional right to a legal judge. Finding a national court in violation of the constitution is about the highest sanction the Constitutional Court can apply and, as a sanction, it stings.[80]

This decision created a constitutional censure for judges who refused the ECJ's authority by either withholding a reference to the ECJ or rejecting an ECJ decision. But the threshold to sanction a national court is high. It is not enough to question the national court's decision; one must prove that the national court acted 'arbitrarily'. Other cases where the Federal Tax Court has refused to make a reference to the ECJ have been appealed to the Constitutional Court, languishing on its docket for years (recall that the BVerfG does not have to hear individual appeals).[81] The main influence of the BVerfG's *Kloppenburg* ruling is that now no German high court will reverse or refuse to apply an ECJ preliminary ruling decision directly. Lower courts can go to the ECJ when they disagree with a higher court's decision, knowing that if they are applying an ECJ decision, they will not be overturned on appeal.

Taking advantage of this situation almost immediately, a lower tax court in Düsseldorf referred to the ECJ a case where its ruling had twice been quashed by the Federal Tax Court. The lower court found that it did not have to follow a Federal Tax Court interpretation when the ECJ made a different interpretation of the same law.[82]

Why did the Constitutional Court take the side of the ECJ in this dispute? It has been argued that the Constitutional Court was in a more ECJ-friendly mode under the tutelage of Constitutional Court judge Steinburger, who as an international law specialist 'understood' European law. But 'understanding' ECJ jurisprudence had nothing to do with it. The BVerfG had no direct interest at stake in the debate over directives, so it was willing to accept the ECJ's *Van Duyn* jurisprudence. While Steinburger may have been somewhat more Euro-friendly than previously BVerfG judges, neither the BVerfG's

---

[80] Ibid.

[81] Based on an interview with a German lawyer who had appealed a few cases where the national court refused to make a reference to the ECJ, 10 Jan. 1994, Cologne.

[82] FG Düsseldorf decision of 6 Sept. 1989, [1990] RIW 230.

decision on the direct effect of directives nor the *Solange II* decision qualified the Constitutional Court's position on the ultimate supremacy of the constitution and the ultimate authority of the BVerfG to determine the limits of European law in the national realm.

The BVerfG's decision contributed directly to European legal integration and the supremacy of European law. It put an end to challenges to the ECJ's jurisprudence on the direct effect of directives. More importantly, by rejecting the Federal Tax Court's attempt to interpret the German ratification texts, and by declaring that national courts are bound by ECJ interpretations of European law, it essentially obliged the courts below it to follow the substantive interpretations of the ECJ. Meanwhile, it reserved for itself the exclusive authority to find limits to the reach of European law based on constitutional provisions. While the BVerfG accepted the ECJ's 'development of the law' regarding the direct effect of directives, it was clear that the ECJ's power to develop the law had limits. In its *Kloppenburg* decision it argued:

The community has not been given adjudicative power by the EEC Treaty to extend its jurisdiction limitlessly. The Community is not a sovereign State within the meaning of international law, which would have authority to resolve conflicts concerning responsibilities for internal matters. Neither the territorial sovereignty nor the personal jurisdiction of Member-States has been transferred to the Community; its external powers cover limited fields even though they may not be restricted by the principle of special authorization as they are in relation to other Treaty objectives. In the framework of the general law of international treaties, the Member-States are now, and always have been, the masters of the Community treaties . . .[83]

Thus even in this friendly decision made with the presence of a friendly judge, the consistent position of the BVerfG was affirmed. As far as the BVerfG is concerned, EC law is international law. There are limits to the authority of the ECJ to expand its jurisdiction through interpretation. And member states are the masters of the treaty.

Round 5: Creating a role for the constitutional court in monitoring the expansion of European law

In its *Kloppenburg* ruling on the direct effect of directives, the BVerfG refused to allow the Federal Tax Court to use the ratification texts of the EC Treaties to find limits to European law's expansive reach. In its *Maastricht* decision, issued just 5 years later with four of the same judges from the *Kloppenburg* and

---

[83] 'Kloppenburg', *Frau Kloppenburg v. Finanzamt Leer*, BVerfG decision 2 BvR 687/85 of 8 Apr. 1987, BVerfGE 75, [1988] 3 CMLR 1. Quote p. 18.

Solange II decisions, the Constitutional Court claimed this power for itself.[84] The *Maastricht* ruling was the BVerfG's most defiant and critical commentary on the ECJ's international legal order. The *Maastricht* decision arose out of a constitutional complaint against the law ratifying the Maastricht Treaty on a European Union (TEU). The complainants, four members of the European Parliament from the Green party and a high-ranking civil servant of the European Commission, hired law professors to write the appeals. The court dismissed as inadmissible all of their arguments except the charge that the TEU so reduced the German parliament's legislative autonomy that it violated the claimant's constitutional right to vote for representatives governing the polity.[85] Some thought that even this complaint should have been ruled inadmissible.[86] But the Constitutional Court was not going to pass up a captive audience and an opportunity to review the Maastricht Treaty in detail. The German President refused to sign Germany's ratification law until the Constitutional Court decision had been rendered; thus ratification of the Maastricht Treaty became dependent on the BVerfG's decision.

The *Maastricht* decision's main message was to the Court of Justice. In *Kloppenburg* the BVerfG had allowed the ECJ to 'develop' the Treaty of Rome through legal interpretation. But in its *Maastricht* ruling, the BVerfG made it clear that it would not be so accommodating in the future. In a thinly veiled critique of the ECJ, the BVerfG fingered specific expansions of EC authority from the past that it felt had gone too far. While some of the expansions arguably came from political bodies, the ECJ had allowed these expansions.[87] If the ECJ would not constrain political bodies, the BVerfG made it clear that it would:

Whereas a dynamic extension of the existing Treaties has so far been supported . . . in future it will have to be noted as regards interpretation of enabling provisions by

[84] *Brunner and others v. The European Union Treaty*, '*Maastricht* decision' 2 BvR 2134/92 and 2 BvR 2159/92, [1994] CMLR 57.

[85] The charges that were inadmissible included: (1) that the Maastricht Treaty obliged Germany to proceed with integration even if later changed its mind (especially in terms of monetary integration); (2) that it was unconstitutional to turn over control of the currency; (3) that even a democratic EU could not fully protect the basic rights of Germany since only rules voted by Germans would serve to protect German rights; (4) that the Maastricht Treaty itself violates basic rights; (5) that the exclusion of the ECJ from the two pillars in the TEU created a lacunae in the protection of basic rights; and (6) that European integration is designed to eliminate the constitutional order of the Basic Law.

[86] See e.g. Streinz (1994).

[87] The BVerfG was critical of the Council's use of Article 235 EEC. As Joseph Weiler has argued, Article 235 has become an elastic clause that member states have used to justify EU level actions in areas unrelated to the common market (Weiler 1991: 2435–50).

Community institutions and agencies that the Union Treaty [creates] . . . interpretation may not have effects that are equivalent to an extension of the Treaty. Such an interpretation of enabling rules would not produce any binding effects for Germany.[88]

The BVerfG argued that the Act of Accession defines the limits of what has been agreed to by the German parliament.[89] Any European level decision or action exceeding the transfer of sovereignty agreed to in the Act of Accession would be considered an 'ausbrechender Rechtsakt' (ultra vires) and would be inapplicable in Germany.[90] As one commentator put it, 'in other words the Community legal order is subject to the approval of the Federal Constitutional Court' (Foster 1994: 404).

The *Maastricht* decision also seemingly reversed the Constitutional Court's *Solange II* position that it would not exercise its right to review whether or not European law violated German basic rights, as long as the ECJ was sufficiently protecting these rights.[91] In its *Maastricht* ruling, the BVerfG implied that any encroachment of international law of constitutional relevance 'will be subject to review in full by the German courts'.[92] If European law infringed on basic rights, it said, 'then the European Court or alternatively the Federal Constitutional Court would offer adequate protection of those rights. Here, too, the Constitutional Court and the European Court are in a relationship of co-operation for the guarantee of constitutional protections, under which they compliment each other.'[93]

The BVerfG's second message was to Germany's governing bodies. During the ratification process for the TEU, a new Article 23 was created for the German constitution, requiring a two-thirds vote from the parliament to transfer more sovereignty to the EC. This ensured that parliament (and the *Länder*) would be consulted and that the government would need the support of opposition parties to grant the EC new powers. This new article did not

[88] N. 84 above, *Maastricht* decision (1993), p. 105.

[89] This is the technique used by the BVerfG to interpret international treaties.

[90] The Constitutional Court argued: 'if European institutions or agencies were to treat or develop the Union Treaty in a way that was no longer covered by the Treaty in the form that is the basis for the Act of Accession, the resultant legislative instruments would not be legally binding within the sphere of German sovereignty. The German state organs would be prevented for constitutional reasons from applying them in Germany. Accordingly the Federal Constitutional Court will review legal instruments of European institutions and agencies to see whether they remain within the limits of the sovereign rights conferred on them or transgress them.' N. 84 above, *Maastricht* decision (1993), p. 89.

[91] As will be discussed, the BVerfG's third banana ruling has established that the *Solange II* doctrine has not in fact changed.

[92] N. 84 above, *Maastricht* decision (1993), p. 80.   [93] Ibid. 82.

convince the BVerfG that German democracy was protected. In interviews, members of the German Constitutional Court expressed concern that most politicians hardly understood the Maastricht Treaty and that they did not fully appreciate how much of their own authority they were giving away.[94] To keep the parliament from giving away too much German sovereignty, the BVerfG created a constitutional limit on the transfer of national political authority to the EC level based on the inviolability of German democracy. It developed a problematic and much criticized theory of the state and the people, identifying the German people as the true source of German sovereignty.[95] Germans, it argued, have a constitutional right to participate in their government, and thus the constitution mandates that national political authority can only be transferred when there is real democracy at the European level. Real European-level democracy requires certain 'pre-legal' social conditions to exist, including:

continuous free debate between opposing social forces, interests and ideas, in which political goals also become clarified and change course and out of which comes a public opinion which forms the beginning of political intentions [*politischen Willen*].[96]

Until the 'factual conditions' fulfilling the 'pre-legal conditions' are realized, democratic legitimization can only be maintained by giving national parliaments a substantial role in the integration process. The BVerfG's argument implied that if transferring legislative authority to the European level undermined the ability of the German people to articulate their political will through the legislative process, this transfer would be unconstitutional despite parliamentary assent. This theory lent a nationalist tone to the decision. Its ultimate affect was to install the BVerfG as the final protector of the *demos*, and the final arbiter of national sovereignty.[97]

The Constitutional Court's *Maastricht* decision created leverage the BVerfG could use to influence not only the ECJ but also the German and

[94] Interviews with the author of the *Maastricht* decision at the German Constitutional Court, and his law clerk, 8 Dec. 1993, Karlsruhe.

[95] N. 84 above, *Maastricht* decision (1993), p. 88.

[96] The BVerfG ruled: 'If the peoples of the individual States provide democratic legitimization through the agency of their national parliaments (as at present) limits are then set by virtue of the democratic principle to the extension of the European Communities' functions and powers. Each of the peoples to the individual States is the starting point for a state power relating to the people. The states need sufficiently important spheres of activity of their own in which the people can develop and articulate itself in a process of political will-formation which it legitimates and controls, in order thus to give legal expression to what binds the people together (to a greater or lesser degree of homogeneity) spiritually, socially and politically' (ibid. 87).

[97] For an excellent critique of this theory, see Weiler (1995).

European policy-making processes. Throughout its decision, the Constitutional Court signalled to German political organs, European institutions, and the German government which actions would be unconstitutional. To defend the charge that the TEU unacceptably transferred policy-making power from the German parliament to unaccountable European political institutions, the German government and the Commission had emphasized how real political power remained at the national level. The BVerfG documented these arguments in its decision; they would be the benchmark from which the ECJ's interpretation could not stray. In the end of the judgment, the Constitutional Court actually spelt out the role each political institution should play in ensuring that European integration remained constitutional and limited.[98] If the European Council, the German government, the *Bundestag*, or the *Bundesrat* do not exercise their legal obligations, constitutional challenges to European policy can be raised in front of the Constitutional Court.

The defiant language in the *Maastricht* ruling invited German litigants to use the German legal system to influence policy and politics. The Broadcasting Directive dispute and the banana dispute are direct results of this invitation. They show how the German judicial system has become part of the political game. In the Broadcasting Directive case (1995), the Bavarian government challenged the applicability of the EC Directive in Germany on the grounds that it encroached into the *Länder*'s legislative authority. The ECJ had yet to hear a challenge to the directive. Instead of pre-empting the European Court, the BVerfG declared that the extent of Germany's obligation under the directive was not clear enough to indicate whether the directive constituted a violation of the constitutional separation of powers.[99]

[98] The BVerfG argued: 'How far the subsidiarity principle will counteract an erosion of the jurisdictions of the member-states, and therefore an exhaustion of the functions of and powers of the Bundestag [these are code words meaning how long EC legislation remains constitutional], depends to an important extent (apart from the case law of the European Court relating to the subsidiarity principle) on the practice of the Council as the Community's real legislative body. It is there that the Federal Government has to assert its influence in favour of a strict treatment of Article 3b(2) of the EC Treaty and so fulfill the constitutional duty imposed on it by Article 23(1), first sentence, of the Constitution. The Bundestag for its part has the opportunity, by using the right of cooperation in the formation of Germany's internal political intentions established by Article 23(3) of the Constitution, to have an effect on the Council's practices and to exercise and influence on them within the terms of the subsidiarity principle. In so doing the Bundestag will also be performing a constitutional duty incumbent upon it under article 23(1), first sentence, of the Constitution. In addition, it is to be expected that the Bundesrat, too, will pay particular attention to the subsidiarity principle' (n. 84 above, *Maastricht* decision (1993), pp. 106–7).

[99] The 1995 decision was actually the second case on the issue. In the first BVerfG case, Bavarian officials tried to force the Federal government to vote against the EC's broadcasting

While the decision left the EC directive intact, it essentially voided the directive of having a legally binding effect within Germany.[100] In the text of the decision, the BVerfG also laid out exactly what the Federal Government had to do to avoid a negative decision in the future. The Federal Government must determine if the legislation is important for the communal interests of member states and if the Federal government can support the measure, and defend EC authority in front of the *Bundesrat*, giving the *Länder* the opportunity to offer legal opinion and to ensure no encroachment of *Länder* legislative authority occurs. The Federal government must then represent the *Bundesrat* opinion at the EC level, and if it is outvoted, it must do everything in its power to change or overturn the Council decision, if necessary bringing a case to the ECJ. The decision also made it clear to the ECJ that if the directive were to be found valid and legally binding, it would violate the separation of powers clause in the German constitution. Finally, the decision established consultative rights which the *Länder* could demand in future European policy-making, including the right to demand the German government challenge questionable European laws in front of the ECJ.

The Broadcasting Directive decision was seen as a peace offering to the ECJ because the BVerfG did not find the directive to be unconstitutional. How much peace the decision offered is questionable. The decision is remarkable for making the Government's actions in the Council a subject of constitutional review (Herdegen 1995). And the BVerfG's banana decisions, issued in the same year, show that the BVerfG was still quite willing to challenge European law and ECJ jurisprudence.

---

directive on the basis that it encroached on *Länder* prerogatives in the area of television and radio policy. At that time, the BVerfG refused to order the Federal government to vote against the directive, on the grounds that such a decision would undermine the bargaining leverage of the Federal government. Seemingly granting the government licence to give away *Länder* legislative authority, the BVerfG found that even if the German government failed to influence the EC not to legislate, it would have encroached on the authority of state governments, but it would nonetheless have used its freedom of manoeuvre to bring the final text as close as possible to the wishes of the *Länder* (this decision was issued in 1989, four years before the *Maastricht* decision). In negotiations on the broadcasting directive, the German government won concessions in the form of protocols attached to the directive. Protocols 4 and 5 declared that the directive was only binding in the end to be achieved, and Protocol 7 made the end of the directive relatively vague and unenforceable, implying that the goal was simply to achieve a higher audiovisual capacity in Europe 'with each member state working towards the goal within their constitutional capacities to do so'. (Directive 89/552 OJ L298/23) *Bayerische Staatsregierung v. Bundesregierung*, BVerfG decision 2 BvG 1/89 of 11 Apr. 1989, [1989] EuR 266, [1990] 1 CMLR 649.

[100] BVerfG decision 2 BvR 1/89 (re: Broadcasting Directive) of 22 Mar. 1995, [1995] EuR 104, [1995] EuGRZ 125, [1995] EuZW 77.

The banana conflict stemmed from a 1993 European regulation (404/93) which was designed to assist inefficient banana manufacturers in former European colonies—the so-called ACP (African–Caribbean–Pacific) countries—as part of a development arrangement agreed to in the Lomé conventions.[101] This regulation replaced the previous non-harmonized system under which a special protocol allowed Germany to import inexpensive Latin American bananas duty-free. The new regime hit German banana importers especially hard. They had few trade contacts with ACP banana exporters, and the Latin American bananas they had imported duty free were now subject to significant tariffs. Some importers also found that their past record in importing Latin American bananas did not situate them well when quotas for importing bananas at favorable rates were distributed.

The German government had opposed the regulation from the beginning. Taking on the role prescribed by the German Constitutional Court, it immediately challenged the regulation in front of the ECJ. In the first *Germany v. Council* case, the German government argued that the regulation violated importer's fundamental rights (the prohibition against discrimination, the individual's right to property, and the principle of proportionality); that the regulation was ultra vires in exceeding the EC's authority under the Common Agricultural Policy; and that it violated General Agreement on Tariff and Trade (GATT). The ECJ upheld the directive, saying that it did not violate basic rights and was not ultra vires.[102] The ECJ refused to review the compatibility of the regulation with the GATT, denying any internal legal effect for the GATT.[103]

This ECJ decision was strongly criticized in Germany, where its decision was taken by some as further evidence that the ECJ does not take rights seriously (Everling 1996). German importers challenged the regulation directly in front of the ECJ (under Article 173 EEC, now Article 230), asking for invalidation of the regulation, and later asking for individual relief. Their appeals were dismissed because the litigants could not show that the EC

---

[101]   Lomé Conventions: OJ 1976, L25/1; OJ 1980, L347/1; OJ 1986, L86/1; OJ 1991, L229/1.

[102]   The ECJ found that the right to property and the freedom to pursue a trade were not absolute rights: they could be restricted by rules of a 'general interest' so long as the rules did not constitute 'a disproportionate or intolerable interference, impairing the very substance of the rights guaranteed'. It also argued that importers could not claim a right 'to property in a market share'. It found that the regulation was allowable under the CAP, hence it was not ultra vires. *Germany v. Council*, ECJ C-280/93, [1994] ECR I-4973. See para. 78.

[103]   In a second case, the German government challenged the Commission's system for implementing the disputed regulation, but the ECJ dismissed this case on a technicality. Opinion 3/94, [1995] ECR I-4577.

regulation affected them differently from importers in a similar situation.[104] Importers also continued to challenge the regulation in German courts, raising the same legal arguments the German government had used, and demanding interim relief while the disputes were processed. The litigants and a number of German judges clearly gained strength from the BVerfG's *Maastricht* decision. They challenged ECJ precedent in the belief that, as per the *Maastricht* decision, they and the BVerfG could rule inapplicable any European law that violated the German constitution or exceeded European authority. The BVerfG stoked the flames in a number of rulings, keeping the pressure on the German government and the ECJ.

The German Constitutional Court's first ruling in a banana case (January 1995) was issued in response to an individual constitutional complaint against a German appeal court ruling that refused to grant interim relief from the EC's banana regulation.[105] T. Port believed that the quota allocated to him under the regulation was unfair and invalid. He claimed that applying the regulation would create irreparable harm to his business in violation of his right to property guaranteed by the German constitution. The appeal court had dismissed his application for interim relief because such a ruling would anticipate a finding from the European Court that his quota allocation was invalid. Given that the ECJ had already upheld the validity of the regulation in *Germany v. Council*, there was little reason to think that the regulation or the allocation of the quota was in fact invalid.

It was significant that the BVerfG decided to rule on the constitutional complaint; ruling on it implied that its *Solange II* decision had indeed been reversed. While the BVerfG refused to review the validity of the regulation itself at that time, it interpreted the regulation on its own and found that the regulation had provisions to allow for a transitory regime. It ordered the appeals court to consider whether the fact that the litigant was faced with bankruptcy constituted an irreparable infringement on his right to property, implying that interim relief was warranted. Some analysts saw this ruling as ordering the administrative court to provide relief that had no basis in

---

[104] In the words of the ECJ, from importers 'who fulfilled the same objective criteria defined by the regulation'. There were a number of cases raised by litigants from various countries. See e.g. *Leon van Parijs v. the Council*, ECJ Case 257/93, [1993] I ECR 3335, and *Chiquita Banana Company v. the Council*, ECJ Case 276/93, [1993] I ECR 3345. The ECJ dismissed the applications for interim relief on the grounds that the applicants were basically asking for suspension of key elements of the directive (on the basis that they were invalid). See e.g. *Leon van Parijs v. the Council*, ECJ Case 257/93, [1993] I ECR 3917.

[105] *Firma T. Port v. Hauptzollamt Hamburg-Jonas*, (*T. Port I*, Banana I) BVerfG decisions of 25 Jan. 1995, first chamber of the second senate, 2 BvR 2689/94 and 2 BvR 52/95, [1995] EuZW 126.

European law (Foubert 1996: 131). Significantly, the BVerfG relied on the German constitution to provide basic rights protection, rather than looking for an answer in the ECJ's jurisprudence on basic rights or on interim relief.

This ruling, issued by a three-judge chamber and not by the full senate, was criticized because it refused to defer to the ECJ's authority, and did not specify any limits regarding when the BVerfG would interpret European law or conduct a constitutional review of European law. By insisting that national courts had to protect the basic rights of individuals, the BVerfG also implied that this obligation took precedence over complying with an ECJ decision (Pache 1995).

The appeals court did indeed grant temporary relief, but it stipulated that the increased quota allocation would be subtracted from future quotas should the regulation's application be upheld by the ECJ.[106] It also referred the issue to the ECJ, asking whether or not the EC's banana regulation allowed for interim relief, and under what conditions a national court could award this relief.[107]

While the case was pending, T. Port imported more bananas from Ecuador without an import licence, and audaciously demanded that the German authority lift his quota on tariff-free imports. This time he charged that the banana regulation was invalid because it violated the GATT. A Hamburg authority refused this demand, and T. Port again appealed to the BVerfG. In its second banana ruling (April 1995) the BVerfG declined to intervene because T. Port had not exhausted his legal remedies under German and European law.[108] But it did suggest that it was not impossible that the regulation could be ruled inapplicable because it conflicted with Germany's obligation under GATT. It also noted that the court of 'appropriate jurisdiction' had not yet ruled on this issue. Following this decision, the Hamburg tax court ordered customs officials to allow the banana shipment without an import licence,[109] and at the lower import rate and it referred the case to the ECJ, challenging the ECJ's earlier interpretation which implied that GATT does not have precedence over secondary European law.[110] This (and three other similar rulings) were reversed by the Federal Tax Court because no

[106] *Firma T. Port v. Hauptzollamt Hamburg-Jonas*, Verwaltungsgerichtshof Hessen decision of 9 Feb. 1995, [1995] EuZW 222.

[107] Ibid.

[108] *Firma T. Port v. Hauptzollamt Hamburg-Jonas* (*T. Port II*, Banana II), BVerfG decisions of 26 Apr. 1995, first chamber of the second senate, 2 BvR 760/95, [1995] EuZW 412.

[109] *Firma T. Port v. Hauptzollamt Hamburg-Jonas* (*T. Port II*) order 19 May 1995, [1995] EuZW 413.

[110] ECJ case C-182/95, still pending.

final decision on the Hamburg court's *T. Port* case had been made.[111] The Federal Tax Court's ruling was appealed to the BVerfG, but the BVerfG did not rule on it.[112]

The ECJ ruled on the issue of national courts granting interim relief in its *Atlanta* ruling (November 1995).[113] It found that national courts can grant interim relief if there are serious doubts as to the validity of a Community act, if the validity of the contested act is not already at issue before the Court of Justice, if the court itself refers the question to the ECJ, if there is urgency (i.e. if interim relief is necessary to avoid serious and irreparable damage), if the court takes due account of community interest, and as long as the court respects the rulings of the ECJ. The BVerfG's first banana ruling would not qualify under these conditions because the BVerfG did not take into account the ECJ's jurisprudence, did not consider community interests, and did not refer the issue to the ECJ. Shortly thereafter, the ECJ ruled on the *T. Port* reference that had been prompted by the BVerfG's first banana ruling.[114] Here the ECJ found that the regulation in question did allow for transitional measures but that the proper way to elicit these measures was to go through the EC's legal system. In other words, the plaintiff has to rely on the Commission to implement the transitional measures. Should the Commission fail to act, either the member state can raise a failure to act suit on the litigant's behalf or the litigant can directly challenge the Commission's failure to act in front of the ECJ. National courts cannot hear such suits, nor can they themselves award interim relief when it is the Commission's responsibility to do so. This decision was a compromise. It implied that the BVerfG did not have the authority to issue the order it did in its first banana ruling. At the same time, however, it created an obligation for the Commission to protect litigants' rights to property by instituting transitional measures when justified.

The *Atlanta* ruling and the ECJ's first *T. Port* ruling were issued in November 1996. Shortly before, on 24 October 1996, the administrative court of Frankfurt sent to the BVerfG a constitutional challenge to the banana regulation aimed at forcing the BVerfG to assess the validity of the regulation, and thus confront the issues it had ducked in its previous banana

---

[111] *Firma T. Port v. Hauptzollamt Hamburg-Jonas* (*T. Port II*), BFH decision 22 Aug. 1995. Cited in ECJ decision C-364/95 and C-365/95, [1998] ECR I-1023, para. 46.

[112] Cited ibid. para. 47.

[113] *Atlanta Fruchthandelsgesellschaft v. Bundesamt für Ernahrung und Forstwirtschaft*, ECJ Case 465/93, [1995] I ECR 3761. This decision built on the ECJ's earlier jurisprudence from Zuckerfabrik Suderdithmarschen and Zuckerfabrik Soest, [1992] I ECR 3761.

[114] *T. Port GmbH & Co. KG v. Bundesanstalt für Landwirtschaft und Ernährung*, ECJ Case 68/95, [1996] ECR I-6065.

rulings. In its reference to the BVerfG, the administrative court made it clear that it thought that the ECJ's banana rulings did not sufficiently protect basic rights.[115] The administrative court challenged the *Solange II* position that as long as the ECJ was 'generally' protecting basic rights, the BVerfG would not intervene. Protecting basic rights is a national obligation, it asserted. Furthermore, the court claimed, there is a 'structural deficit' between the rights protected by the ECJ and the rights protected by the German constitution, so that there is no way for the ECJ to 'generally protect' German basic rights. The administrative court asked the BVerfG to speak directly about 'the limits of the application of European law supremacy'. If it should avoid this question, the administrative court asked the BVerfG to decide if the German ratification law for the EC Treaties is compatible with the German constitution, so far as it gives to the EC powers to pass binding laws in violation of the German constitution. This was the same question raised by the Rhineland-Palatinate tax court in 1965.

In the meantime, a GATT/WTO dispute resolution panel twice condemned the EU banana regime, and the US government began Super 301 hearings against the EU's banana regime (Cassia and Saulnier 1997: 539).[116] In response to the WTO rulings, the EU revised its banana regime.[117] It also struck a deal with a number of Latin American exporters of bananas, removing them and their bananas from the dispute over the EU's banana regulation. The EU still has preference for ACP bananas, and thus has not satisfied the victors of the WTO rulings (at this point the US and Ecuador).[118] Ecuador— the country involved in the Hamburg court's *T. Port II* case— was not party to this agreement. The ECJ used the fact that Ecuador entered the WTO in 1994 (after the banana regulation came into effect) to escape the conflict between the banana regulation and Germany's membership in GATT. The

---

[115] The administrative court also raised the issue of whether the regulation is ultra vires, and if it violates GATT; but it ruled that the regulation is not ultra vires and that the EC now has jurisdiction over GATT issues so that Germany is not directly responsible for GATT compliance. *Atlanta v. Bundesamt fuer Ernaehrung und Forstwirtschaft "Banana III"* Verwaltungsgericht reference 1 E 798/95 (V), 1 E 2949/93 (V) to the BVerfG of 24 October 1996. [1997] EuZW 182.

[116] The EU blocked the first GATT decision, so it was never adopted (or published). Because it was never adopted, the Commission had said it had no legal value (Cassia and Sulnier 1997: n. 115). The first formal report (second condemnation) was the panel report from 25 Sept. 1997 (WTO DSU report DS 27/R, Appellate Body Report, WT/DS27/AB/R). A third condemnation came on 17 July 2000 (WTO DSU report DS 165/R).

[117] For more on the EU–WTO dispute, see Peers (1999).

[118] For a summary of the state of play, see 'Overview of the State of Play of WTO Disputes', available at the WTO's website at http://www.wto.org/english/tratop_e/dispu_e/dispu_e.htm The latest update of 15 Jan. 2001 discussed the banana dispute on pp. 4–5.

issue of whether individuals have rights to use the GATT accord to challenge European laws in national courts remains open, with a constitutional complaint on this issue lodged before the BVerfG.[119]

The German Constitutional Court left the Frankfurt court's reference on its docket for nearly four years. Was it giving the ECJ time to reassess its *Germany v. the Council* ruling? Was it waiting for its most anti-ECJ member to leave? Did it hope the EU would change the banana regulation under pressure from the US and the WTO? The BVerfG's long-awaited ruling was issued in June 2000, after Judge Kirchhof had left the bench,[120] after the ECJ qualified the legal basis on which it was upholding its ruling in *Germany v. the Council*, after the EU had settled with a number of Latin American exporters, but before the WTO–EU dispute was resolved. Its third banana decision was strongly critical of the Frankfurt court, dismissing its reference as invalid and stating that the Frankfurt court had misread its *Maastricht* decision.

This ruling clarified what the BVerfG meant by a 'cooperative relationship' with the ECJ. As long as basic rights are protected sufficiently by the ECJ, the BVerfG will not exercise its right to ensure that European law respects German basic rights. The Frankfurt court's reference would only be valid if the claim were that the ECJ's protection had sunk below a sufficient level, or that a particular right guaranteed by the German basic law was not protected under European law. Not only was this claim not being made, but in this particular case the ECJ *had* recognized in European law a fundamental right to property. The BVerfG noted that one month after the Frankfurt court's reference (and four years before its own ruling, one might add), the ECJ had decided the *T. Port* cases; it had affirmed the plaintiff's right to property and the Commission's responsibility to consider the hardship the plaintiff was facing. The German Constitutional Court chastised the administrative court for not withdrawing its reference once the ECJ had created constitutional protections for German importers. The final sentence of its third banana ruling is that both decisions (the BVerfG's first banana decision, and the ECJ's *T. Port I* decision in response) 'clarify the interaction between the legal protection of basic rights at the European level through national and community courts'.

How do these rulings clarify the 'cooperative' relationship between the ECJ and the BVerfG? The BVerfG did not make a reference to the ECJ in any

---

[119] *T. Port v. Hauptzollamt Hamburg-Jonas* (*T. Port II*), ECJ decision C-364/95 and C-365/95, [1998] ECR I-1023. This case, and the reference, was discussed above.

[120] Judge Kirchhof left the bench in Nov. 1999. Bananamarktordnung (Banana III) BVerfG decision 2 BvL 1/97 of 7 June 2000. [2000] EuGRZ 328. Also available at the BVerfG's web site at: http://www.bverfg.de.

of its banana cases. It did not follow the ECJ's jurisprudence in its first banana ruling. The BVerfG did not cede its authority to review the compatibility of European law with German basic rights protections, or its claim to the power of *Kompetenz-Kompetenz*—the power to decide the boundaries of European authority. And it has left open the possibility that European law that conflicts with Germany's other obligations under international law may be inapplicable.[121] The only thing this decision clarified was that German litigant challenges to European law need to be based on the claim that ECJ protections have sunk below an acceptable level, or that the ECJ does not recognize a basic right that is protected by the German constitution.

The BVerfG's *Maastricht* decision, the broadcasting decision, and the BVerfG's banana decisions upheld European policies. As long as the German Constitutional Court does not reverse European policy, pundits claim victory for the German government and the European Union. But is it really a victory? The BVerfG clearly avoids overruling the ECJ or invalidating the application of European law in Germany. Perhaps it is motivated by respect for the ECJ, but then one might wonder why it is so willing to reject ECJ jurisprudence in its obiter dictum. Perhaps it is being deferential to the executive's foreign policy prerogatives and Germany's commitment to the European Union. Or perhaps it believes that the European laws in question represent complex political deals, deals which are best negotiated by political bodies and which the German government is realistically unable to improve.

While none of these decisions invalidated European law or Germany's right of membership in the Community, the BVerfG's *Maastricht* decision, the *Broadcasting* decisions, and the *Banana* rulings represent a significant expansion of the powers the BVerfG had declared in the *Solange I* and *Solange II* decisions, and an extension of the national legal tools which can be used in Germany to challenge European laws. To use a Constitutional Court judge's own metaphor, the new powers mean that BVerfG can play a role refereeing the rules of the European policy-making game.[122]

Another consequence of these rulings is that once again the BVerfG has shown that a threatening stick creates influence. The *Maastricht* decision has encouraged other high national courts to assert their own powers of constitutional review.[123] The Italian Constitutional Court and French *Conseil Constitutionnel* were already well on their way in this direction, and observers

---

[121] This was left open in its *Banana II* decision, n. 108 above.

[122] This metaphor was used in an interview with a judge at the *Bundesverfassungsgericht*, Karlsruhe, 8 Dec. 1993.

[123] For a recent study of this issue, see Mayer (2000).

expect them eventually to follow the German Constitutional Court's lead.[124] Under the influence of the *Maastricht* ruling (Olsen-Ring 2000), the President of the Danish Supreme Court signalled his intention to 'play a more active role . . . assuming a law creating function beyond what was customary [in Denmark] in this respect'.[125] In a revolutionary ruling, the Danish Supreme Court, asserted for the first time a power to conduct abstract review of the Danish act of accession to the TEU (Høegh 1999: 87–8).[126] And other national courts may well follow this direction too.

On the positive side, the interaction between German courts and the ECJ has forced all courts involved to clarify, limit, and better justify the legal reasoning underpinning their jurisprudence. The BVerfG ended up once again limiting its role in ensuring basic rights protection in European law (though its power to review whether or not European law is ultra vires has not been limited). And the ECJ forced European institutions to protect the basic rights of European citizens, and limited its jurisprudence regarding European law and the GATT.

The *Maastricht* decision also triggered an academic and political debate about what type of polity the European Union is. To be sure, there were other forces contributing to this debate. But the German Constitutional Court decision has been a focal point of this debate because it provided legitimacy to actors concerned about advances in European integration, and because it articulated a controversial vision about what it would take for 'real democracy' to exist at the European level. The outcome of this debate is far from certain. But we can be sure that courts will play a role in defining this outcome.

Summarizing the five rounds of doctrinal change

German positions regarding European law supremacy have evolved over time. Each round of integration took a number of years because it took many

---

[124] The Italian Constitutional Court gave itself the authority to review acts of accession with the constitution in *Fragd*, but not the power to review ultra vires secondary acts of the EC (Laderchi 1998: 170). The French *Conseil Constitutionnel* gave itself the power to review the 'framework agreements' under the Schengen accord, but not secondary acts of EC institutions. Both courts face procedural difficulties in claiming this power. *Fragd SpA v Amministrazione delle Finanze*, Italian Constitutional Court Decision 232 of 21 Apr. 1989, [1989] 72 RDI. *Conseil Constitutionnel* decision 91-294 DC of 25 July 1991, 'Schengen Decision', [1991] *Recueil des Décisions du Conseil Constitutionnel* 91, [1991] R. Fr. D. Admin. 173.

[125] From an interview in 1996. Transl. and quoted in Rasmussen (1998: 80).

[126] *Hanne Norup Carlsen and Others v. Prime Minister Poul Nyrup Rasmussen*, '*Maastricht* decision' of 6 Apr. 1998, Ugeskrift for Retsvaesen H 800, [1999] 3 CMLR 854.

years for legal cases to work their way through the system and because doctrine was refined and developed across a number of related cases. Table 3.2 summarizes the changing doctrine in each round of integration, highlighting the areas of substantial agreement, and aspects of a growing disagreement between the ECJ and national courts.

III. Conclusion

At the end of the day, what do the disagreements between the ECJ and German courts mean? How are they significant? On the one hand it is absolutely clear that European law takes precedence over conflicting national parliamentary law and government policy. The German government is bound to its European legal obligations. This was the fundamental idea behind the ECJ's *Costa v. ENEL* decision. The fact that despite the conflicts between the ECJ and the German Constitutional Court this principle has never been questioned reveals of how firmly entrenched this principle remains.

But the remaining disagreements are also significant; they directly influence political outcomes. Erhard Blankenburg observed that the BVerfG rarely finds a national law unconstitutional. But its rulings have a 'much larger anticipatory effect. No major legislative project proceeds without prior "informative consultation" by government departments, as well as opposition parties, with a judge or their collaborators at the constitutional court' (Blankenburg 1996: 309). One can see the 'anticipatory effect' extend into European policy-making. Constitutional constraints directly shape German positions in the Council, and *Länder* governments and parliamentary actors now have more say in negotiations over specific European policies.[127] The BVerfG's rulings also encourage the German government to make more vigorous use of the EC legal system to challenge EC policy.

The doctrinal disagreements also influence how European law is interpreted, once it is created. The differences between national and European legal doctrine influence the types of case litigants bring and the way lawyers frame challenges to national and European laws. When victorious, litigants

---

[127] Applying Robert Putnam's two-level game analysis, domestic constraints can be a source of leverage in international negotiations. If other member states believe that the German government is truly constrained by constitutional/domestic-political factors, they are more likely to concede certain points in negotiation (Putnam 1988).

can reopen the political process to create a new policy outcome. To avoid a conflict with national courts, the ECJ also clearly adjusts its jurisprudence. In all these ways, the disagreements between German doctrine and ECJ doctrine changes the nature of political and legal discourse, and the future trajectory of legal interpretation and of European integration.

The German experience also highlights both the great strengths and weaknesses of European integration. The fact that the basic supremacy of European law remains so entrenched shows real progress in the process of European integration. The weakness in the process, however, is revealed in the trend-line of rising disagreements over time. The substance of disagreement—the threat European law creates to basic rights protection and democracy—is of great concern. And the trend raises the danger of serious popular backlash against the European Union.

In retrospect, early acceptance of European law supremacy was all too easy. It was readily granted in part because it looked as though very little sovereignty was being handed over and because the BVerfG's own constitutional authority was not at stake. But as integration progressed, discord grew. The more European law expanded and the more the ECJ expanded its claims regarding European law supremacy, the more European law encroached on the prerogatives of national actors, including national courts. References to the ECJ grew as the body of EC law grew. But willingness to refer a case does not necessarily mean support for the ECJ. It seems that familiarity with the EC legal process brings knowledge of weaknesses in the system. German courts most involved with interpreting European law have been its strongest critics.

An effective rule of law should influence the political process, making political actors more accountable to legal, procedural, and constitutional requirements. A secondary effect of this process is the expanded influence of law and legal actors in the political process. On the positive side, the legal process is used to keep the EU and the ECJ accountable to national actors, while at the same time keeping national governments accountable to European legal and political bodies. Not to be forgotten, however, is that the legal process creates certain biases.

The legal process can be used to challenge policy passed in the general interest by public bodies. Those groups most able to use the legal system effectively can gain a disproportionate influence over public policy. Given the strongly liberal nature of European law, legal interpretation can expand the liberalizing influence of European integration in the national realm. Unorganized groups and those who lack legal expertise or financial resources

Table 3.2. The process of doctrinal change in Germany, divided into rounds of legal integration

Year of legal decisions in doctrinal debate	National doctrine regarding European law supremacy established in round	Growing consensus between ECJ and German courts	Points of disagreement between ECJ and German courts
Round 1, 1963–7 1963: ECJ *Van Gend en Loos* 1964: ECJ *Costa v. ENEL* 1963: FG Rhineland-Palatinate 1967: BFH 1967: BVerfG (July and Oct.)	German sovereignty has been transferred to the EC, giving the EC authority to issue binding regulations. Whether individuals can draw on European laws in national courts was never an issue. The direct effect of European law is tacitly accepted. German courts are not competent to assess the validity of European regulations (this position will be reversed).	Agreement regarding the ECJ's doctrine of direct effect. Agreement regarding the supreme authority of the ECJ to review the validity of European law. Language in BVerfG decisions seems to concur with the ECJ's interpretation in the *Costa v ENEL* ruling.	
Round 2, 1965–71 1965–8: FGs turnover tax decisions 1966: ECJ *Lütticke* 1967: BFH *Firma Molkerei Zentral* 1969: BFH *Lütticke* 1971: BVerfG *Lütticke*	European law is supreme to subsequent national law. German courts must hold the government accountable to its EC legal obligations.	Agreement regarding the ECJ's doctrine of direct effect. Agreement regarding the supreme authority of the ECJ to review the validity of European law. Agreement that European law is supreme to German law, and national courts have an obligation to enforce European law supremacy.	
Round 3, 1971–85 1970: ECJ *International Handelsgesellschaft* 1971: VW Frankfurt ref. to BVerfG 1974: BVerfG *Solange I* 1979: BVerfG *Vielleicht*	ECJ declares that EC Treaty is supreme to national constitutions. The German Constitutional Court declares that the EC Treaty is a treaty like all others. It gains its authority in Germany by virtue of Article 24 of the German constitution. The German Constitutional Court declares that the	Agreement regarding the ECJ's doctrine of direct effect. Agreement that European law is supreme to German law, and that national courts have an obligation to enforce European law supremacy.	Disagreement about the special nature of European law. Disagreement regarding the supremacy of European law over the German

Round / Cases	Court rulings	Agreement	Disagreement
(continued from previous round)	...review the compatibility of European law with the German constitution, and thus the validity of European law in Germany (a reversal of the position in round 1).		*(continued)* ECJ's exclusive capacity to evaluate the validity of European law with respect to basic rights protections. Disagreement about the special nature of European law. Disagreement regarding the supremacy of European law over the German constitution.
Round 4, 1981–7 Direct effect of directives 1974: ECJ *Van Duyn* 1981: BFH *Becker* 1985: BFH *Kloppenburg* 1987: BVerfG *Kloppenburg*	Federal Tax Court's attempts to refute the direct effect of directives, and to reject an ECJ decision, are reversed by the German Constitutional Court. The German Constitutional Court declares the ECJ the legal judge (*gesetzlicher Richter*) for EC legal issues. German courts must refer questions about European law to the ECJ, and enforce ECJ rulings regarding European law. Acceptance of the ECJ's interpretation allowing that directives can create direct effects.	Agreement regarding the ECJ's doctrine of direct effect, including the direct effect of directives. Agreement that European law is supreme to German law, and that national courts have an obligation to enforce European law supremacy. Agreement about the binding nature of ECJ rulings. Agreement about when national courts should refer EC legal issues to the ECJ, except with respect to the German Constitutional Court.	Disagreement over the ECJ's exclusive capacity to evaluate the validity of European law with respect to basic rights protections.
Round 5, 1993–8 Article 23 added to German Constitution 1993: BVerfG *Maastricht* 1994: ECJ *Germany v. Council* 1995: BVerfG broad-casting directive	German Constitutional Court seeks to create limits to broad ECJ interpretations and to new parliamentary powers (new Article 23 GG) finding. There are immutable constitutional limits on the ability of the government to transfer authority to the EC. European law and ECJ interpretations which violate the German constitution or exceed the power explicitly transferred to the EC are not binding in	Agreement regarding the ECJ's doctrine of direct effect, including the direct effect of directives. Agreement that European law is supreme to German law, and that national courts have an obligation to enforce European law supremacy. Agreement about when national courts should refer European legal issues to	Disagreement about the special nature of European law. Disagreement regarding the supremacy of European law over the German constitution. Disagreement over the

Table 3.2. *cont.*

Year of legal decisions in doctrinal debate	National doctrine regarding European law supremacy established in round	Growing consensus between ECJ and German courts	Points of disagreement between ECJ and German courts
1995: BVerfG *Banana I, II* 1996: BFH *Banana I* 1996: VW Frankfurt Banana reference to BVerfG 1996, 1998: ECJ *T. Port* 1998: ECJ *Germany v. Council* 2000: BVerfG *Banana III*	Germany. The Constitutional Court is the final arbiter of the limits of European authority in Germany, thus the Kompetenz-Kompetenz resides with the German Constitutional Court. The Constitutional Court clarifies that it will hear basic rights challenges only when the ECJ's standard of protection has sunk below a certain level, or when a specific right protected by the German constitution is not protected under European law.	the ECJ, except with respect to the German Constitutional court.	ECJ's exclusive authority to evaluate the validity of European law with respect to basic rights protections. Disagreement over the ECJ's exclusive authority to determine the limits of European authority, and thus disagreement over whether the ECJ or the German Constitutional Court has the ultimate *Kompetenz-Kompetenz*. Disagreement over the binding nature of EC laws and ECJ decisions which are seen as ultra vires by German courts.

may be unable to use European law to their advantage. And the structure of the German legal system (namely the ability of *Länder* and individuals to raise constitutional challenges to European laws through national courts or by direct appeal), combined with the Germans' experience in using the legal system as a tool of political influence, gives German actors a greater influence over European policy-making than similar actors in other countries.

4

French Judicial Acceptance of European Law Supremacy

Of the original member states, French national courts had the hardest time embracing the ECJ's supremacy doctrine. It took until 1989 for all three of France's supreme courts to accept a role enforcing European law supremacy, and there were significant and enduring disagreements between these on this issue. There were also a number of challenges to the ECJ's jurisprudence and authority during the twenty-five-year process of doctrinal change.

The French case illustrates the limits of legalist accounts, which rely on compelling legal logic to explain judicial preferences *vis-à-vis* European law. The French constitution clearly allows for the supremacy of international law, but this did not guide judicial behaviour. French courts also remained unconvinced by the legal logic of the European Court's position. The French case also contradicts neo-functionalist expectations; from the beginning European law offered French courts a new power of judicial review, yet this opportunity was eschewed by French administrative courts for many years.

Adopting a legal-culture explanation, scholars claim that French judicial reticence towards European law supremacy comes from the French Revolution and the laws of 16 and 24 August 1790, in which a sanction against activist judges was inscribed into the French penal code.[1] According to some, the failure to repeal these provisions made French judges hesitant to accept a role enforcing European law supremacy hundreds of years later and even after the French constitution had been reformed to explicitly allow the supremacy

---

[1] Judges 'shall be guilty of an abuse of their authority and punished with loss of their civil rights' for interfering with the legislature or administration 'by issuing regulations containing legislative provisions, by suspending applications of one or several laws, or by deliberating on whether or not a law will be published or applied' Act of 16 and 24 August 1790 Title II, Art. 13 (translation from Stone (1992: ch. 2, n. 10 for more on the historically limited role of judges in France, see Merryman (1996: 109, 111) and Dadomo and Farran (1996: 47).

of international law over national law (Manin 1991: 500). For others, it was less the formal legislative restraints on judicial review than the larger spirit behind these provisions. French laws, it was argued, are the embodiment of *la volonté générale* (the general will). It would be undemocratic if they could be set aside by judges (Jacqué 1981; Lachaume 1990: 386). Both explanations have clear limits. First, they cannot account for the divergent positions French courts took on European legal issues over a fifteen-year period. Second, French courts have long been interpreting French law in ways that challenge the authority of French political bodies.[2] Third, the argument that parliamentary laws are sacrosanct because they embody the *volonté générale* has for years made little sense. In the Fifth Republic most of the parliament's legislative power was given to the executive branch, which is able freely to circumvent the parliament (Lagneau-Devillé 1983: 470). The *Conseil d'État* has not hesitated to control the legal edicts of the executive branch and to blur the line between parliamentary law that it could not review and executive acts which it could (Cappelletti 1989: ch. 2). If a revolutionary tradition was impeding judicial change, why did this tradition run out when it did? Why did three high French courts respond so differently to this tradition?

The French experience is more consistent, however, with the expectations of neo-realist scholars. Judicial reticence was in part a response to Gaullist concerns about national sovereignty and national interests. But it is not clear that government's growing support for European integration and its prodding of the judiciary was caused by geopolitical calculations. Party politics provide a more convincing explanation. As the power of Gaullist parties weakened, French judges started asserting more independence. The socialists, after their failed attempt to reflate the economy, embraced European integration, and this change contributed to a change in French legal doctrine regarding European law supremacy, although it was not the only factor pushing in this direction.

How judicial rivalries manifested themselves in the process of doctrinal change was different in France from the situation in Germany. Because the structure of the legal systems differed, the institutional incentives of courts also differed. But in both countries, doctrinal change was a process of courts positioning themselves against one another and *vis-à-vis* political bodies in

---

[2] According to Alec Stone, the taboo against judicial review has been challenged throughout post-Revolution France (ibid. 23–45). Mauro Cappelletti has argued that the French discovered fairly early that allowing the government to control itself did not work, which is why the *Conseil d'État* became increasingly independent and took on the role of a court controlling governmental excesses of power (Cappelletti 1989: 197).

order to maximize their independence, influence, and authority. When the *Cour de Cassation* broke ranks and accepted a role enforcing European law supremacy, it brought European law into France, facilitating the expansion and penetration of European law into the French legal system. The *Cour de Cassation*'s actions created pressure on the *Conseil Constitutionnel* and the *Conseil d'État* to change their European law supremacy jurisprudence. Ultimately, the other two high courts changed their positions because it became clear that their strategy had not kept European law out of the national system, had not protected national sovereignty, and instead had undermined their influence in the EC legal and political process. The recalcitrant French courts brought their jurisprudence more into line with the doctrinal position accepted by all the other member states and, at this point, by the French government, in order to establish an influence parallel to that of high courts in other member states. Accepting a role enforcing European law supremacy was only one of the strategies the *Conseil d'État* and *Conseil Constitutionnel* employed in the late 1980s and early 1990s to increase their influence in the process of European integration. They also lobbied for structural reforms that have contributed to a new political situation in France where the French parliament, the *Conseil d'État*, and the *Conseil Constitutionnel* are more involved in the EC policy-making process.

The *Conseil d'État* and *Conseil Constitutionnel* were the last national high courts to refuse to enforce European law supremacy. Their conversion made the construction of an international rule of law complete; the supremacy of European law became an unquestioned cornerstone of the EC legal order, binding national courts and governments alike. The doctrinal reversal in France does not mean that judicial barriers to the uniform application of European law have been entirely surmounted. Indeed, French courts also claim the right to find limits to the authority of European law. As in Germany, there is arguably a salutary side to the disagreements between French courts and the ECJ. The remaining judicial divergences force the French government to respect the French constitution and French parliament, and keep the ECJ receptive to national political and legal concerns.

This chapter traces the negotiation regarding doctrinal change in France. Section I identifies the main judicial actors in France and their preferences in EC legal issues. Section II explains the evolution of the French doctrinal debate over time, divided into rounds in which the debate evolved.

I. The main judicial actors in the legal debate

Most of the pressure for doctrinal change in France came horizontally—from the other high courts—rather than from lower courts. This contrast can be explained by the structure of the French legal system, which led French courts to adopt different strategies from their counterparts in Germany, still with the same objective of protecting their influence, independence and authority. This section introduces the key judicial actors in the French supremacy debate, providing background on the different institutional contexts of the courts to help understand the discussion of doctrinal change that follows.

The French legal system is divided into three branches, with no hierarchical overlap but with significant jurisdictional overlap. Fig. 4.1 shows the French judiciary's organization. In contrast to the German system, where there is a clear hierarchy leading to the Federal Constitutional Court at the apex, the French judicial system is relatively unhierarchical.[3]

While they are all supreme courts, the different jurisdictions of the *Conseil Constitutionnel*, *Conseil d'État*, and *Cour de Cassation* create different roles for each court in European law debates. The French *Conseil Constitutionnel* is the body authorized to conduct constitutional review of national laws. Recall that the similar court in Germany, the German Constitutional Court, has the power of *abstract judicial review* in cases raised by the government, members of parliament or *Länder* government, and *concrete judicial review* in cases raised by private litigants, or in cases referred by other courts in the judiciary.[4] The French *Conseil Constitutionnel*, by contrast, only has the power of abstract judicial review. All the German Constitutional Court cases involving EC law discussed in Chapter 3 were concrete judicial review cases raised by private litigants and national judges. None of these cases would have reached the *Conseil Constitutionnel*; indeed, most of them could not have been raised in France at all. In other words, the institutional structure of the French legal system does not allow the *Conseil Constitutionnel* to be seized by private

---

[3] Not on the table is the *tribunal de conflits*, a judicial body that can be called upon to resolve interpretive divergences across branches when inconsistencies arise (the German system has a similar body.) The *tribunal de conflits* was never asked to resolve the conflict over European law supremacy, even though this was perhaps the most significant existing difference between the two branches. For more on the role of the Tribunal de Conflit in France, see : Dadomo and Farran (1996: 107–11).

[4] The term 'abstract judicial review' applies to cases where there is no actual dispute before the court. In concrete judicial review cases, there is a dispute which gives rise to a legal question. See above, Ch. 3, sect. II for a complete description of the powers of the German Constitutional Court.

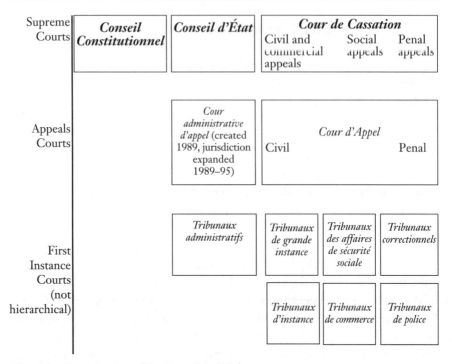

Fig. 4.1. Organization of the French judicial system

litigants to challenge European or national policies, leading the *Conseil Constitutionnel* to respond to the ECJ and European law supremacy differently from its German counterpart.

The *Conseil Constitutionnel* is seized when political actors (the President, the Prime Minister, the President of the Assembly or Senate, or sixty members of parliament) oppose a law that has recently been passed, and not yet promulgated (Stone 1992). Until recently, those political actors disagreeing with European law and European policy lacked the numbers or the power to raise a constitutional challenge. Because its ability to influence European law debates is so limited, and out of a fear that a law it approved could be interpreted in an unconstitutional way and later invalidated by the ECJ, the *Conseil Constitutionnel* for many years refrained from becoming involved in debates over European law. It later changed its jurisprudence to allow it to review treaty amendments and certain European laws, but its involvement in European law debates remains circumscribed and limited.

The *Conseil d'État*, the highest administrative court, is the court charged with reviewing the actions of the French government. It is the only court in

France where private litigants can directly challenge national policies, including government administration of European policy. But its close links to the government have kept it from pursuing this role vigorously. The *Conseil d'État* also serves an adviser to the state (hence the name *Conseil d'État*), reviewing legal aspects of proposed legislation and regulations. Its advising role brings members of the *Conseil d'État* (*Conseillers d'État*) into daily contact with administrators and government officials.[5] *Conseillers d'État* also come from the same elite academic establishment as most high government officials, the prestigious *École Nationale d'Administration* (*ENA*), and they float between the *Conseil d'État*, the private sector, and governmental appointments throughout their career. The close relationship between *Conseillers d'État* and public actors is meant to, and does, influence how the *Conseil d'État* executes its judicial role, creating what some see as a conflict of interests (Radamaker 1988: 144). In European legal issues, the *Conseil d'État* has identified strongly with the French state. It has shared the government's anger against ECJ rulings, and for many years refused to become the policeman of government compliance with European law. It changed its jurisprudence regarding the primacy of European law because it became clear that not being involved in enforcing European law was undermining its own power and France's influence over European legal interpretation.

Given that the *Conseil d'État* is the only court where private litigants can challenge government policy, one would expect most references to the ECJ to come from administrative courts. Yet 90 per cent of referrals to the ECJ come from the judiciary branch (see Table 4.1).[6] The dearth of references from administrative courts and the doctrinal positions taken by the *Conseil d'État*, are indicative of the unfriendly attitude taken by the *Conseil d'État* towards the ECJ.

The relatively large number of references from the judiciary branch, the so-called 'ordinary courts', might give the impression that this branch is very involved in European law debates. But as with the *Conseil Constitutionnel*, the way the jurisdiction of the *Cour de Cassation* is defined keeps it from being a key player. Except with respect to social security and a few other issues,

---

[5] *Conseillers d'État* participate in judicial and advising functions simultaneously, and thus it is impossible analytically to separate the functions when considering the interests and incentives of the *Conseil d'État* regarding European law.

[6] It is hard directly to compare reference rates of the French administrative branch to those of the German administrative branch because in Germany there are other courts which can hear direct challenges to government and legislative rules. Even by this crude measure, however, the total number of references is very low: 53 French references (10% of French references) compared to 195 references (22% of German references). (See Tables 3.1, p. 69 and 4.1. p. 130)

Table 4.1. French preliminary ruling references, 1960–1964[a]

	Civil/commercial		Social		Penal		Administrative		Other		Total	
	No.	%[b]	No.	%	No.	%	No.	%	No.	%	No.	%
	Cour de Cassation, civil and commercial		Cour de Cassation, social		Cour de Cassation, penal		Conseil d'État		Cour de Cassation (plenary)		Total supreme courts	
	19	4	18	4	8	2	13	3	2	*	60	12
	Cour d'Appel, civil and commercial		Cour d'Appel, social		Cour d'Appel, penal		Cour admin. d'appel (since 1989)				Total appeals courts	
	38	7	49	10	15	3	2	*			104	20
	Tribunal de grande instance		Tribunal des affaires de sécurité sociale		Tribunal correctionnel		Tribunal admin.					
	146	29	11	2	3	*[c]	39	8				

Court	Number	%
Tribunal de 1ère instance	66	13
Commission de 1ère instance du contentieux de la sécurité sociale	30	6
Tribunal de police	27	5
Tribunal de commerce	22	4
Other lower courts	3	*
Total lower courts	347	68
Total civil/commercial	291	57
Total social courts	108	21
Total penal courts	53	10
Total admin. courts	54	10
Other	5	*
Total	511	

[a] The figures in this chart are based on data provided by the research and documentation division of the Court of Justice. Included are references for opinions even if the opinion did not result in an ECJ decision reported in the ECJ's Annual Report. Hence the total number of references varies slightly from the number reported by the ECJ.
[b] Percentage of total references by French courts.
[c] * = <1%.

judiciary courts cannot hear direct challenges to government policy. Conflicts between European law and national policy, when raised, enter the case indirectly. Either the compatibility of government policy with European law must be at issue in a case between two private parties (in which case the government policy is probably not the direct target), or the compatibility issue arises when a private *defendant* in a case raises a European law *defence* against a government official pursuing legal action against the private litigant. European law supremacy was indirectly raised in a case brought by the government against an importer of coffee in 1976, and the *Cour de Cassation* used this case to challenge the *Conseil d'État*'s European law jurisprudence. But there were no cases involving European law supremacy before 1976, and few cases after that.

As Chapter 2 argued, when there is jurisdictional overlap competitive tension between courts is heightened. In Germany, because the branches of the judiciary are divided by subject matter, there is little jurisdictional overlap and little threat that one branch's jurisdiction over a category of cases might be transferred to another branch. In France there is overlap, and this threat is real. Formally, the administrative branch has jurisdiction over public law issues, while the judiciary branch deals with private law issues. In practice, however, the distinction between what is public and what is private law is hazy. Indeed, in some areas of law administrative and judiciary courts could well be applying the same legal texts, and applying them differently.[7] The rationale for having two branches deal with often similar issues is continually questioned. The *Conseil d'État* is more politically influential than its judiciary counterpart, and because of the elite selection process for the *Conseil d'État*, and the access of its members to high government positions, it is more prestigious.[8] But it is less popular among lawyers because its decision-making is

[7] e.g. the administrative branch deals with legal issues that are essentially private in nature except that the plaintiff is a public actor. Thus, administrative courts hear malpractice cases against public hospitals while the judiciary branch hears malpractice cases against private hospitals. There are also a number of public law areas that are decided by the judiciary branch, including certain questions of taxation, competition policy, and social security benefits (a publicly administered system). As mentioned above, judiciary courts can also hear indirect challenges to government policy raised in the context of a civil case, or criminal proceedings. For more see: Dadomo and Farran (1996:50).

[8] Members of the *Conseil d'État* come from the best of the elite *École Nationale d'Administration*. According to Doris Marie Provine , 'The Council of the State is a sought-after assignment because of its centrality and significance to the national government. It is an inside player, assisting the President and sometimes parliament in preparing legislation and examining it for constitutional defects.' The ordinary judiciary, on the other hand, 'is widely regarded as an occupation for those who lack the ambition to be practising lawyers or academics'. Its members are poorly paid, and have little prestige (Provine 1996: 187, 204).

cryptic and only a few lawyers are licensed to raise cases before the *Conseil d'État*. Subject to constant attack from lawyers, and plaintiffs, the *Conseil d'État* has feared that it would be eliminated, or that its jurisdiction would be transferred piecemeal to the judiciary branch. Judiciary courts, meanwhile, have resented the superior attitude of *Conseil d'État* judges.

There is also jurisdictional overlap between the constitutional and administrative branches. When the *Conseil Constitutionnel* was created in 1958, it filled a role interpreting the French Constitution that the *Conseil d'État* had informally occupied.[9] The *Conseil Constitutionnel* was much maligned in its early years, accused of being a political body in the pocket of its creator, Charles de Gaulle (Stone 1992: ch. 2).[10] Only after the *Conseil Constitutionnel*'s legal and political stature grew did it become a rival of the *Conseil d'État*. The *Conseil Constitutionnel* came into its own during the period of time that European law supremacy was being debated. This change in status was hard for the *Conseil d'État* to accept, but it was a reality. As constitutional law expert Louis Favoreau noted:

The process of integrating the *Conseil Constitutionnel* in the judiciary system has largely commenced and is in practice irreversible . . . It is not to deny the jurisdictional character of the *Conseil Constitutionnel* that one [meaning the *Conseil d'État*] attempts to stop the process and avoid the reversal of the equilibrium which is occurring in the legal system. One could say that it is somewhat surprising to see a battle over a terrain which was never, in reality, claimed by the administrative jurisdiction; all legislative acts, parliamentary acts and government acts were always considered to be outside of the authority of the administrative court. But in reality what is at stake is the orientation and even the direction of the legal order: until now the *Conseil d'État* was assured of an important influence if not a decisive influence in this domain; but for some time the influence of the *Conseil Constitutionnel* has tended to substitute for that of the *Conseil d'État*. (Favoreau 1988: 155)

---

[9] The *Conseil d'État* never really had the authority to conduct constitutional review, but until the *Conseil Constitutionnel* was created it was the only judicial body practising any sort of judicial review of government policy. And it often interpreted the constitution in order to understand the limits of its own powers, and of the government's powers.

[10] It is significant that the *Conseil Constitutionnel* is called the 'Constitutional Council' rather than the 'Constitutional Court'. The *Conseil Constitutionnel* was created by General de Gaulle to be more of a political than a legal body. In its early years it was used by de Gaulle to strip bills of compromises the executive had reached with the parliament. When the *Conseil Constitutionnel* failed to stop the clearly unconstitutional efforts of De Gaulle to amend the constitution through referendum, most politicians and legal scholars lost faith in the institution. Its political nature made it very unpopular among members of parliament. Within the legal community, it was not even considered to be a legal body (Stone 1992: 60–6).

The debate over European law supremacy was one of the key places that this changing role was apparent. Indeed, the debate over European law supremacy, because of its legal and political significance, became part of the larger judicial rivalry between the three supreme courts in France.

Lower courts were not key players in the process of doctrinal change. The structure of the French judiciary helps explains why French lower courts played a lesser role than their German counterparts. The *Conseil d'État* was the first and last instance court for challenges to government policy (this changed recently).[11] Lower administrative courts (which heard challenges to the regional and local administrative actions) had no real means to challenge the *Conseil d'État*'s European law jurisprudence. Only in the judiciary branch could the EC legal system be used to circumvent higher court jurisprudence. But given the willingness of the *Cour de Cassation* to accept ECJ jurisprudence, appealing to the ECJ was not an effective means to escape higher court doctrine.

French judges were clearly less bold than their German counterparts. The wariness of French judges was probably influenced by the political intervention in the judicial process in France in the 1960s.[12] There is also clearly a greater public wariness about judicial intervention in the political process. As Mary Provine has said: 'Courts in France are not known for standing up to other government officials, and no one expects them to play an active role in governance' (Provine 1996: 177). Public wariness and judicial conservatism

Table 4.2. Domestic civil litigation rates compared: civil litigation per 100,000 inhabitants

Country	Civil procedures	Cases heard in first instance legal bodies	Cases heard on appeal
West Germany (1989)	9,400	4,911	251
England and Wales (1982)	5,300	1,200	16
France (1982)	3,640	1,950	250

[11] In 1989 administrative courts of appeal were created, and gradually a significant amount of the *Conseil d'État*'s first instance authority was devolved to courts below it. This only happened in the mid-1990s, but already we can see that lower administrative courts are now pressuring the *Conseil d'État*. See further n. 127 below.

[12] See n. 17 below.

perhaps explains why French lawyers seem less aggressive at pursuing legal challenges to government policy. French litigation rates are one third those of found in Germany (see Table 4.2).[13] And a number of scholars have lamented the failure of French lawyers to embrace European law in their practice, at least in the 1960s and 1970s (Touffait 1975; Buffet-Tchakaloff 1984: 376; Lecourt 1973). The next section shows how the interests of national courts *vis-à-vis* European law evolved over time, and how the interactions of these high courts influenced the debate over European law.

II. The process of doctrinal change regarding European law supremacy

The main legal issue in France was not really whether European law was supreme to French law but rather *whether national judges had the authority* to enforce the supreme European law over subsequent French law. France has a monist constitution. Article 28 of the 1946 French constitution clearly grants international law primacy over national law. Article 55 of the 1958 French constitution reasserted and qualified the 1946 provision, stating that 'treaties or agreements duly ratified or approved have . . . an authority superior to that of laws, subject, for each separate agreement of the treaty, to reciprocal application by the other party'. While the constitution is clear, there was a legal debate about whether the constitutional provisions were addressed only to political bodies or whether they also authorized judges to ensure the compatibility of French law with international law. If Article 55 is addressed only to political bodies, then French judges lack the authority to consider whether French law is compatible with European law.

Many French scholars and judges hoped the postwar constitutions would be seized as a legal and political opening to reinterpret French legal precedents of the interwar years. For the *Conseil d'État*, the precedent was the 1936 *Arrighi* decision in which it refused the authority to examine the validity of a statute, for any reason.[14] This doctrine amounted in practice to the German dualist position *lex posteriori derogat legi prior* (last law passed trumps all previous laws);

[13]   The total volume of litigation initiated by private actors (civil litigation) is unusually high in Germany. If the procedures raised in administrative and labour courts were added to the German figures, the rate of civil procedures would increase by another 1,350 per 100,000, and the appeal rate would rise accordingly (Blankenburg 1996: 295; repr. in Conant 2001).

[14]   Arrighi decision. *Conseil d'État* decision of 6 Nov. 1936, [1936] Recueil Lebon 966.

the *Conseil d'État* would apply the last statute passed, but it would not examine whether French statute conflicted with previously passed international rules, or with the French constitution. For the *Cour de Cassation*, the precedent was the 1931 *Matter* Doctrine, which implied that judges should assume that legislators did not intend to contravene international law unless the law specifically said otherwise, in which case the legislative will should be followed over international law. This doctrine was a more flexible version of the *lex posteriori* doctrine, allowing greater room for judges to reconcile national law with international law.

After the 1946 French constitution established the supremacy of international law, some judiciary court judges began according treaties supremacy over posterior laws.[15] In 1950 André Pepy, *Procureur Général* at the *Cour de Cassation*, argued that the new clause in the 1946 constitution was a sign of the legislative will that judges apply international law over national law:

> Tribunals, confronted with two juridical rules, one inscribed in a treaty, the other defined by internal law, are advised by the French legislator himself, expressing his will in the form of a constitutional principle, saying that in a conflict between two laws, it is the first which they should apply.[16]

This argument did not, however, create a new doctrinal precedent. In the late 1950s (before the 1958 constitution had been written) there was a judicial debate regarding whether a Spanish treaty concluded in 1862 had precedence over a subsequent French law. Different courts took different positions about whether French courts were competent to set aside conflicting national laws. In the end, the old doctrine prevailed; the Foreign Ministry was asked to interpret the Treaty, and precedence was given to the subsequent French law. This meant that before the issue of European law supremacy even arose, it had been determined that the constitutional provision regarding international law supremacy did not empower judges to set aside national laws. This experience led scholars to predict that the 1958 constitution would not change anything, and that the *Arrighi* and *Matter* doctrines would continue as the basis for French legal practice regarding international law (Constantinesco 1968: 324–5). They were right for many years.

In the 1980s, Pepy's thirty-year-old argument was resurrected and accepted as the legal basis for European law supremacy by all of the high

---

[15]   Cour d'Aix (10 Nov. 1947, S. 1948.2.83), and Lyon (16 Feb. 1953, D. 1952.801), cited in Druesne (1975: 379).

[16]   Argument by Procureur-Général Pepy in 'Matter Doctrine', *Cour de Cassation* (criminal branch) decision of 3 June 1950, [1951] I Sirey 109. Quoted and cited in Kovar (1975: 645). My translation.

French courts. Article 55 was from then on interpreted as empowering judges to enforce the supremacy of international law over national law. From a formal legal standpoint, nothing had changed. The constitution was not amended to spell out that judges were to apply Article 55. The revolutionary 1790 prohibition against judges practising judicial review had not been repealed. French judges just decided to interpret Article 55 differently, adopting an interpretation they had rejected for years.

The change in French doctrine from the *Arrighi/Matter* doctrines to seeing Article 55 as empowering ordinary court judges emerged over twenty-five years. This section divides the process of doctrinal change into five separate 'rounds' during which key issues of French doctrine evolved. During Round 1 (1960–9), the *Conseil d'État* declared that only the *Conseil Constitutionnel* could enforce European law supremacy, establishing a clear precedent against referring cases to the ECJ and against national court enforcement of European law supremacy. During Round 2 (1970–6), the *Conseil Constitutionnel* declared that enforcing international law supremacy was not part of its constitutional mandate, and the *Cour de Cassation* used the constitutional vacuum to assert for itself the authority to enforce European law over subsequent national law. Undeterred by these changes, during Round 3 (1977–81) the *Conseil d'État* became even more defiant of the ECJ, repudiating the latter's jurisprudence on the direct effect of directives. In Round 4 (1982–9) the *Conseil Constitutionnel* qualified its earlier supremacy jurisprudence, and when it was acting as an election judge (thus not as a constitutional body) it embraced the *Cour de Cassation*'s solution of enforcing the supremacy of international law. Round 4 ends with the *Conseil d'État* reversing its opposition to enforcing European law supremacy. Having both accepted a role enforcing European law supremacy, in Round 5 (1990–8), the *Conseil Constitutionnel* and *Conseil d'État* sought new powers and means to influence the development of French and European law. The *Conseil Constitutionnel* created for itself a role reviewing the constitutionality of expansions of European Union authority and of new international agreements. The *Conseil d'État* augmented its advising role to include EC policy, and reinforced the administrative court system to protect itself from future attempts to transfer its jurisdiction to the judiciary branch.

Round 1. French judicial refusal to consider European law supremacy, 1962–1969

The political context of the 1960s is important in understanding the early position of French courts on EC legal issues. In the 1960s all three branches of the French judiciary faced serious attacks on their independence and authority, in large part because of their positions on issues related to Algeria.[17] Meanwhile De Gaulle was fighting attempts to give more power to the EC's supranational institutions (Gerbet 1983: 319–20; Van der Groeben 1985: 184). De Gaulle had shown a willingness to exact revenge on the judiciary, and he would not look kindly on a judicial support for the ECJ's position that French sovereignty had been irrevocably transferred to the European level.

The first European law cases to arise were related to France's policy regarding Algeria. In 1964 major international petroleum firms (Shell, Esso, Standard, and Mobil Oil) used European law to challenge the French government's policy for the development of an association of gas stations selling gas from Algeria and Gabon. The oil companies argued that the French government's decree and oil monopoly violated European law. The French government, along with the European Commission, argued that the French regime was consistent with the Treaty of Rome, which had included Article 37 EEC specifically for the French petroleum import regime (Chevallier 1965; Fourré and Wenner 1965). The *Conseil d'État* rejected the oil firm's arguments in a ruling consistent with European law.[18] But the relatively

[17] From 1958 to 1970 there were 7 bills to abolish the *Conseil Constitutionnel*, and while none made it through the legislative process, it was clear that there was little parliamentary support for the *Conseil Constitutionnel* (Stone 1992: 66). Because the criticisms of the special military tribunals in Algeria by the *Conseil Supérieur de la Magistrature*, the body created to promote the independence of judges was reformed to the point that it lost all influence. In addition, there were large changes in the judiciary court system motivated by the government's desire to have a 'more controllable (judiciary) from an ideological point of view' (Lagneau-Devillé 1983: 476). The number of lower courts was reduced to 15% of its pre-1958 level with power devolved to extra-judicial conciliatory bodies, which in some respects became a parallel institution to the judiciary courts (ibid.). The influence of appellate courts and Parisian jurisdictions was also increased, making lower court challenges to traditional high court positions even less likely. The greatest political pressures were against the *Conseil d'État* after its decision in the 'Canal Affair' (1962), where the *Conseil d'État* annulled a government's decree establishing a special military court in Algeria, and de Gaulle threatened to do away with the *Conseil d'État* altogether. A number of proposals were seriously considered, but in the end a more moderate change in the *Conseil d'État*'s personnel, organization and jurisdiction was accepted. Some of the older members retired and members of the *Conseil d'État* were rotated more frequently through the administration to 'improve their chances of gaining experience of active administration outside of the *Conseil* altogether' (Parris 1966: 103). These attacks made judicial evolution regarding European law supremacy unlikely in the 1960s, especially given that the first cases in which jurisprudence might have evolved were related to France's Algeria policy.

[18] When the same plaintiffs challenged the French decree through an Italian court, the ECJ upheld the French decree, lending support to the *Conseil d'État*'s decision. S*ARL Albatros v. SOPECO*, ECJ decision 20/64, [1965] ECR 41. Discussed in Fourré and Wenner (1965).

antagonistic tone of the *Conseil d'État*'s *Commissaire du Gouvernement* was disconcerting.[19]

In the *Shell Berre* case, *Commissaire du Gouvernement* Questiaux addressed the question of whether a reference to the ECJ was obligatory for courts of last instance or whether high courts could interpret clear European law on their own? She argued against referring the case to the ECJ because the *Conseil d'État* was already competent 'to apply the treaty in all the areas in which it appears clear to you'.[20] This position was consistent with the *Conseil d'État*'s well-established Doctrine of *Acte Clair* that was widely used to avoid sending cases involving international law to the Foreign Ministry for interpretation (Lagrange 1971). But the *Acte Clair* argument went against the position advocated by the ECJ, and the EC legal texts at issue were far from clear. Refusing to refer the case was a bad precedent to set in the first European law case to reach a French court, and a number of French scholars felt the *Acte Clair* Doctrine was abused in this case (Chevallier 1965; de Laubadère 1965; De Soto 1964; Wenner 1964; Fourré and Wenner 1965).

Given the political sensitivity of the petroleum regime, it is not surprising that the *Conseil d'État* would not want the ECJ involved. But the sceptical tone was again apparent in the *Conseil d'État*'s 1967 *Petitjean* decision, a far less polemical case.[21] In this case, French tomato growers invoked European law to challenge a French agricultural taxing scheme. At issue was whether the EC articles in question created direct effects. *Commissaire du Gouvernement* Questiaux again discouraged the *Conseil d'État* from making a reference to the ECJ, arguing that the ECJ's jurisprudence regarding when European law created direct effects was clear enough for national courts to apply on their own. In asserting its own authority to determine when European law did and did not create direct effects, the *Conseil d'État* was challenging one of the ECJ's main interpretive roles. Whether a Treaty article

---

[19] Despite what the name might imply, the *Commissaire du Gouvernement* is not a representative of the government, but rather a full member of the *Conseil d'État*, who offers a reasoned opinion for the *Conseil d'État* to consider. Because *Conseil d'État* decisions are short and cryptic, the arguments of the *Commissaire du Gouvernement* are often the best indicator of legal sentiment inside the *Conseil d'État*.

[20] Société des pétroles Shell-Berre et autres, Sociétés 'Les Garages de France', Société Esso-Standard, Société Mobil Oil française, Société française des pétroles B.P., *Conseil d'État* decision of 19 June 1964, [1964] Recueil Lebon 344, [1964] 5 RDP 1019. Quote from RDP, p. 1031.

[21] S.A. des Etablissements Petitjean et autres, *Conseil d'État* decision of 10 Feb. 1967, [1967] Recueil Lebon 63, [1967] AJDA 267, [1967] RTDE 681.

creates direct effects is seldom clear, and the ECJ ultimately did grant direct effects to the treaty articles in question.[22]

Neither case raised the issue of European law supremacy, but these decisions set the tone for how French courts should deal with issues of European law. The *Commissaire du Gouvernement's* arguments in both cases made it seem that a plaintiff's appeal to European law was a back-handed and illegitimate strategy, a dilatory tactic or an attempt to obstruct the legal process. The preliminary ruling reference process was portrayed as if it were long and arduous, and it was suggested that sending the ECJ broad cases to decide could open a Pandora's box which would change the nature of French and European law in unanticipated ways.[23] The rulings created unsettling precedents and were a step away from rather than a step towards building an atmosphere of judicial cooperation between French courts and the ECJ.

The first French case specifically raising the issue of European law supremacy did not arise until 1968.[24] The case, like *Shell-Berre*, involved a politically sensitive issue associated with French Algerian policy. On 4 April 1962, the EC Council had adopted a regulation requiring that non-EC imports have special certificates and creating an EC level tariff regime.[25] Nineteen months later the French Minister of Agriculture unilaterally exempted a large import of Algerian semolina from the EC regulation. Confusing the issue was the fact that the government decree was issued during a period of transition towards Algerian independence when the status of Algeria as an independent non-EC country was still being negotiated. Wanting European tariffs to apply, a French association of semolina producers challenged the government decree, asserting that the Minister of Agriculture had exceeded his power by creating separate trading rules for Algerian semolina. The dispute went to the core of whether France could conduct an independent trade policy, an especially sensitive subject since Algeria had recently been considered part of France itself.

[22] The articles in question were 91, 92, and 93. According to Folsom, these articles do create direct effects (1995: 91–2).

[23] In *Shell-Berre* Questiaux argued that requiring a reference 'would open the door to delaying tactics, overcrowding both jurisdictions'. *Supra Shell-Berre*, RDP, p. 1031. In the *Petitjean* case, Questiaux made the task of a reference sound arduous; first the *Conseil d'État* would have to ask if Article 91 created direct effects. If the answer was yes, then the *Conseil d'État* would have to refer it a second time to ask for an interpretation of the confusing article. See n. 21 above, *Petitjean*, RTDE, pp. 691–2. This perspective was also voiced in an academic article by a member of the *Conseil d'État* (Mazard 1971).

[24] 'Semoules decision', Syndicat Général de Fabricants de Semoules de France, *Conseil d'État* decision of 1 Mar. 1968, [1968] Recueil Lebon 149, [1970] CMLR 395.

[25] EC regulation 19/62 from 4 Apr. 1962.

The legal issue was complex. A few days after the EC regulation was passed, the French parliament had issued a statute stating that during the transition to Algerian independence the old bilateral rules of exchange would apply. According to the ECJ's supremacy doctrine the *Conseil d'État* would have to examine the compatibility of the French law and the decree with European law and grant European law supremacy if a conflict existed. French doctrine was far less clear. There was no question that French courts could enforce European law over any legal text that did not have the force of a parliamentary *loi*, but whether a piece of legislation was based on a *loi*, or based on a *règlement*, *décret*, *arrêté*, or *ordonnance* without the force of a *loi* was often open for interpretation.[26] The *Conseil d'État* could have avoided a conflict if it chose to classify the statute in question as a decree. The *Commissaire du Gouvernement* acknowledged this possibility: 'It is doubtless possible to give [the legislative text] several interpretations.' But Questiaux made it clear that to consider the statute a decree would mean that a reference to the ECJ would be necessary.[27] Finding that the decree was based on a *loi* also allowed the *Conseil d'État* to go on the record in opposition to French scholars advocating judicial enforcement of European law supremacy. Rejecting Pepy's legal argument, which was growing in popularity among academics, Questiaux argued:

To be sure, under Article 55 of the Constitution a treaty which has been duly ratified has . . . an authority superior to that of statutes. The Constitution thus affirms a preeminence of international law over internal law and numerous voices (nearly all of the academic writers) have been raised to say that a provision which makes our Constitution one of the most receptive to an international legal order should not remain a dead letter.

But the administrative court cannot make the effort which is asked of it without altering, by its mere will, its institutional position. It may neither criticize nor misconstrue a statute.[28]

Judges typically use lacunae in legal texts to develop the law or seize new powers for themselves, but the *Conseil d'État* used a gap in the French constitution to argue that no new powers were accorded to French judges. It argued

[26] The executive's authority to act could always be traced back to some parliamentary or constitutional authorization, and in reality the executive's practice of governing by decree in the Fifth Republic meant that the distinction between a *loi* and a *décret* lost all practical relevance. For a discussion of the 'flexibility' of the legal categories, see Loschak (1972: 138–50).

[27] Questiaux noted the advantage of seeing the decree as implementing a *loi*: If 'the decision under attack is in law based on the provisions of national law, and if it is not for you to put aside its application in favour of the provisions of the Community regulation and Treaty, the mere wish to verify its conformity with the international undertakings of France cannot justify sending the case to the European Court.' N. 24 above, *Semoules*, CMLR, pp. 398–9, 403.   [28] Ibid. 403–4.

that because politicians did not explicitly change the role of the courts while they were changing the role of all the other institutions, political bodies had shown that they wanted the French judges to continue to play a 'subordinate [role] of applying the statute'.[29] Indeed, the fact that the *Conseil Constitutionnel* was created while the role of the judiciary remained unchanged showed that the *Conseil Constitutionnel* and not ordinary French courts should be enforcing European law supremacy. Questiaux pointed out that there were other ways to ensure that European law was respected. The *Conseil d'État* could use its advisory role to promote the respect of European law. The EC Commission could use its infringement procedure to ensure that France does not misconstrue its legal obligations. And the *Conseil Constitutionnel* could enforce Article 55.[30] These arguments were somewhat disingenuous. The *Conseil d'État* knew the protections for European law were inadequate, but the situation was not created by the *Conseil d'État*, and it was not for the *Conseil d'État* to resolve.

The *Conseil d'État* signalled its support of the *Commissaire du Gouvernement's* argument by adopting the language and the legal argumentation used by Questiaux. In its nine-sentence decision, it found that the Ministry of Agriculture's decree had the force of *loi*. The *Conseil d'État* did not address the issue of European law supremacy, and thus implicitly accepted Questiaux's argument that it lacked the authority to question a national law. It simply said that 'the complainant syndicate cannot maintain that by taking the attacked decisions the Minister of Agriculture has exceeded his powers'.

Writing on this decision, the French Advocate-General at the ECJ said: 'It is useless to recall that in France tribunals have always refused to recognize their competence to judge the constitutionality of laws. One must note that this is a simple tradition; no formal text, constitutional or legislative, has ever denied or accorded such a competence to the judge.' For Lagrange, 'the truth is that the judges do not dare to enter into open conflict with the parliament which is traditionally considered to be the only body qualified to sovereignly express the national will' (1968: 228).

While maintaining the fiction of parliamentary sovereignty might have lent legitimacy to the *Conseil d'État's* action, the parliament was not the

---

[29] Questiaux argued: 'Certainly it is maintained that the traditional abstention of the courts before acts of the legislature would be less justified once our Constitution no longer recognizes the supremacy of the Parliament. But the Constitution has specifically dealt with the judicial review of legislation by adopting a restrictive view and conferring such review upon the Constitutional Council; above all while modifying the balance of legislative power and regulatory power, it did not think it good to define in a new way the powers of the courts; the task of the latter remains the subordinate one of applying the statute' (ibid. 404).

[30] Ibid. 404.

Conseil d'État's primary concern. Its larger objective in classifying the legal issue as a conflict between an EC regulation and a French *loi* was to keep legal issues out of the EC legal system, to protect its own authority over such issues, and to assure that it could find in favour of French policy. Questiaux argued:

It is difficult to imagine that there should be created in all areas affected by an international treaty whole zones in which the laws would be deprived of effect by the [national] judge, *and on the basis of texts which he is not fully entitled to interpret*. The argument is enticing in order to encourage the development of a Community legal order; its evolution is more difficult to imagine if it withdraws from the action of the legislator whole sections of the life of the country because treaties have appeared in the area in question . . .[31]

Indeed Questiaux saw the existence of the ECJ as an impediment to French courts finding creative ways to enforce international law. She argued that because the ECJ has to be consulted when there is a question about European law, the *Conseil d'État* was forced to choose between a straightforward interpretation not to apply the regulation, or an interpretation 'in the Community spirit' where the ECJ is consulted and the national court has to enforce the ECJ's decision.[32] When the German Constitutional Court rejected the supremacy of European law over the German constitution in its *Solange I* decision, Darras and Pirotte compared the German Court's action to the *Conseil d'État's Semoules* decision:

The *Semoules de France* decision of the *Conseil d'État* and the *Internationale Handelsgesellschaft (Solange I)* decision are very comparable. They both have as their underlying motivation a defensive reflex against a power which pretends to exclude their control and which puts in check the hierarchy of norms in the internal law of which these jurisdictions are the supreme guardians. (Darras and Pirotte 1976: 420)

---

[31] Ibid. 405–6 (my emphasis).

[32] Questiaux argued: 'It is perfectly conceivable, as we have said, that in the interpretation of statutes the judge should reason with regard to Community law just as he reasons with regard to general principles and start from the idea that the legislator did not intend to derogate from it. The only obstacle to such an unofficial collaboration of the national judge in the building of Community law is that it comes up against the problems of interpretation of that law, and that such rearrangements are easier when the powers of interpretation of the judge are undivided. But such was the desire of the negotiators of the Treaty. The present case well illustrates these difficulties since it leads you to be the arbitrator between a simple and almost simplistic interpretation, which from the beginning is opposed to the application of the Community regulation, and a more hazardous interpretation which immediately poses problems of interpretation of the Treaty. The effort of interpretation would in any case be frustrated by the redoubled inconvenience of having to compare the national statute once the European Court has given its reply' (ibid. 405).

While the *Conseil d'État's* attitude towards European law was not necessarily indicative of a broader judicial antagonism among French courts, judiciary courts were no more enthusiastic regarding European law or the preliminary ruling process at the time. Between 1965 and 1969 only seven references were sent to the ECJ by French judiciary courts. None of them was sent by a first instance court. None involved a law passed subsequent to an EC regulation. And all but one dealt with the complicated technical issue of social security for migrant workers. In more political issues, courts were deciding the cases on their own, invoking *Acte Clair* even when European law was not clear (Constantinesco 1968). The *Cour de Cassation* also seemed unenthusiastic about European law. One insider thought that the *Cour de Cassation* had 'calculat[ed] that their jurisdiction would no longer be the supreme and exclusive interpreter of the new texts' (Touffait 1975) and was thus only lukewarm about European law supremacy. Constantinesco included the judiciary courts in his assessment:

Oddly there remains the conclusion that despite the confirmation of their authority to decide on conflicts between national and EC law, French courts seem to do everything to avoid deciding between such conflicts, using sham arguments or circuitous reasoning to content themselves, and to guarantee the application of national law. (Constantinesco 1968: 325)

Rather than antagonize French judges, pro-integration scholars characterized early French decisions as well-intentioned misunderstandings of the law. But it seemed that the only endorsement of the ECJ's jurisprudence came from French courts staffed with pro-integration advocates. In 1967, for example, the *Cour d'Appel* in Paris made a reference to the ECJ without being requested to do so by the disputants. Also in 1967, the Parisian *Cour d'Appel* made a decision enforcing European law over national law based on the special nature of the EC legal order. At the time, pro-integration advocate Adolphe Touffait was president of the court.[33]

The *Semoules* case involved a national government unilaterally breaking European law by decree. By refusing even to question the validity of this decree, the *Conseil d'État* was condoning the type of situation the ECJ was trying to avoid though its supremacy doctrine. Despite what Questiaux claimed,

---

[33] Touffait (1975: 827–9). In an interview, a French legal scholar discussed how Touffait used his position at the *Cour d'Appel* in the late 1960s to send references to the ECJ (interview with a French professor of law specializing in EC law, Paris, 6 June 1994). Indeed, between 1965 and 1969 nearly half of the references by French courts (3 out of 7) to the ECJ came from the *Cour d'Appel* in Paris.

denying a judicial role in enforcing European law did allow the French government to ignore European law. The *Semoules* case did more than leave established legal precedent intact. It asserted orthodoxy once again in what was clearly a new legal situation created by EC membership and by Algerian independence, seizing a chance to close the door on the possibility of doctrinal evolution in light of the ECJ's supremacy doctrine.

Round 2. The Cour de Cassation *breaks ranks and accepts a role enforcing European law supremacy, 1970–1976*

French politics changed rapidly in light of the student revolts in 1968 and De Gaulle's departure from politics. As the Algerian conflict faded, a new sentiment emerged within the constitutional and judiciary branches. In a 1971 decision, the *Conseil Constitutionnel* incorporated preambles of previous French constitutions and statutes into French constitutional doctrine, basically creating for itself a bill of rights to enforce.[34] This decision marked a huge expansion of *Conseil Constitutionnel's* jurisdictional authority, introducing into French politics the notion of judicial review. In addition, it marked the first time the *Conseil Constitutionnel* decided against the executive (Stone 1992: 66–9). In 1974, the Parliament amended Article 61 of the constitution so that sixty senators or deputies could raise constitutional challenges to laws and regulations before the *Conseil Constitutionnel* (still before the statute was actually promulgated). Expanding access to the *Conseil Constitutionnel* led to more constitutional cases, and thus more opportunities for the *Conseil Constitutionnel* to develop constitutional law and influence national policy. Hitherto it had tended to support the policy of the government. After these changes, it began to create constitutional limits on public policy, and to build its legal and political authority (Stone 1992: ch. 3).

The *Conseil Constitutionnel's* new willingness to use its constitutional powers did not, however, extend to enforcing the supremacy of international law. When asked in 1975 to examine the compatibility of a French abortion law with the European Convention on Human Rights, the *Conseil Constitutionnel* refused. Its ruling was based on a number of questionable arguments. The *Conseil Constitutionnel* argued that while Article 55 of the Constitution clearly made international law superior to national law, it did not imply that the *Conseil Constitutionnel* was to enforce this provision. According to the *Conseil Constitutionnel*, because the supremacy of international treaties is limited and

---

[34] *Conseil Constitutionnel*, decision 71-44 DC of 16 July 1971, [1971] *Recueil des Décisions du Conseil Constitutionnel*, 29.

contingent on reciprocal application by other states, it could not enforce this provision. Furthermore, it made the perplexing assertion that a law contrary to a treaty is not necessarily contrary to the constitution.[35]

The 1975 ruling did not concern European law per se. In 1976, the *Conseil Constitutionnel* made a decision that contravened ECJ doctrine on European law supremacy. It determined that the EC Treaty is a treaty just like any other, and that the EC does not participate in the exercise of French sovereignty. It asserted that the constitution did not allow for a transfer of sovereignty, although 'limitations' of sovereignty were constitutional.[36] For many this distinction between a 'transfer' and a 'limitation' of sovereignty was dubious, if not euphemistic. But as Jacqué observed, it allowed the *Conseil Constitutionnel* to be the 'the master of the decision' regarding if and when limitations of French sovereignty could occur (Jacqué 1981: 4–7). The 1976 decision was also somewhat surprising in its reasoning. The case involved whether direct election of members to the European Parliament undermined the exercise of French national sovereignty. The *Conseil Constitutionnel* claimed that directly electing a parliament was not equivalent to transferring French sovereignty because the European parliament was not part of the French Republic and did not exercise French sovereignty. Vedel saw the *Conseil Constitutionnel* as saying that 'the election by universal suffrage is, at least from a juridical point of view, without importance' (1987: 14).

In its *Semoules* decision, the *Conseil d'État* claimed that the *Conseil Constitutionnel* was the appropriate legal body to enforce Article 55 of the French constitution and keep it from becoming 'a dead letter'.[37] But by refusing this power, the *Conseil Constitutionnel*'s 1975 decision *did* in practice make Article 55 a dead letter. Some have argued that by refusing to enforce Article 55 itself, the *Conseil Constitutionnel* was implicitly sending a message to other French courts to enforce European law supremacy. But scholars commenting on the decision at the time noted it was not intended nor could it necessarily be taken as a signal to other French courts that they should enforce European law supremacy (Boulouis 1975: 572; Favoreau and Loïc 1975).[38]

---

[35] This is perplexing because the constitution accords international law supremacy over national law. *Conseil Constitutionnel* decision 74-54 of 15 Jan. 1975, [1975] *Recueil des Décisions du Conseil Constitutionnel* 19 [1975] D. Jur. 529. See 3rd, 4th, and 5th 'considerations'.

[36] *Conseil Constitutionnel* decision 76-71 DC of 29/30 Dec. 1976, [1976] *Recueil des Décisions du Conseil Constitutionnel* 15.

[37] N. 24 above, *Semoules*, CMLR, pp. 398–9.

[38] This position was confirmed in interviews with members of the *Conseil Constitutionnel*, 30 May and 23 June 1994, Paris.

While the *Conseil Constitutionnel* was not sympathetic to European law supremacy, there were strong signs that judiciary courts were becoming more favourably disposed to enforcing European law over conflicting national law. In 1970, the *Cour de Cassation* acknowledged the supremacy of European law over a subsequent national act.[39] The *Ramel* case was not politically controversial. The government had decided not to defend the French regulation after losing in the first instance and what was at stake was a French regulation, not a *loi*. But, for the first time a French court used European law supremacy to set aside a national policy, and in its obiter dictum the *Cour de Cassation* boldly declared that national laws 'cannot overrule international law whose authority must prevail by virtue of constitutional law'.[40]

Following the *Ramel* decision, French judiciary courts began to apply European law supremacy.[41] These were promising advances, but none of the decisions invoked the supremacy of European law over French *loi*. French courts took this step in the *Jacques Vabre* case.

The coffee firm *Jacques Vabre* had refused to pay a French import tax, arguing that the tax exceeded similar taxes on domestic products and thus violated Article 95 EEC, which prohibits import taxes having the effect equivalent of a tariff. No reference to the ECJ was made, but the ECJ had established the direct effect of Article 95 in its 1966 *Lütticke* decision and there was a well-developed EC jurisprudence regarding the limits created by Article 95 for national import tax schemes.[42] The *tribunal d'instance* and the *Cour d'Appel* had decided in favour of *Jacques Vabre*, but they used circuitous arguments to avoid contradicting jurisprudential orthodoxy. The *tribunal d'instance* boldly asserted that European law is supreme over French statutes, but the legal basis for its ruling against the French government was that the customs authority had made an inaccurate calculation based on the wrong text.[43] The

---

[39] *Administration des contributions indirectes et comité interprofessionnel des vins doux naturels v. Ramel, Cour de Cassation* decision of 22 Oct. 1970, [1971] 14 DS Jur. 221, [1971] 1 CMLR 315. [40] Ibid. CMLR 317.

[41] In 1971 the *Jacques Vabre* case was decided in favour of EC law in a ruling by the *tribunal d'instance*. In 1972 the *Cour de Cassation* and the Parisian *Cour d'Appel* issued decisions according European law supremacy over French policy, relying on the EC Treaty as the basis for the supremacy of European law. *Administration des Douanes v. Société Cafés Jacques Vabre and J. Weigel et Compagnie S.à.r.l.*, Tribunal d'instance decision of 8 Jan. 1971, [1976] 1 CMLR 43. *Guerrini* decision, *Cour de Cassation* decision of 7 Jan. 1972, [1972] II JCP 17158, [1972] D. Jur. 497. *Joseph Aim and Société SPAD v. L'Administration des Douanes, Cour d'Appel* decision of 12 Apr. 1972, [1972] 1 CMLR 901.

[42] *Alfons Lütticke GmbH v. Hauptzollamt Saarlouis*, ECJ Case 57/65, [1966] ECR 205.

[43] N. 41 above *Jaques Vabre*.

Cour d'Appel sided with the plaintiff but insisted that what was at stake was a French regulation, not a *loi*.[44] The French government thought that the judiciary courts lacked the authority to set aside French law, and it appealed its loss.

The *Cour de Cassation* avoided detours that would have weakened the force of its decision. It classified the government act as a *loi* and declared that European law takes precedence over French law.[45] The decision's notoriety comes in large part from the strong arguments made by *Procureur Général* Adolphe Touffait.[46] Touffait wanted the *Cour de Cassation* to make a path-breaking decision that would encourage the *Conseil d'État* and the *Conseil Constitutionnel* to follow its lead. He argued that the *Conseil d'État*'s *Semoules* decision was really an exceptional situation given Algeria's young independence, and he made it seem like the *Conseil Constitutionnel*'s 1975 abortion decision was intended to resolve the longstanding debate over whether French courts could enforce Article 55. Touffait made the questionable claim that the *Conseil Constitutionnel*'s 1975 decision showed that controlling the compatibility of national law with European law was not constitutional review, but simply *applying* a clear provision of the French constitution.

Touffait had a long history of pro-integration politics, and as President of the *Cour d'Appel* he had issued the most supportive European law decisions in France to date.[47] Given his prior inclination, it is unlikely that he was inspired by the *Conseil Constitutionnel*'s decision. But drawing on the recent *Conseil Constitutionnel* decision lent an air of constitutional legitimacy to the *Cour de Cassation*'s actions, and put the *Conseil Constitutionnel* in the position of either explicitly opposing the decision, or letting the precedent stand. Touffait needed to address the issue of Article 55 because that was the central question for most French judges. Really he wanted to get away from French constitutional terms entirely, and shift the debate to the terms of the ECJ's doctrine. He argued:

If I have directed your attention for so long on Article 55 of our Constitution, it is because the argument of the appeal in discussing its scope relies on the authority of a judgment of the *Conseil d'État* and has led us to follow the plaintiff (the government)

---

[44] Ibid., *Cour d'Appel* decision of 7 July 1973, [1975] 2 CMLR 223.

[45] Ibid., *Cour de Cassation* decision of 24 May 1975, [1975] 2 CMLR 343.

[46] The *Procureur-Général* serves the same function as the *Commissaire du Gouvernement*, but unlike the *Commissaire du Gouvernement*, whose position is rotated among *Conseil d'État* members, the *Procureur-Général*'s position is permanent.

[47] Buffet-Techakaloff (1984: 273). See further n. 34 above.

onto the ground chosen by him . . . It would be possible for you to give precedence to the application of Article 95 of the Rome Treaty over the subsequent statute by relying on Article 55 of our Constitution, but personally I would ask you not to mention it and instead base your reasoning on the very nature of the legal order instituted by the Rome Treaty.[48]

Touffait drew on the argument of pro-integration scholars that basing European law supremacy on the special nature of the EC Treaty (the ECJ's judicial reasoning) would improve the likelihood of reciprocal enforcement of European law supremacy in other countries, especially in countries lacking a constitutional provision such as Article 55. Appealing to the pride of the *Cour de Cassation*, Touffait closed by arguing: 'It is in this context that the judgment you are to deliver will be read and commented upon; its audience will extend beyond the frontiers of our country and spread over the whole of the member-states of the Community.'[49]

The *Cour de Cassation*'s *Jacques Vabre* decision firmly endorsed the supremacy of the EC Treaty over national law. The *Cour de Cassation* did not follow Touffait's plea to base its decision on the nature of the EC Treaty itself. It referred to Article 55 of the constitution, but it also noted that the separate nature of the EC legal order was directly applicable to nationals of member states and binding in national courts.[50] This decision was widely anticipated, and interpreted as a fundamental breakthrough. Why was the *Cour de Cassation* willing to go where other French courts were not? Part of the reason is that the *Cour de Cassation* is not the main articulator of French law and thus it felt less threatened by the ECJ. As Vedel argued:

A judge [like the *Conseil d'État*] which sets outs texts of principle, forging over tens and even hundreds of years an autonomous public law, would find it more difficult to integrate a new body, coordinated and hierarchical, of law and would have a tendency to

---

[48] N. 45 above, CMLR, p. 364.

[49] Ibid. 367.

[50] Many pro-integration scholars were disappointed that the *Cour de Cassation* had not followed Touffait's plea to base European law supremacy on the special nature of the EC legal system (Boulouis 1975; Jeantet 1976; Pirotte-Gerouville 1976; Ruzié 1975). The *Cour de Cassation* seemed to go more in the direction encouraged by Touffait in the *Von Kempis* decision (Mar. 1976), where it set aside a French law by referring to European law and ECJ jurisprudence, but not to the French constitution. The *Jacques Vabre* and *Von Kempis* decisions were the only cases, however, where the EC Treaty and doctrine were relied on. When the *Conseil Constitutionnel* ruled in Sept. 1976 that the EC Treaty was a treaty like any other, without a greater or a lesser duty to be followed, the *Cour de Cassation* stopped referring to the EC Treaty as a basis for European law supremacy, instead relying on the French constitution to support its actions. *Von Kempis (Clave Bouhaben) v. Geldof, Cour de Cassation* decision of 12 Mar. 1976, [1976] 2 CMLR 152. *Conseil Constitutionnel* decision 76-71 of 29/30 Dec. 1976, [1976] *Recueil des Décisions du Conseil Constitutionnel* 15.

defend the judicial principles which it authored and which, even more than the rules, are the substance of the law which it applies. Whatever the importance of the jurisprudence of the *Cour de Cassation* is, it deals mainly with codes, and notably of civil codes. The *Cour de Cassation* has created many less juridical norms than the *Conseil d'État*: it has not operated in the vast legislative 'no man's land'. It is thus more used to the idea that a jurisprudence can change when the texts change and esteems such a change to be the adoption of the European treaties. (Vedel 1987: 27–8)

It is also clear that the *Jacques Vabre* case presented the *Cour de Cassation* with a rare opportunity to make a very significant decision that would, as Touffait said, extend beyond the frontiers of France. One should also not underestimate the pride at stake when the *Cour de Cassation* introduced an alternative interpretation regarding the supremacy of European law over that of the *Conseil d'État*. The judiciary branch is the poor second cousin to the administrative branch, without the same prestige as the elite *Conseil d'État* and without the same professional opportunities or chance to influence policy.[51] To be a creator of French law was to seize the initiative from the *Conseil d'État*, which fancied itself the most serious and important of the French high courts. Indeed, the *Cour de Cassation*'s decision establishing the supremacy of European law over subsequent national law was one of its most important decisions in years, and gained the court an international profile which it had rarely achieved before.

A few academics hailed the *Jacques Vabre* decision as a breakthrough for the entire French legal system (Hummings 1975; Simon 1976), but this was more wishful thinking than reality. The *Jacques Vabre* decision introduced into the French legal context a strong and authoritative alternative view to that of the *Conseil d'État*, and put the onus on politicians and the *Conseil Constitutionnel* to tell ordinary court judges that they could *not* enforce European law over French law. But it did not directly affect the jurisprudence or behaviour of the other French courts. The *Jacques Vabre* decision was dismissed by the *Conseil d'État* as a political move by Touffait, who at the time was a candidate to be an ECJ judge. The *Conseil d'État* held firmly to its *Semoules* doctrine.[52] Indeed, it never accepted the *Cour de Cassation*'s argument that enforcing European law

---

[51] According to Boigel, with the creation of the *École Nationale d'Administration*, the prestige associated with being a judge in the judiciary branch declined (Boigel 1995: 39). See further n. 8 above on the different prestige of these two legal bodies.

[52] When the *Conseil d'État* was presented with an opportunity to reverse its *Semoules* jurisprudence in 1979, and was even nudged to do so by lower administrative tribunals that were starting to review posterior law in light of international treaties, it continued to apply its *Semoules* jurisprudence. Union Démocratique du Travail, *Conseil d'État* decision of 22 Oct. 1979, [1979] *Recueil des Décisions du Conseil d'État* 385.

supremacy was simply 'applying' the constitution.

By 1976 a significant divergence within the three branches of the French judiciary had emerged. The *Conseil d'État* refused to enforce the supremacy of European law—insisting that was the *Conseil Constitutionnel*'s job. The *Conseil Constitutionnel* refused its authority to enforce European law supremacy. And the *Cour de Cassation* said that the fact the *Conseil Constitutionnel* was not reviewing the compatibility of French law with international treaties showed that enforcing European law supremacy was not constitutional review, it was simply *applying* the EC Treaty. Members of the *Conseil d'État* called for political bodies to resolve this divergence by indicating through law if judicial bodies had the authority to enforce European law supremacy. They also hoped that the *Conseil Constitutionnel* would make it clear to the *Cour de Cassation* that its 1975 decision did not authorize ordinary courts to enforce Article 55 (Galmont 1990). These hopes seemed realistic in the context of the late 1970s, when anti-integration sentiments were being roused within French judicial and political bodies.

Round 3. Encore Non!—*The* Conseil d'État *steps up its opposition to ECJ jurisprudence, 1977–1981*

The *Conseil d'État*'s 1960s jurisprudence was hardly friendly towards the ECJ, but it was not angry or upset with the ECJ either. In an interview, a French negotiator of the Treaty of Rome and a Former *Conseil Constitutionnel* judge explained the mentality inside the *Conseil d'État* in the 1960s:

When the EC legal system came along, the *Conseil d'État* could not imagine that the ECJ could somehow be supreme to the *Conseil d'État*. Add to this assumption a bit of nationalism, and the *Conseil d'État* could not see any room for European law or the ECJ, unless it was a technical question.[53]

What was mostly a lack of imagination, however, turned to hostility in the 1970s. The change began with the ECJ's 1974 *Charmasson* decision.[54] The *Conseil d'État* had referred the case to the ECJ expecting it to uphold the French government's position. By making a reference to the ECJ in a case where the outcome was practically assured to be positive, the *Conseil d'État*

---

[53] Interview with a negotiator of the Treaty of Rome and a former *Conseil Constitutionnel* judge, 23 June 1994, Paris. This argument was reiterated in an interview with a member of the *Conseil d'État* since 1959 (27 June 1994, Fiesole), and in an interview with the Secretary-General of the *Conseil d'État* (5 July 1994, Paris).

[54] *Charmasson v. Ministre de l'économie et des finances*, ECJ Case 48/74, [1974] ECR 1383.

hoped to counter the academic criticism that it abused the *Acte Clair* doctrine, and reinforce the French position that their special banana import agreement with France's former colonies was, in fact, compatible with European law. But contrary to the *Conseil d'État*'s expectations, the ECJ ruled that as of 1974 French sovereignty over bilateral trade agreements had been ceded.[55] The *Conseil d'État* had finally made a reference to the ECJ, and now it was stuck with a binding and 'higher' ECJ decision with which it disagreed.

Conseil d'État judges were further annoyed with the audacity of the ECJ's assertion of the supremacy of European law over national constitutions in its 1970 *International Handelsgesellschaft* decision,[56] and the ECJ's 1978 *Simmenthal* decision,[57] which authorized lower courts to ignore higher court jurisprudence on European law supremacy.[58] And the *Conseil d'État* was upset about the increasing specificity of EC directives. The more laws drafted in Brussels, the more foreign legal texts were implemented in France without the *Conseil d'État*'s review, and thus the less influence it had in its advising role.

Disenchantment with the EC and the ECJ was also growing in the French administration. Political bodies were angry about the ECJ's 1971 *ERTA* decision, where it asserted the EC's exclusive legislative authority in external economic policy matters (Jacqué 1981: 4-1).[59] The ECJ's 1974 *Charmasson* decision that so angered the *Conseil d'État* had also provided a wake-up call to the French government, which had until then seen the ECJ as a relatively limited institution (Buffet-Tchakaloff 1984: 18). The National Assembly also disliked the increasing specificity of EC directives, which gave it less influence over national legislation implementing EC directives. In 1976 the National Assembly passed a law that would allow it to nullify European laws and ECJ interpretations that encroached on its prerogatives (Jacqué 1981: 4-7, 4-8). While the parliament has yet to use this procedure, in 1978 it refused to adopt an EC directive, calling it a 'misappropriation of the procedure of the directive and a veritable usurpation of the legislative powers of the Member States'.[60] For the first time in the Fifth Republic, the National

[55] The ECJ's decision did not apply to the case at hand, since it was concerned with a period before the expiration of the transition period.

[56] *Internationale Handelsgesellschaft GmbH v. Einfuhr- und Vorratsstelle für Getreide und Futtermittel*, ECJ Case 11/70, [1970] ECR 1125.

[57] *Amministrazione delle Finanze dello Stato v. Simmenthal SpA (II)*, ECJ Case 106/77, [1978] ECR 629, [1978] CMLR 263.

[58] Based on interviews with members of the *Conseil d'État* involved in EC legal issues, including some of the *Commissaires du Gouvernement* who had argued European law cases, 30 May 1994, Paris; 27 June 1994, Fiesole; 7 and 11 July 1994, Paris.

[59] *Commission v. Council (ERTA)*, ECJ Case 22/70, [1971] ECR 263, [1971] CMLR 335.

[60] JO Ass. Nat. Deb. of 30 Nov. 1978, p. 8571.

Assembly declared an act of government (namely the government's attempt to reform value added tax through the EC) to be unconstitutional (Weill 1978). Also in 1978, after a shrill debate in which the ECJ was vilified for its 'fraud and excesses of power', the French parliament passed into law an act incompatible with an ECJ decision regarding Euratom (Jacqué 1981: 4-1).

These political protests made the *Conseil d'État* think it would have support in challenging the ECJ's ever-expanding authority. It also thought it would have the support of the *Conseil Constitutionnel*, which seemed also to want to keep the process of legal integration from encroaching on national sovereignty (Vedel 1987). As mentioned, the *Conseil Constitutionnel*'s 1975 and 1976 decisions had openly rejected the ECJ's doctrine on the special nature of the EC treaties.[61] In addition the *Conseil Constitutionnel* made two decisions in 1977 and 1978 that implied that it would review the constitutionality of EC obligations.[62] These decisions were derided at the time as a usurpation of the powers of the ECJ, since the ECJ was the only body authorized to consider the validity of EC rules. But the decisions were consistent with the German Constitutional Court's *Solange I* position that national constitutions are superior to European law (Zoller 1992: 272).

Emboldened by this support, the *Conseil d'État* began intentionally and explicitly to issue decisions contradicting ECJ jurisprudence. Its best-known defiance was the *Cohn-Bendit* decision, which repudiated the ECJ's jurisprudence on the direct effect of directives. In this case, *Commissaire du Gouvernement* Genevois acknowledged that this ECJ's jurisprudence was legally questionable, but argued that the only way to resolve the issue was to engage in dialogue with the ECJ. He defined for the *Conseil d'État* three options: (1) accept the ECJ jurisprudence even if there was a disagreement over legal interpretation;[63] (2) ignore ECJ jurisprudence to 'draw attention to the fact that the case law of the Court of Justice . . . puts the national judge in a difficult position' and to 'mark clearly that case law which departs somewhat from the letter of the Treaty can be usefully contested by national

[61] Nn. 35 and 36 above, *Conseil Constitutionnel* decisions 74-54 and 76-1.

[62] In these cases parliamentarians had asked the *Conseil Constitutionnel* to review the constitutionality of EC regulations. The *Conseil Constitutionnel* could have dismissed the referral because the regulations did not have to be passed by the parliament, and thus there was no French law to review. Its willingness to hear the cases was taken as a sign that the *Conseil Constitutionnel* would review the constitutionality of EC obligations. *Conseil Constitutionnel* decision 77-89 of 30 Dec. 1977, [1977] *Recueil des Décisions du Conseil Constitutionnel* 46. *Conseil Constitutionnel* decision 77-91 of 18 Jan. 1978, [1978] *Recueil des Décisions du Conseil Constitutionnel* 19. *Conseil Constitutionnel* decision 78-93 of 29 Apr. 1978, [1978] *Recueil des Décisions du Conseil Constitutionnel* 23.

[63] 'Cohn-Bendit', *Minister of Interior v. Daniel Cohn-Bendit*, *Conseil d'État* decision of 22 Dec. 1978, [1978] Recueil Lebon 524, [1980] 1 CMLR 545. See CMLR, p. 560.

courts';[64] or (3) reject extreme positions and enter into a dialogue with the ECJ by raising the concerns in a reference to the Court.[65] For Genevois, the third option was the only valid one.[66] Not making a reference, he argued, would be an affront to the ECJ:

[i]t would be singularly lacking in respect for the Community Court, which by the EEC Treaty has the task of ensuring a uniform application of community law over the territory of the Member-States of the Community, to interpret the Treaty in a sense which is diametrically opposed to a well-established case law of the Court of Justice of the European Communities.[67]

What is more, it would be hypocritical:

You cannot in my view give absolute priority to the literal interpretation of the text when your own case law itself gives many examples of cases in which you have indulged in constructive interpretation.[68]

The *Conseil d'État*, he argued, might simply 'have to give way, in the same way as, in exceptional cases, the duty of obedience of an official may have to give way'.[69] Dialogue with the ECJ would be a more productive approach, one that would allow the *Conseil d'État* more influence over ECJ decisions.

   The Interior Minister had relaxed his contested decision against Cohn-Bendit two days earlier, and the *Conseil d'État* could have dismissed the case because it was no longer legally relevant. But the *Conseil d'État* took the provocative approach of refusing to refer the issue to the ECJ and explicitly challenging the ECJ's doctrine on the direct effect of directives. Most legal scholars interpreted the *Conseil d'État's Cohn-Bendit* decision as a politically inspired attack on the ECJ. European Court judge Kapteyn summarized the situation this way:

After the not very constructive decisions of the *Conseil d'État* in the Shell Berre case and the Syndicat de Fabricants de Semoules case the judgment in the [*Cohn-Bendit*] case openly impairs the authority of the Court of Justice. Here the very system of judicial cooperation of courts in a Community context is deliberately broken: The *Conseil d'État* substitutes its own interpretation of a Treaty provision for that of the Court of Justice and on its part refrains from a dialogue with the Court on the difference of

---

   [64] Ibid., CMLR, pp. 560, 561.

   [65] N. 63 above, *Cohn-Bendit*, CMLR, p. 561.

   [66] He argued: 'in my opinion, in the field of Community law you have no valid reason for departing from the case law of the Court of Justice unless it requires you to act against the Constitution of the French Republic, which it would not do': ibid. 564.

   [67] Ibid. 562.

   [68] Ibid. 562.   [69] Ibid. 564.

opinion that has arisen . . . Has the 'guerre des juges' feared by the *Commissaire du Gouvernement* become a fact with this decision? . . . it hardly appears possible to avoid the conclusion that a declaration of war was involved. (Kapteyn 1979: 704)

The issue was clearly greater than a disagreement over legal interpretation. The decision had no practical impact, since the French government had already rescinded its contested decision. And the *Conseil d'État* actually left open a door through which individuals could challenge improperly executed EC directives, implying that all Cohn-Bendit had needed to do was to argue that the Minister's action was illegal.[70] More important than the legal issue, the *Conseil d'État* was trying to show the ECJ what could happen when it exceeded its interpretive authority. According to Dutheillet de Lamothe and Robineau, both *Conseillers d'État*,

In refusing to bend before the jurisprudence of the Court on directives, the *Conseil d'État*, it seems to us, in return showed that the absolute authority which is attached to decisions rendered by the Court under the auspices of Article 177 does not permit [the Court] to impose on national jurisdictions, by way of its authority, an interpretation of the treaty going far beyond [the treaty's] stipulations. Such a remark does not in any way put into question the liberty, seen in some cases as a necessity, for the Court to do its praetorian [meaning institution-building] work . . . [The *Conseil d'État*] is showing simply that this praetorian work must, as far as it is bold, correspond to a certain consensus in national jurisdictions. (Dutheillet de Lamothe and Robineau 1979: 30)[71]

As Kovar put it, the *Conseil d'État* was trying to influence the ECJ to stop its integration-oriented jurisprudence, a jurisprudence that was 'systematically favourable to increasing integration to the detriment of the rights of states' (Kovar 1979: 19158 p. 1).[72] The *Cohn-Bendit* decision is the most celebrated example of defiance, but not the only one (Buffet-Tchakaloff 1984: 310–15). One year later the *Conseil d'État* refused to make a reference to the ECJ, and refused to apply an ECJ ruling to a case at hand.[73]

---

[70]   The *Conseil d'État* had said in its decision: '*in absence of any dispute on the legality of the administrative measure taken* by the French government to comply with the directives enacted by the Council of the European Communities, the solution to be given to the action brought by M. Cohn-Bendit may not in any case be made' (ibid. 563; my emphasis). Indeed, in subsequent decisions the *Conseil d'État* developed this loophole to bring its jurisprudence into line with that of the ECJ (Tatham 1991: 919). Féderation Française des sociétés de protection de la nature. Conseil d'État decision of 7 Dec. 1984 [1985] RFDA. 303.

[71]   My translation.

[72]   My translation.

[73]   The *Conseil d'État* refused to apply a regulation the ECJ had deemed invalid—a practice it would not apply under French legal doctrine. Syndicat National des Fabricants de Spiritueux Consommés à l'Eau, *Conseil d'État* decision of 27 July 1979, [1980] RDP 219.

At first it seemed that the *Conseil d'État's* strategy was having the desired effects. The German *Bundesfinanzhof* followed the *Conseil d'État* in its defiance of the direct effect of directives.[74] Former Gaullist Prime Minister Michel Debré organized *Le Comité pour l'indépendance et l'unité de la France*, which made the ECJ one of its principal targets. In a parliamentary debate in 1979, Debré accused the ECJ 'not for the first time or the last' of having 'pathological megalomania . . . declaring what is and is not European law based on pure inventions of law'.[75] He urged the government to take action against the ECJ, and to declare ECJ decisions in which France was not a party to be non-binding within France. In September 1980 Debré's group sponsored a conference on the 'Sovereignty of French Law', to create an alternative anti-European supremacy view to that of the prevailing academic literature. Participants (which included former members of the *Conseil Constitutionnel*) challenged what they called ideological jurisprudence, which did not look to existing law but tried to create new law based on a particular ideology of Brussels bureaucrats. The conference's consensus was that the ECJ had gone well beyond its Treaty mandate, and that when the ECJ engaged in its 'fantasy exegesis', it went well beyond Article 55 of the French constitution (B.L.G. 1980; Duverger 1980). Participants called for a constitutional revision and a revision of the Treaty of Rome to make it clear that national judges should not apply European law supremacy.

Three weeks after this conference, the National Assembly acted by attaching to a judicial reform bill an amendment explicitly designed to counter the *Cour de Cassation's Jacques Vabre* decision and make national court enforcement of European law supremacy illegal. When proposing his amendment, M. Aurillac presented the 'problem' this way; it was clear from both the *Conseil d'État's* jurisprudence and the *Conseil Constitutionnel's* 1975 decision that French judges could not set aside national law in favour of international law. But

unfortunately, to complicate things, the jurisprudence of the *Cour de Cassation* [came out] rigorously opposed . . . This contrary jurisprudence presents numerous inconveniences; this is all the more true because the *Cour de Cassation* can intervene in commercial law, the regulator of economic life. What is more, through this jurisprudence the *Cour de Cassation* contorted one of the foundations of French law: the prohibition against tribunals getting involved in the exercise of legislative power.[76]

[74] *Re: Value Added Tax Directives*, BFH decision (Case V B 51/80) of 16 July 1981, [1982] I CMLR 527. See further above, Round 4.

[75] JO Ass. Nat. Deb. of 1 June 1979, p. 4610. My translation.

[76] Ibid. 9 Oct. 1980, p. 2637. My translation.

The solution suggested was to reinstate and modernize the law of 16 and 24 August 1790 by inserting in a proposed judicial reform the statement: 'Judges cannot, directly or indirectly, take any part in the exercise of legislative power, nor can they hinder or suspend the execution of laws regularly promulgated for whatever reason, without abusing their authority.'[77] This solution was endorsed by the *Garde des Sceaux* (Guard of the Seals), Alain Peyrefitte of the Ministry of Justice:

> One could think that the *Conseil d'État* better respected the provisions of the law of 1790 . . . than the *Cour de Cassation*. . . . The Government could not be anything but favourable to the amendment of the commission which is nothing more than a reaffirmation of a great republican tradition.[78]

The law was passed overwhelmingly in the National Assembly, but the executive branch got the senate to block debate on the amendment to avoid problems for France at the European level. Since the issue was not debated in the senate, the amendment never gained legal force.[79]

The failure to have this amendment adopted into law had the opposite effect to that intended by M. Aurillac and his supporters. It signalled clearly that neither the parliament nor the government would act against courts applying European law supremacy. After the failed Aurillac amendment, the political context was changed. While political bodies did not legitimate the *Cour de Cassation*'s *Jacques Vabre* decision, it was clear that politicians would tolerate judges reviewing the compatibility of French law with European law.

Round 4. The Conseil d'État *and* Conseil Constitutionnel *accept a role enforcing European law supremacy, 1982–1989*

The political and legal context in France changed significantly in the 1980s. The political allies supporting the *Conseil d'État*'s legal orthodoxy were the Gaullists, who had used appeals to national sovereignty as an attempt to undermine support for the other party of the Right, the *Union pour la démocratie française* (UDF). Their opposition to European integration helped to split the vote on the right and contributed to the first election of a government of the Left in the Fifth Republic. The 1981 Socialist victory had two impacts with respect to the debate over European law supremacy. First, after

---

[77] JO Ass. Nat. Deb. of 1 June 1979, p. 4610. My translation.

[78] Ibid. 2644. My translation.

[79] For more on the failed Aurillac amendment, see Buffet-Tchakaloff (1984: 346), Galmont (1990), Isaac (1980), Jacqué (1981: 4–14). For more on conflicts between the French parliament and the ECJ, see Buffet-Tchakaloff 1984: 341–8.

Mitterrand's economic experiment failed in 1982–3, the Socialists turned to European integration as a means of promoting economic prosperity (Moravcsik 1998: 333). For the first time since the Treaty of Rome had been negotiated, European integration became a priority for the French government.

Second, the role and jurisprudence of the *Conseil Constitutionnel* began to change because of the party realignment. The Socialists were now in power, but the *Conseil Constitutionnel* was still dominated by Gaullist appointments and was a helpful tool to challenge laws passed by the Left-dominated parliament. The strategic use of the *Conseil Constitutionnel* by the minority Right transformed the *Conseil Constitutionnel* into a player in French politics (Stone 1992: ch. 3). Through time, the Socialists appointed their own judges to the *Conseil Constitutionnel*, including judges more positively disposed to European legal integration.[80] The changing appointments also brought new priorities to the legal body. According to Alec Stone (1992: 100), beginning in 1981 the *Conseil Constitutionnel* started explicitly to court the legal community, 'recogniz[ing] and actively [seeking] the legitimating power of legal discourse and the judicial function . . . The Council's work . . . became more attendant to judicial norms, its decisions lengthened, [and] developed into a technical and closely argued jurisprudence'. Winning support in the scholarly community became a priority, as did getting other French courts to accept its jurisprudence.

There had been wide criticism of the *Conseil Constitutionnel*'s 1975 decision rejecting a role enforcing the supremacy of international law because of the 'contingent' nature of international law. The Secretary-General of the *Conseil Constitutionnel* pointed out that many international legal texts, such as the Convention on Human Rights, have a constitutional status and are not contingent (Genevois 1988a: 213–14). As *Procureur-Général* Touffait and the *Cour de Cassation* also indicated in the *Jacques Vabre* case, the issue of reciprocity can be addressed through the EC's infringement procedure, thus EC legal obligations are not contingent.[81] Also criticized was the *Conseil Constitutionnel*'s dubious distinction between 'transfers' and 'limitations' of sovereignty. This distinction had been called illusory. If the *Conseil Constitutionnel* wanted to bolster respect for its international law jurisprudence, it had to find more compelling legal argumentation.

---

[80] e.g. George Vedel, who was the French representative negotiating the sections of the Treaty of Rome pertaining to the ECJ, and Robert Lecourt, a former ECJ justice who is reputed to be the architect of the ECJ's supremacy doctrine and who had actively encouraged French judges to help promote integration through law (Lecourt 1964; 1965).

[81] N. 43 above. See pp. 345–6, 369.

But the *Conseil Constitutionnel* was still hesitant to take on a role enforcing the supremacy of international law because of procedural limitations. Since laws cannot be questioned before the *Conseil Constitutionnel* once they are promulgated, the *Conseil Constitutionnel* faced the very real possibility that the ECJ, or even worse, the European Court of Human Rights would later reject a law it reviewed.[82] The *Conseil Constitutionnel* did not want to be the enforcer of European law supremacy. The *Jacques Vabre* solution of having national courts enforce European law supremacy ensured that Article 55 was not a dead letter.[83] And the failed Aurillac amendment revealed that political bodies had accepted this position too.

In 1986 the *Conseil Constitutionnel* endorsed the *Jacques Vabre* precedent and started to push the *Conseil d'État* to change its position as well. It did not endorse the claim that judges were simply 'applying' the constitution. It argued instead that 'it was the responsibility of the different organs of the state to protect the application of international conventions in the cadre of their respective competences',[84] which was another way of saying that the *Conseil d'État* should enforce European law supremacy in its jurisdictional realm too (Bonichot 1989). In 1988, the *Conseil Constitutionnel* made it even clearer that the *Conseil d'État* should change its jurisprudence. Acting in its capacity as an election judge, the *Conseil Constitutionnel* applied the *Cour de Cassation*'s *Jacques Vabre* jurisprudence, acknowledging its duty to enforce international law supremacy.[85] Writing on the decision, Genevois commented:

[This decision] cannot but re-enforce the doctrinal current which . . . implicitly authoriz[es] the administrative judge, like the judiciary judge, to assure the respect of the hierarchy of norms which it edicts . . . one can thus hope that the solution adopted

[82] The *Conseil Constitutionnel* was concerned especially about the ECHR because a condemnation would mean that it had not sufficiently protected basic rights. Based on interviews with the Secretary-General of the *Conseil Constitutionnel*, 30 May 1994, Paris. This argument was published in Genevois (1988a).

[83] In an article, the Secretary-General of the *Conseil Constitutionnel* argued that while the *Conseil Constitutionnel* did not necessarily intend by its 1975 decision that the ordinary courts should exercise control of national laws with treaty obligations, 'how could it not be noticed the application made by the judiciary judge in the *Jacques Vabre* jurisprudence gave good results at least as far as Community law was concerned? It then realized that any reversal of this jurisprudence . . . would have a destabilizing effect' (Genevois 1989: 828).

[84] *Conseil Constitutionnel* decision 86-216 of 3 Sept. 1986, [1986] *Recueil des Décisions du Conseil Constitutionnel* 135, [1987] JDI 289. My translation.

[85] *Conseil Constitutionnel* decision 88-1082/1117 of 21 Oct. 1988, [1988] *Recueil des Décisions du Conseil Constitutionnel* 183, [1988] R. Fr. D. Admin. 908.

by the *Conseil Constitutionnel* will lead the *Conseil d'État* to reconsider its traditional jurisprudence, that it even recently abstained once again from doing. (Genevois 1900b. 915)

The message was heard. In an interview the *Conseil d'État*'s Secretary-General said: 'The idea that the *Conseil Constitutionnel* could decide one way when it worked as an electoral court, and the *Conseil d'État* another way was not acceptable.'[86]

The *Conseil Constitutionnel*'s support of European law supremacy helped to tip the balance in favour of the *Cour de Cassation*'s supremacy, isolating the *Conseil d'État* within the French legal system and undermining the legal validity of arguments the *Conseil d'État* had used to deny itself a role enforcing European law supremacy. Members of the *Conseil d'État* began openly to call for a change in *Conseil d'État* jurisprudence, publishing articles and books that highlighted the disadvantages of the *Conseil d'État*'s *Semoules* jurisprudence (Genevois 1988a; Abraham 1989; Bonichot 1989; Hubac 1988). They pointed out how the divergence in legal outcomes revealed a breach of legal logic and made the legal process look subjective:

a disputant can receive a different solution depending on if the case involves administrative or civil jurisdiction: in one case it will be decided by the rules of the legislature and in the other by rule of the treaty. But intellectually, such different treatment is not justified by any account . . . That one jurisdiction would apply private law and the other public law, that corresponds to the logic of the system. But that one would apply the treaty and the other national law, that doesn't correspond to any logic. (Abraham 1989: 120)

Practically speaking, the divergence was creating disparities in the administration of French law.[87]

The *Conseil d'État*'s jurisprudence and attitude also created problems for the French government. In 1983, France was condemned by the ECJ for setting prices for tobacco imports.[88] The government ignored the ruling, and a case was brought in front of the *Conseil d'État* challenging the government's price setting rules. The *Conseil d'État* refused to review the legality of the French law that was posterior to the EC statutes, but granted it had the authority to review the application of the law by the Ministry. In a ruling that

[86] Interview with the Secretary-General, chief administrative officer of the *Conseil d'État*, 5 July 1994, Paris.

[87] Questions dealing with indirect taxation were sent to the judiciary branch, and questions dealing with direct taxation (VAT etc.) went to the administrative branch. Depending on which type of tax was at stake, the legal result differed.

[88] *Commission v. French Republic*, ECJ case 90/82, [1983] ECR 2011.

directly contradicted the ECJ's finding, the *Conseil d'État* found that the Ministry had applied French law correctly and had not violated European law.[89] On 13 July 1988, France was condemned again by the ECJ for the same law.[90] The tobacco case showed the costs of the *Conseil d'État*'s *Semoules* position. With the French government now wanting to be a model leader in the process of integration, the official condemnation and the *Conseil d'État*'s intransigence towards the ECJ was counterproductive.

Pressure on the *Conseil d'État* increased when in 1987 the *Conseil d'État*'s jurisdiction was attacked by Parisian lawyers, who wanted its authority to hear appeals against Council of Competition decisions to be transferred to the judiciary branch. The lawyers had a general dislike of the *Conseil d'État*, but the latter's anti-ECJ stance fuelled the lawyers' actions since much of French competition law was made at the EC level (Galmont 1990). The issue of transferring powers to the judiciary branch was especially sensitive for the *Conseil d'État*. There had been a clear trend since 1957 towards transferring more and more powers from the administrative branch to the judiciary branch (Combarnous 1995: 176), and there was long-standing support for eliminating the administrative branch altogether (Galmont 1990: 19–20). The success of the lawyers was only the latest example of the problem, and it was noteworthy that this time the *Conseil d'État*'s anti-EC stance was behind the lawyer's actions.

The law transferring competition jurisdiction was appealed to the *Conseil Constitutionnel*, which upheld the transfer—reinforcing the *Conseil d'État*'s sense that no one would come to its defence.[91] But the *Conseil Constitutionnel* did offer the *Conseil d'État* a carrot to facilitate change in the *Semoules* jurisprudence. Before the *Conseil Constitutionnel*'s 1987 decision, the legislature had the power to eliminate the *Conseil d'État* as an institution by passing a simple law. In its decision upholding the transfer of jurisdiction, the *Conseil Constitutionnel* stated that the existence and role of the *Conseil d'État* was itself part of the constitutional guarantee of a separation of powers. The meant that eliminating the *Conseil d'État* would require the higher threshold of a constitutional amendment.

[89] Société Internationale Sales and Import Corporation BV, *Conseil d'État* decision of 13 Dec. 1985.

[90] *Commission v. French Republic*, ECJ Case 169/87, [1988] ECR 4093.

[91] *Conseil Constitutionnel* decision 86-224 of 23 Jan. 1987, [1987] *Recueil des Décisions du Conseil Constitutionnel*, 8, [1987] 1 RJC 303, [1987] R. Fr. D. Admin. 287. For commentary on this decision, see Genevois (1987).

This decision weakened another argument used by the *Conseil d'État* to support its *Semoules* jurisprudence. *Commissaire du Gouvernement* Questiaux had claimed that enforcing European law supremacy would put the *Conseil d'État* in conflict with the legislature, which would be hazardous, since the legislature had the power to eliminate the *Conseil d'État*. After the failed Aurillac amendment, after the *Conseil Constitutionnel* had itself signalled that ordinary courts should enforce European law supremacy in their areas of jurisdiction, and after the *Conseil Constitutionnel*'s 1987 decision helped shore up the *Conseil d'État*'s constitutional standing in the legal order, Questiaux's argument was no longer very compelling.

The government also pushed jurisprudential change in the *Conseil d'État* through its 1987 appointment of Marceau Long as the new Vice-President of the *Conseil d'État*.[92] Long had a more open attitude towards Europe, advocating that 'one should not be cold in the face of European law, but come to know it and contribute to its creation' (Dauvergne 1989).[93] The government also pushed for a reconsideration of the *Semoules* position by commissioning the *Conseil d'État* to do a thorough study of the relation between international law, national law, and European law. In a letter of 21 November 1988, Prime Minister Rocard stressed:

The construction of Europe is of paramount importance for the whole French society. The government wishes to consider all the elements necessary to take decisions in this matter. The realization of the internal market . . . requires in particular that we pursue and amplify efforts to adapt our internal law to the demands of the Community. It would be fruitful if state actions in this area were guided by a synthetic vision, the creation of which it seems to me falls within the vocation of the *Conseil d'État* . . .

This commission signalled the government's desire that the *Conseil d'État* be part of its commitment to European integration. Rocard suggested that it would be desirable to have the first reflections in the spring of 1989, during the French presidency of the EC.[94]

By 1988 it was clear that the *Conseil d'État*'s attempts to contest and stop the encroachment of European law and ECJ authority into its domain had failed. Judiciary courts from the first instance upward were applying European law

---

[92] The President of France is the president of the *Conseil d'État*. The vice-president is the actual head of the *Conseil d'État*, and the head of the elite *École Nationale d'Administration* as well. See further n. 8 above.

[93] My translation.

[94] Letter from Prime Minister Michel Rocard to M. Marceau Long, Vice-President of the *Conseil d'État*, Paris, 21 Nov. 1988, Document 978/SG.

supremacy. The *Conseil Constitutionnel* had taken the *Cour de Cassation*'s side on the supremacy issue, and strongly signalled that the *Conseil d'État* should change its jurisprudence. Parisian lawyers had succeeded in having powers transferred from the administrative to the judiciary branch in large part because of the *Conseil d'État*'s anti-European law position. In an interview, the Secretary-General of the *Conseil d'État* noted:

[*Semoules*] was designed to protect the law, but in the end the law wasn't protected, but rather was more vulnerable. Other French courts were setting aside the law, as well as international courts. The law was becoming fragile and vulnerable to these other courts, and the *Conseil d'État*'s refusal to review the compatibility of the law with international treaties only exacerbated the problem. It was better that the *Conseil d'État* reviewed the law and establish its compatibility with international treaties than to let international courts do this.[95]

The *Conseil d'État* chose to issue what was by now a long-awaited reversal in a case where the *Conseil d'État*—like the *Conseil Constitutionnel*—sat as an election judge.[96] The substance of the case was insignificant, and the plaintiff's arguments were quite easy to dismiss. As *Commissaire du Gouvernement* Frydman put it:

the whole difficulty is then to decide whether, in conformity with your settled case law, you should dismiss this second argument by relying on the [French] 1977 Act alone, without even having to verify whether it is compatible with the Treaty of Rome, or whether you should break fresh ground today by deciding that the Act is applicable only because it is compatible with the Treaty.[97]

So as not to antagonize older members of the *Conseil d'État*, Frydman refrained from questioning the logic of the *Semoules* position. But he argued: 'Nevertheless, it seems to me that a different reading of Article 55 is certainly equally conceivable in law and is infinitely preferable from the viewpoint of expediency.'[98] A different interpretation was expedient because the legal foundations of the *Semoules* jurisprudence had been eroded. The *Conseil Constitutionnel* had not taken for itself the power to control the compatibility of French law with European law, and had instructed French courts 'to protect the application of international conventions in the cadre of their respective competences'.[99] According to Frydman, the *Conseil Constitutionnel* 'could

[95] Interview with the Secretary-General of the *Conseil d'État*, 5 July 1994, Paris.

[96] '*Nicolo*', *Raoul Georges Nicolo & another*, *Conseil d'État* decision of 20 Oct. 1989, [1989] Recueil Lebon 190, [1990] 1 CMLR 173.

[97] Ibid., CMLR, 177.   [98] Ibid. 179.

[99] N. 84 above, *Conseil Constitutionnel* decision 86-216.

not . . . express itself more clearly in condemning your traditional [*Semoules*] reply'.[100]

The political foundations had also eroded. The old *Semoules* doctrine had failed to keep European law out of the French system. In 1968, *Commissaire du Gouvernement* Questiaux had argued that it was hard to imagine that the legislator should be denied the authority to act in 'whole sections of the life of the country because treaties have appeared in the area in question'.[101] In 1989 Frydman acknowledged:

It cannot be repeated often enough that the era of the unconditional supremacy of internal law is now over. International rules of law, particularly those of Europe, have gradually conquered our legal universe, without hesitating furthermore to encroach on the competence of Parliament . . . In this way certain entire fields of our law such as those of the economy, employment or protection of human rights, now very largely originate genuinely from international legislation . . .[102]

The idea that not enforcing European law supremacy avoided conflict with the legislature also seemed 'less urgent than in the past'. The *Conseil Constitutionnel* had guaranteed the constitutional existence of the *Conseil d'État* in the French separation of powers.[103] The attempt to sanction the *Cour de Cassation* through the Aurillac amendment had failed. Indeed, it had become 'somewhat paradoxical to see the *Conseil d'État* refusing to [enforce Article 55 of the Constitution] because of its humility with regard to the legislature when every day ordinary courts of first instance examine, by this indirect approach, the validity of the laws which they have to apply'.[104]

Maintaining the *Semoules* jurisprudence also created legal inconsistencies within the French system that were becoming more problematic. The doctrinal divergence between the *Cour de Cassation* and the *Conseil d'État* had become 'the most serious now existing between your two courts, lead[ing] to absurd practical consequences'.[105] The *Conseil d'État*'s position also led to the 'shocking' situation that citizens could not rely on regulations in French administrative courts when they would be able to in other countries 'solely on the ground that, in our country, the regulation has been set aside by a contrary statute'.[106]

Changing its *Semoules* jurisprudence would eliminate these inconsistencies, and actually help the *Conseil d'État* regain influence lost to international courts. Frydman pointed out that in refusing to control the compatibility of

---

[100] N. 96 above, '*Nicolo*', CMLR 186.
[101] N. 24 above, '*Semoules*', CMLR 405.
[102] N. 96 above, '*Nicolo*', CMLR 183.
[103] Ibid. 184.   [104] Ibid. 184–5.   [105] Ibid. 182–3.   [106] Ibid. 183.

French law with European law, the *Conseil d'État* was in practice ceding the issue to international tribunals:

At a time when the European Commission and the European Court of Human Rights are for their part beginning occasionally to examine the compatibility of French laws, with the 1950 convention . . . you should yourselves assume this function and break their monopoly.[107]

Indeed, a large part of the *Commissaire du Gouvernement*'s argument seemed to be designed to seize the interpretive initiative from international courts. While Frydman recommended that the *Conseil d'État* change its jurisprudence, he did not recommend that it should adopt the ECJ's interpretation of the legal basis for European law supremacy. Indeed, he asserted that the ECJ's supremacy jurisprudence had 'no legal foundation whatever'.[108] Article 55 of the French constitution was the *only* legal basis for national judges to enforce European law supremacy. His total repudiation of the ECJ's 'supranational way of thinking' was designed to show the ECJ that national courts remain independent from it. Dehaussy noted:

'Internationalism' is imprinted in the Nicolo decision, as opposed to 'Community'. Once again the independence of the national judge is affirmed not only with regard to other state powers, but also with regards to the ECJ: [the ECJ] cannot be taken for a supreme federal court whose decisions impose themselves on national courts, even in the limited competences of the Communities. The independence of the judge is also a manifestation of the national independence in the face of possible encroachments. (Dehaussy 1990: 29)

Ending his address, Frydman said: 'if you agree [with my arguments], you should then, in the case before you today, take care to point out that the Act of 7 July 1977 is compatible with the Treaty of Rome before relying on its provisions against Mr. Nicolo's arguments.'[109] The *Conseil d'État* did just this. First it affirmed the compatibility of the disputed act with the French 1977 act, and then it said:

Pursuant to Article 227(1) of the Treaty of 25 March 1957 establishing the European Economic Community, 'this Treaty shall apply to . . . the French Republic'. The rules set out above, laid down by the Act of 7 July 1977, are not incompatible with the clear stipulations of the above-mentioned Article 227(1) of the Treaty of Rome.[110]

The legal interpretation advocated by Frydman, and accepted by the *Conseil d'État*, was that Article 55 empowered national judges to set aside statutes that are contrary to treaties. This was the same argument that *Procureur* Pepy

---

[107] Ibid. 189.   [108] N. 96 above, '*Nicolo*', CMLR 189.   [109] Ibid. 191.   [110] Ibid.

had used in 1950, that *Commissaire du Gouvernement* Questiaux had rejected in 1968, and that the *Conseil d'État* had refused throughout the 1970s and 1980s. Nothing in the legal texts had changed, and it is doubtful that the *Conseil d'État* had suddenly become convinced by legal argumentation that had been around for thirty years and that it had rejected once again only a few years earlier.

The *Conseil Constitutionnel* changed its European law jurisprudence to win support in the legal community and to strengthen respect for Article 55 of the French constitution. The reversal of the *Conseil d'État's* opposition to European law supremacy was based on a new strategic calculation in a new institutional context, where the *Conseil Constitutionnel* was the authoritative interpreter of French constitutional law, where first instance judiciary courts were shaping the interpretation of European law, and where the government was tolerating judicial review and advocating greater European integration. By 1989 all French courts had accepted a role enforcing European law supremacy. Disagreement regarding the direct effect of directives had all but disappeared.[111] The ECJ had also made an overture, coming closer to the *Conseil d'État's* position regarding the ability of national courts to interpret clear European law on their own.[112]

The *Nicolo* decision signalled that the *Conseil d'État* was relenting in its opposition to enforcing European law supremacy. It did not, however, mean that the *Conseil d'État* would accept all ECJ jurisprudence. The *Conseil d'État* can still claim that European law is sufficiently clear and thereby avoid a reference to the ECJ. And there remain outstanding disagreements between the ECJ and French courts regarding the issue of the supremacy of European law over the French constitution, whether the EC legal order is a 'special' legal order distinct from traditional forms of international law, and who has the final authority to interpret the limits of European law authority in France. On these issues, the French supreme courts remained united in their opposition to the ECJ's jurisprudence.

[111] See n. 70 above.

[112] According to Hjalte Rasmussen (1984: 256–9), the ECJ's *CILFIT* decision was designed to acknowledge high court concern that the ECJ was interfering in their domain, while at the same time creating criteria about when high courts could interpret European law on their own. This move is seen as an ECJ effort to encourage high courts to constrain their use of the doctrine of *Acte Clair*.

Round 5. 1990–1998: the Conseil d'État *and* Conseil Constitutionnel *reposition themselves to influence the development of European law*

Accepting a role enforcing European law supremacy was but one piece of the overall strategy of the *Conseil Constitutionnel* and *Conseil d'État* to increase their influence in European integration. In the 1990s both institutions sought to reposition themselves in the French legal and political order so as better to limit the expansion of EC authority into the French political system.

The 1974 expansion of access to the *Conseil Constitutionnel* that allowed sixty senators or deputies to challenge the constitutionality of national laws did not include challenges to treaties. Article 54 of the French constitution authorized only the President of the Republic, the President of the Senate, and the President of the National Assembly to refer questions concerning treaty and treaty amendments to the *Conseil Constitutionnel*. These actors tended to be in agreement regarding European integration (they were usually from the same party), and thus the *Conseil Constitutionnel* had been excluded from most of the political debates over EC authority.[113] But the Schengen agreement was not a Treaty amendment, and thus fell under Article 61 of the French constitution, which allows sixty members of parliament to seize the *Conseil Constitutionnel* to review the constitutionality of a French law. Thus the *Conseil Constitutionnel* was brought into the debate about expanding European powers.

From the referent's perspective, delegating authority over the sensitive issues of border control and immigration policy was an unacceptable transfer of French sovereignty to the EC. In their reference, the appellants asked the *Conseil Constitutionnel* to review the issue of what was an illegal 'transfer' of sovereignty and what was a legal 'limitation' of sovereignty. The nature of the Schengen agreement meant that the *Conseil Constitutionnel* had either to reject the constitutionality of the entire agreement or to accept the agreement—it could not accept only parts of the agreement (Vedel 1992). In addition, by the time the *Conseil Constitutionnel* was asked to rule on the Schengen agreement, the Treaty on the European Union (TEU or the Maastricht Agreement) had already been drafted. The creation of a monetary union was obviously a much bigger transfer of sovereignty than the Schengen agreement, and the *Conseil Constitutionnel* wanted to wait to define better what

---

[113] The exception was with respect to the direct election of members of the European parliament. It is noteworthy that the Single European Act (SEA) was not referred to the *Conseil Constitutionnel*, even though it is likely that the switch to qualified majority voting required a constitutional amendment.

constituted a 'transfer' of sovereignty until it could examine the more significant agreement. Thus it avoided speaking to the main issue at stake, and instead used the *Schengen* decision to lay the groundwork for a later review of the TEU.[114]

The *Schengen* decision expanded the *Conseil Constitutionnel*'s power to review all questions about the conformity of international obligations with the constitution, including any important act that modifies an international treaty. It also served notice to the Executive Authority of the Schengen Accord that its acts were subject to *Conseil Constitutionnel* review, regardless of whether they required parliamentary assent. Laying the groundwork for a reference regarding the Maastricht Treaty, the decision declared that France cannot be bound by unconstitutional obligations. As a result, parliament could not ratify, validate, or authorize an international engagement contrary to the constitution. This ruling established clearly what had already been accepted: the French constitution is supreme over European law. After this ruling, it would be hard for President Mitterrand to avoid sending the Maastricht Treaty to the *Conseil Constitutionnel* for review (Zoller 1992: 280–2).

There were ultimately three separate decisions regarding the ratification of the Maastricht Treaty. The most significant decision was the first ruling, *Maastricht I*. Here the *Conseil Constitutionnel* evaluated whether the Treaty on a European Union (TEU) was contrary to the French constitution. The *Conseil Constitutionnel* revised its much-contested jurisprudence that 'transfers of sovereignty' were unconstitutional. Many had argued that there was no clear difference between a 'limitation' of sovereignty and a 'transfer of sovereignty'. In *Maastricht I*, the *Conseil Constitutionnel* adopted a middle language:

> the respect for national sovereignty cannot be an obstacle to . . . France being able to conclude, under the reserve of reciprocity, international engagements with a view to participating in the creation or the development of a permanent international organization, with legal personality and invested with the power of decision by the effect of a *transfer of competences* consented to by the member states.[115]

The difference between a transfer of *competence* and a transfer of *sovereignty* was also not so clear, but the ECJ had used the term 'transfer of competence'

---

[114] '*Schengen* Decision', Case 91-294 DC, *Conseil Constitutionnel* decision of 25 July 1991, [1991] *Recueil des Décisions du Conseil Constitutionnel* 91, [1991] R. Fr. D. Admin. 173.

[115] *Maastricht I*, *Conseil Constitutionnel* decision 92-308 DC of 9 Apr. 1992, [1992] *Recueil des Décisions du Conseil Constitutionnel* 55, [1992] RJC I-496 (my emphasis).

in its *Costa v. ENEL* decision, and thus it had been accepted in the legal community.[116] The *Conseil Constitutionnel* reviewed all the ways in which the TEU implied a transfer of competences to the EC level, finding that the constitution had to be amended before the TEU could be ratified.

Using the *Conseil Constitutionnel*'s new language, the French parliament inserted a new clause (Article 88) into the constitution that allowed France to consent to transfers of competences necessary for the establishment of an economic and monetary union, and to create common rules regarding external borders of the member states. It also authorized EC citizens who were residents in France to vote in certain elections (Stone 1993: 75–7).[117] The *Conseil Constitutionnel*'s ruling stuck closely to the terms of the TEU, as did the constitutional amendment. The implication was that further transfers of competences must be reviewed by the *Conseil Constitutionnel* and inscribed into the constitution on a case-by-case basis. Thus *Maastricht I* set the precedent that the *Conseil Constitutionnel* was to be permanently involved whenever there was an expansion of EC authority (Schoettl 1998: 142).

As had happened in Germany, the National Assembly used the requirement for constitutional amendment to force the executive branch to include it in the process of EC policy-making. The new Article 88-4 requires the government to consult the National Assembly about European law being negotiated in the Council of Ministers. The parliament also won a change to Article 54 of the French constitution so that sixty members of parliament could now make a reference to the *Conseil Constitutionnel* during the ratification of international and EC Treaties. This new power was used immediately by opponents of the TEU who wanted the *Conseil Constitutionnel* to reconsider its *Maastricht I* decision and to side with them on points they had lost in parliamentary debate.

The Gaullist minority had tried throughout the parliamentary debate to insert a series of amendments that would establish the inalienability of French sovereignty. They tried to enshrine the Luxembourg compromise (the French veto in EC policy-making) into the French constitution. They also tried to reestablish the supremacy of national law over European law and extend the jurisdiction of the *Conseil Constitutionnel* to control the validity of EC agreements and EC legislation (Stone 1993: 78). The *Maastricht II*

---

[116] The English version states 'transfer of power'; the French version uses the word 'compétences'. *Costa v. Ente Nazionale per L'Energia Elettrica (ENEL)*, ECJ Case 6/64, [1964] ECR 585, [1964] CMLR 425. Quote from ECR, p. 593.

[117] Law 92-554 of 25 June 1992, 'Des Communautés européennes et de l'Union européenne', new title XVI of the Constitution revising Article 88 of the Constitution.

reference came after the Danish rejected the TEU and after a referendum on the Maastricht Treaty had been called. Thus the *Conseil Constitutionnel* had to consider the Gaullist challenge in the middle of a political debate over ratification of the TEU. The referents asked the *Conseil Constitutionnel* to articulate a constitutional theory of state sovereignty to serve as a guide in the future process of European integration. They noted:

Of the twelve states of the Community, France is the one most attached to its identity and national unity. It is undeniable that the constitutional order rests on the central idea of national sovereignty. But if sovereignty is no longer anything but an *addition des compétences*, if one can remove successively these *compétences* as one would the leaves of an artichoke, at what point or at what degree do we arrive at the heart?[118]

Wanting to reserve for itself the right to define the inalienable limits of national sovereignty, the *Conseil Constitutionnel* refused to reopen its *Maastricht I* decision. It declared the issue of the constitutionality of the TEU to be *chose jugée* (already decided) and not subject to reexamination. It did, however, examine the constitutionality of the law authorizing the ratification of the TEU, and found that it met the constitutional requirements for treaty ratification.[119] The Gaullists tried once more to open the issue by challenging the constitutionality of the referendum law, but in keeping with its earlier jurisprudence, the *Conseil Constitutionnel* refused to review the constitutionality of public referendums.[120]

A final noteworthy point about the *Maastricht* decisions is that the *Conseil Constitutionnel* continued to insist that reciprocity was required to make EC obligations binding. This language was inscribed into the constitutional amendment in Article 88-4, reinforcing the position that the EC treaties are international treaties like all others.

The French *Maastricht* decisions were issued before the German Constitutional Court issued its defiant ruling on the Maastricht Treaty. If the *Conseil Constitutionnel* had decided after the German Constitutional Court, it might have been even bolder. As it was, its *Maastricht I* decision shored up the new role of the *Conseil Constitutionnel* in the ratification process. When the Treaty of Amsterdam was considered in the French parliament, the *Conseil*

---

[118] Cited in Stone (1993: 82).

[119] *Maastricht II, Conseil Constitutionnel* decision 92-312 DC of 2 Sept. 1992, [1992] *Recueil des Décisions du Conseil Constitutionnel* 76, [1992] RJC I 505.

[120] *Maastricht III, Conseil Constitutionnel* decision 92-313 DC of 23 Sept. 1992, [1992] *Recueil des Décisions du Conseil Constitutionnel* 94, [1992] RJC I 511.

Constitutionnel was dutifully asked to review the constitutionality of the Treaty, and it required certain constitutional amendments.[121]

Many scholars remain unsatisfied with the *Conseil Constitutionnel*'s definition, or rather lack of definition, on the limits of EC authority. Alain Pellet argues that what the *Conseil Constitutionnel* considers to be part of French national sovereignty is not clear. For example, why is monetary policy part of French sovereignty and other policies not? The rule Pellet deduces is that when France is forced to adopt measures she does not agree with, sovereignty is compromised. As long as she agrees, or has agreed, sovereignty is not compromised (Pellet 1998: web p. 12). Also ironic for Pellet is that the *Conseil Constitutionnel* seems unconcerned about the loss of parliamentary sovereignty to the executive branch. It does, however, seem very concerned about its own loss of influence in the process of European integration. Pellet points out: 'the indifference shown by the guardian of the constitution with respect to the preservation of the rights of Parliament contrasts with the jealous (and justified) care with which it takes to safeguard its own rights' (1997: web p. 15).

Gaullist members of parliament have not given up hope of defending French national sovereignty. They continue to highlight the insufficient constitutional protections for European law in reports to parliament (Mazeaud 1996). They have also proposed constitutional amendments that would clarify the supremacy of the French constitution over European law, make the Luxembourg Compromise part of the French constitution, grant the French government the right to renounce all or part of EC Treaties, and give the French government the right to renounce any ultra vires ECJ decisions (Berthu 1997).

The *Conseil d'État* has also sought to create for itself a larger role influencing the future of European integration. Following the *Nicolo* decision, the *Conseil d'État* issued a series of decisions more 'friendly' to European law and to its own authority *vis-à-vis* international law. Its 1989 *Alitalia* decision enabled individuals to draw directly on EC directives to challenge national policy.[122] In 1990, the *Conseil d'État* issued its first decision applying European law over a subsequent French *loi*.[123] The subsequent *GISTI* decision gave administrative judges the authority to interpret EC treaties

---

[121] *Treaty of Amsterdam Conseil Constitutionnel* decision DC 97-394 of 31 Dec. 1997, [1997] *Recueil des Décisions du Conseil Constitutionnel* 344, [1997] RJC, p. I-727.

[122] *Compagnie Alitalia, Conseil d'État* decision of 3 Feb. 1989, [1989] Recueil Lebon 44, [1990] 1 CMLR 248. For an analysis of the *Alitalia* decision, see Tatham (1991).

[123] *'Boisedet', Conseil d'État* decision of 24 Sept. 1990, [1990] Recueil Lebon 251.

without referring them to the Foreign Ministry.[124] And the *Sociétés Rothman et Philip Morris* decision ended the tobacco controversy with the EC and signalled the acceptance of the ECJ's *Francovich* jurisprudence which allows national courts to find state liabilities when EC directives are improperly implemented.[125]

The *Conseil d'État* also worked with political bodies to increase the role it played in the process of European integration. In its study of the relation between international law, national law, and European law, the *Conseil d'État* found that more than half of all new French laws originate in Brussels.[126] As part of the *Maastricht* reforms, the *Conseil d'État* convinced the government to give it new authority to review all EC drafts sent to the French cabinet to see if they are of a legislative nature and thus need to be referred to Parliament. The *Conseil d'État* does more than simply decide on procedural rules; it also reviews the utility of the draft legislation identifying areas of national law that the proposed legislation might affect, and assessing the benefits and costs of such legislation. This allows the *Conseil d'État* to help frame how the proposed law is interpreted by political bodies before EC legislation is negotiated and agreed to. According to the *Conseil d'État*'s Vice-President, Marceau Long, this new role means that European law is not elaborated by specialists but rather by those who prepare and judge national law on the same issues, and it allows the *Conseil d'État* to 'preserve the balance of the French legal system' by contributing to the elaboration of European law (Long 1994).

It is difficult to tell how these new powers are affecting European policy-making or the interpretation of European law; the influence of the *Conseil d'État*'s advisory role is always difficult to measure. The *Conseil d'État* reviews about 500 proposals each year. According to one insider, *Conseil d'État* interventions have led to changes in the law, have influenced European negotiations over laws, and have made the Parliament more aware of how European integration is encroaching on its powers. 'There is a shift in the power struc-

---

[124] *GISTI* decision. *Conseil d'État* decision of 29 June 1990, [1990] Rev. gen. droit int. pub. 879. For an analysis of the GISTI decision, see Buffet-Tchakaloff (1991).

[125] *Sociétés Rothman et Philip Morris and Arizona Tobacco, Conseil d'État* decision of 28 Feb. 1992, [1992] Recueil Lebon 78. Since *Francovich* was consistent with the existent French practice regarding state liabilities, accepting this doctrine was not difficult for the *Conseil d'État*. Indeed, members of the *Conseil d'État* take pride in the fact that the *Conseil d'État* has actually been ahead of the ECJ in this jurisprudence, and seemingly influenced the ECJ in this area. As Sabourin trumpeted: 'Ad augusta per augusta, the *Conseil d'État* places its stones in the construction of Community law'(1993: 423). *Frankovich and Bonifaci v. Italian Republic*. ECJ cases C–6 and C–9/90, [1991] ECR I–5357.

[126] *Conseil d'État* (1992: 16–17).

ture of our democracies, giving a network of judges, without consideration of national boundaries, a considerable influence on the evolution of law . . . we have moved a slight step towards "gouvernement des judges" (Questiaux 1998: 486–8, 490).

Finally, the *Conseil d'État* has tried to improve its position *vis-à-vis* the judicial branch, and the changes it has orchestrated will affect its future role interpreting European law. At the same time as the *Conseil d'État* was reversing its *Semoules* jurisprudence, Vice-President Marceau Long gained support for creating a new tier of Administrative Courts of Appeal and for hiring more administrative court judges. The restructuring of the administrative court system was designed to shorten the wait for administrative court decisions, thus removing a large complaint against the administrative branch and stopping the trend towards transferring power to the judiciary branch (Combarnous 1995: 176). With this reform, the number of lower administrative court judges has doubled.[127] Certain areas of the *Conseil d'État*'s jurisdiction have devolved to the new administrative appeals courts, lightening the *Conseil d'État*'s workload and giving the *Conseil d'État* a real legal hierarchy over which to preside. In 1995, administrative courts were given the power to issue injunctions against administrative decisions (Pacteau 1996: 5), allowing administrative courts to become part of political negotiations between firms and the French administration.

Summarizing the five rounds of doctrinal change

Compared to Germany, the French process of doctrinal change involved less direct negotiation with the ECJ. Indeed, none of the major cases examined in this chapter was referred to the ECJ for consultation. The lack of direct negotiation is attributable to the refusal of French high courts to refer anything but technical questions to the ECJ (Bebr 1983: 456–7). It is also a testament to the inability of lower courts to use the EC legal system to circumvent or challenge the jurisprudence of higher courts. For lower judiciary courts, there was no advantage to using the EC legal system to challenge the *Cour de Cassation* because the latter enforced ECJ jurisprudence. Within the administrative system, there was little room for lower courts to promote doctrinal change by the *Conseil d'État*, since the latter was the first and last instance court for most challenges to government policy. And there was no way for litigants to appeal High Court decisions to the *Conseil Constitutionnel*, or for lower

---

[127] The number of administrative judges rose from 367 in 1987 to 605 (including the new court of appeals) in 1995, with the expectation of 763 judges by 1999 (Stirn 1995).

Table 4.3. The process of doctrinal change in France, divided into rounds of legal integration

Legal decisions in doctrinal debate	National doctrine regarding European law established in round	Growing consensus between ECJ and French courts	Points of disagreement between ECJ and French courts
Round 1, 1960–8 1963: ECJ *Van Gend en Loos* 1964: ECJ *Costa v. Enel* 1964: CE *Shell-Berre* 1967: CE *Petitjean* 1968: CE *Semoules*	French courts can interpret 'clear' European law on their own, without referring the case to the ECJ; the notion of what is 'clear' is often misused. French courts lack the authority to review the compatibility of French laws with European law; thus no reference to the ECJ is necessary when there is a potential conflict between European law and French law. Direct effect of European law is tacitly accepted.	Agreement with ECJ's doctrine of direct effect, though the *Conseil d'État* applies the doctrine on its own, without asking the ECJ.	Disagreement about when French courts should refer cases to the ECJ. Disagreement over the obligation of national courts to enforce European law supremacy over national law.
Round 2, 1970–6 1970: CdeC *Ramel* 1970: ECJ *International Handelsgesellschaft* 1971: ECJ *ERTA* 1974: ECJ *Van Duyn* 1974: ECJ *Charmasson* 1975: CC abortion decision 1975: CdeC *Jacques Vabre* 1976: CC *re* Elections to the European Parliament 1976: CdeC *Von Kempis*	*Conseil Constitutionnel* refuses its authority to enforce European law supremacy. *Conseil Constitutionnel* determines that the EC Treaty is an international treaty like all others. *Conseil Constitutionnel* finds that France cannot transfer sovereignty to the EC; it can agree to limits of its sovereignty. It is unclear what is a 'transfer' and what is a 'limit' of French sovereignty. *Cour de Cassation* accepts that it has the authority to enforce European law supremacy, by virtue of the French constitution *and* the special nature of European law. *Conseil d'État* continues to refuse its authority to enforce European law supremacy.	Agreement with ECJ's doctrine of direct effect, though the *Conseil d'État* applies the doctrine on its own, without asking the ECJ. *Cour de Cassation* agrees with the ECJ's doctrine of European law supremacy. *Cour de Cassation* seems to agree about the special nature of EC Treaty.	Disagreement about when French courts should refer cases to the ECJ. Disagreement on the part of the *Conseil Constitutionnel* and *Conseil d'État* over the obligation of national courts to enforce European law supremacy. Disagreement about the special nature of European law and whether sovereignty has been transferred to the EC. Disagreement regarding the supremacy of European law over the French constitution.

Round 3, 1977–81		
1977: CC decision *re* regulations 1978: ECJ *Simmenthal* 1978: CE *Cohn-Bendit* 1979: CE *Syndicat national des fabricants spiritueux consommés à l'eau* 1981: Aurillac Amendment	*Conseil d'État* rejects the ECJ's jurisprudence on the direct effect of directives. French parliament tries but fails to sanction *Cour de Cassation* for accepting a role enforcing European law supremacy (Aurillac Amendment). Failure opens door to other courts to follow the *Cour de Cassation*'s lead. *Conseil d'État* refuses to apply an ECJ ruling to a case at hand (*Syndicat national des fabricants spiritueux consommés à l'eau*).	Agreement with ECJ's doctrine of direct effect, though the *Conseil d'État* applies the doctrine on its own, without asking the ECJ, and will not apply the direct effect of directives. *Cour de Cassation* agrees with the ECJ's doctrine of European law supremacy.	Disagreement about when French courts should refer cases to the ECJ. Disagreement on the part of the *Conseil Constitutionnel* and *Conseil d'État* over the obligation of national courts to enforce European law supremacy. Disagreement regarding the special nature of European law and whether sovereignty has been transferred to the EC. Disagreement regarding the supremacy of European law over the French constitution. Disagreement on the part of the *Conseil d'État* regarding the direct effect of directives.
Round 4, 1982–9		
1982: ECJ *CILFIT* 1983: ECJ condemns France *re* tobacco prices 1985: CE tobacco decision 1986: CC decision 1987: CC decision *re* transfer of competences 1988: ECJ again condemns France *re* tobacco prices	ECJ decides that national courts may interpret clear laws on their own, narrowing but not eliminating the disagreement over when to refer EC legal issues to the ECJ (CILFIT). *Conseil Constitutionnel* rules that all French courts must accord European law supremacy over subsequent national laws in their respective areas of jurisdiction. *Conseil d'État* refuses to apply ECJ infringement ruling regarding tobacco prices leading France to be condemned a second time in front of the ECJ. *Conseil d'État* ultimately accepts that it has the authority to enforce European law supremacy.	Agreement with ECJ's doctrine of direct effect, though the *Conseil d'État* applies the doctrine on its own, without asking the ECJ. Agreement regarding the supremacy of European law over French law. Greater agreement over when national courts should refer legal issues to the ECJ.	Disagreement about the special nature of European law and whether sovereignty has been transferred to the EC. Disagreement regarding the supremacy of European law over the French constitution. Disagreement on the part of the *Conseil d'État* regarding the binding nature of ECJ decisions.

Table 4.3. *cont.*

Legal decisions in doctrinal debate	National doctrine regarding European law established in round	Growing consensus between ECJ and French courts	Points of disagreement between ECJ and French courts
1988: CC decision as election judge 1989: CE *Nicolo*			Disagreement about the special nature of European law.
Round 5, 1989–98 1989: CE *Alitalia* 1990: CE *GISTI* 1991: CC *Schengen* 1992: CE *Sociétés Rothman et Philip Morris* and *Arizona Tobacco* 1992: CC *Maastricht I, II, III* Article 88 of Constitution added 1992–5: CE jurisdiction devolved to administrative courts of appeal 1997: CC Treaty of Amsterdam	*Conseil d'État* jurisprudence on direct effect directives continues to be brought closer to ECJ position. *Conseil d'État* applies ECJ tobacco ruling it had ignored earlier. *Conseil Constitutionnel* finds that it has the authority to review the compatibility of European law with the French constitution. *Conseil Constitutionnel* finds that European laws in violation of the French constitution require a constitutional change before they become effective in France. Constitution is amended to allow for 'transfers of competences' in certain areas of the EC. The *Conseil Constitutionnel* will review on a case-by-case basis if amendments are needed to expand EC authority.	Agreement regarding the direct effect of European law. Agreement regarding the supremacy of European law over French law. Greater agreement over when national courts should refer legal issues to the ECJ. Apparent agreement that French courts are bound by ECJ decisions. French accept idea that the government has transferred competences to EC level.	Disagreement regarding the supremacy of European law over the French constitution. Possibility of constitutional limits to the binding nature of European law in France. If there is a conflict between European law and the constitution, the constitution must be changed. Otherwise the European law is inapplicable in France.

French courts to bring the *Conseil Constitutionnel* into debates over European law. Indeed, there appears to have been little pressure from below on high courts to alter their EC jurisprudence.[128] Given the structure of the French judiciary, and the attitude of the *Conseil d'État*, it was hard for those advocating a change in French doctrine to involve the ECJ or more sympathetic French courts in a debate over the application of European law in France.[129]

It is not yet clear how these reforms within the administrative court system are influencing the *Conseil d'État* with respect to European law. Richard Harmson (1993) argued that already in the *Nicolo* reversal one could see signs of the pressure the new lower administrative courts were putting on the *Conseil d'État*. As the new administrative courts become more established, one may well see lower administrative courts turn to European law as a tool to enhance their independence, influence, and authority *vis-à-vis* the *Conseil d'État*. Working against this development is the small size of the administrative court system, and the fact that the *Conseil d'État* has decisive influence over the career trajectory of administrative court judges (Stirn 1995).[130]

Table 4.3 summarizes the changing doctrine in each round of integration, highlighting the areas of substantial agreement, and aspects of a growing

[128] Add to this that French litigants and lawyers were slow to embrace European law (Touffait 1975). The fact that the *Conseil d'État* would not respond favourably to challenges to government policy based on European law certainly dissuaded litigants from raising cases. Cross-national studies on equal pay litigation explain the lack of French equality cases based partly on the perception that French courts would react negatively to European law challenge to French equality policy (Fitzpatrick et al. 1993). Foreign oil companies failed in their *Shell Berre* challenge to French policy in 1963. The large Leclerc firm tried to use European law to challenge national rules on discounting books and distributing petrol, but the *Conseil d'État* ruled against them in the 1980s (discussed in Errera 1987). Finally in 1992 the tobacco companies' persistence paid off, but only after the French government had ignored two ECJ decisions in 1983 and 1988, and after the *Conseil d'État* had already refused their suit in 1985 (n. 124 above, *Sociétés Rothman et Philip Morris*). Only firms with deep pockets, like tobacco companies, can afford to keep litigating.

[129] There was no way for a private litigant to bring a case to the *Conseil Constitutionnel*. And the only way to use the judiciary branch to challenge a national law would be to provoke the government to pursue a case against the litigant in the hopes of having the judiciary court set aside a government policy on the bases of European law supremacy—a risky strategy, to say the least.

[130] The administrative branch is small, with fewer than 800 members, and the *Conseil d'État* has decisive influence on the body that considers promotions; thus wise administrative judges avoid confrontation. The *Conseil d'État* has already tried to discourage lower courts from sending references to the ECJ. In the *Letierce* case, the *Commissaire du Gouvernement* made it clear that lower courts are under no obligation to refer cases to the ECJ, and that a refusal to refer the case cannot be appealed to the *Conseil d'État*—only the final interpretation can be appealed. *The Commissaire du Gouvernement* went so far as to advocate that the *Conseil d'État* sanction lower courts if they refer to the ECJ cases where the law was clear and could be interpreted without a reference. So far the lower administrative courts have not challenged *Conseil d'État* jurisprudence in references to the ECJ. Affaire Letierce, *Conseil d'État* decision of 1 June 1994, [1994] AJDA 633.

disagreement between the ECJ and national courts. Unlike in Germany, the French case does not show a trend of growing opposition to ECJ doctrine over time. French judicial positions started out so negative that they really could only become more positive. In the end, the French and German views on the key issues of European law supremacy seem to have converged around similar positions.

III. Conclusion

What do the disagreements between the ECJ and French courts mean? How are they significant? It is now clear that the supremacy of European law will be enforced in France. Since this was the fundamental idea behind the EC's *Costa v. ENEL* decision, we can say that, as of 1989, the basic supremacy of European law over national law has been fully accepted in France.

But the possibility for future conflicts cannot be ruled out. The ECJ's extensions of EC authority are not necessarily valid inside France, and French courts are not obliged to follow ECJ decisions that exceed the EC's or the ECJ's authority. We can still expect the *Conseil d'État* to interpret most European law on its own, adopting French solutions when effective and interpreting European law in favour of French policy whenever possible. We can also expect the *Conseil Constitutionnel* to continue developing its jurisprudence on the constitutional limits to European law in France. Until now, the parliament has responded to *Conseil Constitutionnel* rulings by changing the constitution. But should the *Conseil Constitutionnel* find an EC obligation to be unconstitutional, and should the parliament decide not to change the constitution, the European law under scrutiny would be inapplicable in France. The requirement for reciprocity is another potential stumbling-block. Should the French government determine that another member state is not fulfilling its EC obligations, and should the EC legal system be unable to rectify the situation, the French might also insist that they are not bound by the EC obligation. In either of these cases, French courts would follow the lead of the political bodies.

Compared to German courts, French courts have thus far been less strident in their assertion that European law should be compatible with the French constitution. They have also been less successful in their attempts to influence EC policy or ECJ jurisprudence. The *Conseil d'État* tried to influence the ECJ by flagrantly rejecting its jurisprudence on the direct effect of directives, but defiance did not have the effect the *Conseil d'État* had hoped. This is not to say that French law has had no influence on European law. The structure of the EC legal system is modelled on the French system, and there are areas where the ECJ has adopted legal solutions from French law. But it is hard to find a significant imprint of French *judicial* influence on ECJ jurisprudence or on European policy-making.[131] French courts are less strident and less influential because ultimately they lack the constitutional and legal tools of German courts to use as leverage against political bodies or the ECJ.

German courts can create a real limit to the application of European law in Germany, which is why the German government, European authorities, and the ECJ pay attention to the German Constitutional Court's European law jurisprudence. Because the German Constitutional Court can be seized by national courts, by individuals, and in federal/state disputes, it can count on being invoked whenever there is a serious issue of constitutional concern. Also, amending the German Constitution is difficult, and aspects of the German constitution regarding basic rights, the democratic process and the federal structure cannot be changed. Knowing that an appeal to the German Federal Constitutional Court is likely, and that constitutional constraints are not easily circumvented, political actors at the national and European level must take constitutional concerns into account during the policy-making process. The German Constitutional Court is also in the position of having the final word on the application of European law in Germany, after the policy has been accepted and implemented by national authorities and after the ECJ has ruled. Having this last word gives the German Constitutional Court leverage against the ECJ. By contrast, there is no way in France to use the legal system to reopen political deals reached in Brussels or in Paris because no French courts can hear private litigant complaints about the constitutionality of national or European laws. The *Conseil Constitutionnel* can only be seized before a French law is actually promulgated, and only by a limited number of political actors (the President of the Republic, the President of the Senate, the president of the National Assembly, or sixty deputies or senators). The *Cour de Cassation*, because of its private law jurisdiction, is basically unable to serve as a serious check on the expansion of EC and ECJ authority. While the *Conseil d'État* can create legal and procedural limits to drawing on European law in France, it has chosen not to practise constitutional review, or create constitutional limits to the application of European law in France.

The 1990s have opened a limited means for the *Conseil d'État* and the *Conseil Constitutionnel* to become more active in the political process of EC policy-making, and in assuring that European law respects the French

---

[131] Some might argue that the ECJ has borrowed from the French law on state liabilities. This may be true, but it would not have been French judicial pressure that led to this change.

constitution. But their power remains limited. The *Conseil d'État* can use its enhanced advising role to influence French positions in deliberations in Brussels, and to frame the debate between the parliament and the executive over European law. And in light of its *Schengen* and *Maastricht I* decisions, the *Conseil Constitutionnel* will be invoked increasingly during parliamentary debates over European law and EC Treaty amendments. But most European laws will continue to escape constitutional review in France, and certainly the *Conseil Constitutionnel* cannot count on being invoked except perhaps regarding Treaty amendments. Even if the *Conseil Constitutionnel* does find a European law or Treaty amendment to be unconstitutional, this ruling is unlikely to create much of a constraint on EC and French policy-making. The French constitution can be amended either by referendum or by three-fifths vote in the National Assembly. As long as political actors are willing to change the constitution to make it compatible with EC obligations, a *Conseil Constitutionnel* ruling of unconstitutionality will at most be a procedural limitation that allows for more negotiation about constitutional change.

While the *Conseil d'État* and the *Conseil Constitutionnel* cannot play a role similar to that of the German Constitutional Court, their desire to protect their influence, independence, and authority and to establish limits to EC and ECJ authority is no less strong. If neither the *Conseil Constitutionnel* nor the *Conseil d'État* has attempted to create significant limits on French participation in the EC, or on European law's authority in France, it is because they have correctly fathomed the Government's political sentiment. Thus far, the French government has exercised its influence in Brussels and then successfully forced the parliament, the administration, the population and the judiciary to accept whatever it has agreed to. French courts have created the legal opening to play a larger role in limiting the expansion of and application of European law in the future, but either the political climate or the structure of the judiciary will have to change for this role to become significant.

There are signs that the role and structure of the judiciary in French politics *is* changing. Administrative courts have new power to issue injunctions regarding procurement decisions, and administrative courts of appeal can now decide cases involving government excess of power. These changes could create more legal innovation pushed from below. There are also indications that the *Conseil d'État* might start reviewing the constitutionality of international laws, taking on a role similar to that of the Constitutional Court in Germany.[132] There is continued talk of opening access to the *Conseil*

---

[132] 'Rapport Française', *Cahier de Conseil Constitutionnel* 4, second semester (1998). www.conseil-constitutionnel.fr/cahiers/ccc4/ccc4somm.htm

Constitutionnel for constitutional appeals from private litigants. Perhaps most significantly, within the French population there is a notable shift in public opinion towards having courts enforce political accountability to the law.[133] Parties in favour of protecting French sovereignty against the over-expansive powers of EC bodies are gaining influence on the Right, and they would support more national controls on EC authority. And there are many actors within the judiciary and the administration who would like French courts and French political bodies to have the clout of their German counterparts. If the role of the judiciary changed in France, one could expect far more similarity between French judicial behaviour and that of the German courts, not to mention greater influence on EC policy-making and ECJ decision-making.

---

[133] Pundits and legal observers are noting a rising rule-of-law mentality seizing the French (Questiaux 1995: 247). The number of appeals of administrative court decisions has grown exponentially in the last 10 years (Stirn 1995). There have also been some very famous cases where the public has demanded that the courts hold politicians accountable to the law, such as the cases against Bernard Tapie, against the officials who allowed AIDs-tainted blood to be used in France, and against the abuse of public apartments as political spoils. And in 1998 the French started to enforce anti-doping rules during the *Tour de France*, which some saw as a sign of the changing mentality from expecting rules to be broken by the powerful to holding the powerful accountable to the rule of law (Vincur 1998: 17).

5

Winning Political Support: Why Did National Governments Accept a Judicial Revolution That Transferred Away National Sovereignty?

This book has shown how interactions between the ECJ and national courts resulted in a significant transfer of national sovereignty from member states to the European level. Some have argued that if the member states ultimately accepted this transfer, it must be because at some level they desired it (Rasmussen 1986; Garrett and Weingast 1993). But the fact that member states did not reverse the European legal system's transformation does not mean that the states wanted or preferred it.[1] There is significant evidence that member states did *not* support the transformation of the European legal system. When the issue of the national courts enforcing European law first emerged in front of the ECJ, representatives of the member states argued strongly against any interpretation that would allow national courts to evaluate the compatibility of European law with national law. The European Council has refused attempts to formally enshrine the supremacy of European law in a Treaty revision, or to formally give national courts a role in enforcing European law supremacy.[2] There have also been political challenges to the ECJ and national courts enforcing European law supremacy,

---

[1] As Marks has shown, political bodies may be unable to reverse judicial decisions even if a majority of political actors so desire. For this reason, he argues, 'inaction is neither a sufficient nor necessary condition for acceptability by a majority of legislators. Nor can we conclude that the absence of legislative reaction implies that the court's policy choice leads to a "better" policy in the view of the legislature' (Marks 1989: 6).

[2] Based on an interview with a member of the German negotiating team who put forward the proposal at the Maastricht negotiations for the Treaty on a European Union, 17 Feb. 1994, Bonn.

and numerous battles over extending the right of national courts to refer cases.

How could the European Court and national courts expand the European legal system beyond what member states desired? Why did member states not reassert control and return the system to the one they had designed and intended? If member states failed to control the transformation of the European legal system, what does this mean in terms of their ability to control legal integration in the future? This chapter explains how the ECJ succeeded in transforming the European legal system against the will of member states. Section I explains how the ECJ escaped member state control to orchestrate an institutional transformation that national governments did not desire. Section II explains why member states could not reassert control and change the system back to what they originally planned. While the ECJ was able to transform the European legal system, this does not mean that national governments cannot now influence the ECJ. Section III considers when and how national governments are able to influence and limit the process of legal integration.

I. How did the ECJ escape member state control?

[The Treaties] do not contain but a minimum of supranationalism and no danger of surprise can exist for the contracting states because nothing of substance can escape the control of the national parliament. (from the report of Italian Senator Santero presented in 1957 during the Italian ratification debates over the Treaty of Rome)[3]

Although the Court likes to pose modestly as 'the guardian of the Treaties' it is in fact an uncontrolled authority generating law . . . (from 'More powerful than intended', *Financial Times*, 22 Aug. 1974)

The transformation of the European legal system is no longer seen as controversial. The incredible success of the ECJ makes it hard to imagine a European Union where European law is not supreme over national law. But as Chapter 1 showed, member states intended to create a limited legal system so as to protect national sovereignty. ECJ decisions were made purely declaratory, and the enforcement mechanisms for the Treaty of Rome were actually weakened from what they had been during the Coal and Steel

---

[3] Legisl. Ital. II: 1953–75—Disegni de Legge e Relazione-Documenti Atti Parliamenti, Sennato della Repubblica no. 2107A, p. 51.

Community.[4] Furthermore, during the ratification debates national governments stressed the limits of the European legal system—that only member states or the Commission could raise infringement suits against a state, and that ECJ infringement findings carried no explicit sanctions—as merits of the system.[5] The limits were seen as merits because they protected national sovereignty, while providing a means to resolve disputes over the rules. How could the ECJ go so far beyond what member states had envisioned when they drafted the Treaty of Rome and created the European legal system?

Maybe national governments simply did not understand what was happening?

The legal process has its own dynamic that often leads to interpretations beyond what political actors imagine when they draft legal texts.[6] But the transformation of the European legal system involved far more interpretive licence than is usually the case. Why do political bodies accept legal interpretations that border on judicial lawmaking?

Legal scholars have explained national government acceptance of the ECJ's supremacy declaration based on the compelling nature of legal reasoning, the authority of the legal process itself, and the respect and reverence accorded to the decisions of high judicial bodies (Weiler 1991: 2428). They have also argued that most politicians are only too happy to leave 'technical' discussions about legal language and interpretation to the lawyers to resolve.

---

[4] As discussed in Ch. 1 above, in the ECSC the Commission (then called the High Authority) could levy fines that could be appealed to the ECJ. States could be forced to pay these fines by withholding transfer payments to countries. These mechanisms still exist for the ECSC, but with respect to the Treaty of Rome the Commission lost its sanctioning powers. ECJ decisions were made purely declaratory, and until 1993 violations of European law could not be punished with sanctions (Article 228 TEC, formerly Article 171, came into force as part of the Maastricht Treaty).

[5] Document 5266, annexe to the verbal procedures of 26 Mar. 1957 of the debates of the French National Assembly, prepared by the Commission of the Foreign Ministry; 'Entwurf eines Gesetzes zu den Verträgen vom 25 März 1957 zur Gründung der Europäischen Wirtschaftsgemeinschaft und der Europäischen Atomgemeinschaft', Anlage C; Report of representative Dr Mommer from the *Bundestag* debates of Friday, 5 March 1957, p. 13391; Atti Parlamentari, Senato della Repubblica; Legislatura II 1953–57, disegni di legge e relazioni, document 2107-A, and Camera dei deputati, document 2814 seduta del 26 marzo 1957.

[6] Even the Treaty of Rome's negotiators admit that they did intend the preliminary ruling system, and especially granting the ECJ the power to interpret European laws in preliminary ruling references, to open the door to national court enforcement of European law supremacy (Pescatore 1981). Also based on interviews with 3 negotiators of the legal section of the Treaty of Rome: 3 Nov. 1992, Luxembourg; 7 July 1994, Paris; 23 June 1994, Paris.

They claim that the legal decisions themselves are hard for non-lawyers to comprehend because of their technical and often arcane terminology. Anne-Marie Burley and Walter Mattli make a similar argument in their neo-functionalist account of European integration. They assert that law, with its technical language, serves as a mask obscuring the ramifications of the judicial decisions, and a shield protecting the ECJ from attack by political bodies (Burley and Mattli 1993: 72–3).

But there were many national politicians who saw the ECJ's decisions for what they were: assertions of new powers. The Belgian, Dutch, and German governments participated in the *Van Gend en Loos* case,[7] arguing that the ECJ lacked jurisdiction to respond to the preliminary ruling request. The governments asserted their understanding that a charge against a member state could only be raised by the Commission or another member state. They voiced their fear that if the ECJ were to accept jurisdiction under Article 177, state legal protections would be considerably diminished.

The member states (and the ECJ's Advocate-General) were proceeding from the position that the Treaty of Rome was a standard international treaty that should, following tradition, be interpreted narrowly (De Witte 1999: 178). Because neither the Treaty nor the article in question explicitly granted private litigants the right to draw on European law in national courts to challenge national policies, there was no legal basis to find direct effects. Furthermore, from these government's perspective the ECJ had no jurisdiction to respond to the question of whether European law created direct effects in the Dutch system. Such a question was purely a matter of national law (Stein 1981: 4–6). The Italian government made a similar argument in the *Costa v. ENEL* case, claiming that the case was 'absolutely inadmissible' because the Italian court had to apply the Italian law in question as the latest expression of parliamentary will. The Italian government also argued that only the Commission or another member state could challenge the Italian act (Stein 1981: 11).[8] Indeed, national governments argued against every

---

[7] *Van Gend en Loos v. Nederlandse Administratie Belastingen*, ECJ 26/62, [1963] ECR 1, [1963] CMLR 105.

[8] *Costa v. ENEL*, ECJ Case 6/64, [1964] ECR 585, [1964] CMLR 425. Absent from the whole debate was the sovereignty-jealous French government. According to Buffet-Tchakaloff (1984: 19–21), the French government did not have a system in place for monitoring or participating in ECJ cases, especially in cases that did not involve French courts. But even if they had had a system in place, the lack of French involvement is not surprising. Courts in France are conservative in their legal interpretations. The French government was probably expecting the ECJ (which was after all modelled on the French *Conseil d'État*) to be conservative too, sticking to what the Treaty explicitly said—thus deciding that European law did not grant direct effects, was not supreme to national

significant doctrinal advance the ECJ made in the 1960s and 1970s (Stein 1981: 25).

The position advocated by the national governments lost. Furthermore, the *Van Gend en Loos* and *Costa v. ENEL* decisions included bold assertions that member states had 'limited their sovereign rights', creating a 'new legal order' complete with rights for European citizens and duties for European states. It does not take a legal expert to recognize the potential threat to national sovereignty inherent in such rhetoric. We can perhaps understand why member states had thought their legal arguments would prevail in court. But how can we explain the apparent failure of national governments to respond more forcefully to the early ECJ rulings?

The different time horizons and focus of politicians and judges

While political actors may well understand the long-term doctrinal implications of legal decisions, they have little personal incentive to mobilize to fight problematic legal doctrines. Political actors have short time horizons (Pierson 1996: 135–6). On election day a politician will get credit for saving cherished policies and solving problems of the day. If a legal decision creates an immediately untenable political situation, fighting the decision may be a wise political strategy. However, if a legal decision does not cause a problem today, it is not worth expending political resources to mobilize against it. Even if the decision turns out to be a problem in ten years' time, the chances are that it will be left for other politicians to deal with.

Political actors also interpret the importance of a legal decision differently from judges. For lawyers and judges, legal doctrine and legal precedent is what makes a decision significant—more so than the policy at stake or the material outcome of the case (Alter 1996: 473). Thus for lawyers and judges, the *Van Gend en Loos* and *Costa v. ENEL* cases were very significant because of their doctrinal implications. Political actors, on the other hand, care most about the material or political impact of legal decisions—the policy reversed by a judge or the cost of changing policy to make national law compatible with European law.[9] From a political perspective, the *Costa v. ENEL* and *Van*

---

law, and that national courts could not raise questions about the compatibility of national law in preliminary ruling references.

[9] If a legal doctrine is so politically contestable that the electorate cares about the doctrine, political actors might be mobilized to contest the opinion. US decisions on abortion, and the Italian decision that it is impossible to rape a woman wearing jeans, are examples of decisions that by virtue of their doctrinal implications mobilize public opinion. On the rape and jeans case, see A. Stanley, 'Ruling on Tight Jeans and Rape Sets off Anger in Italy', *New York Times*, 16 Feb. 1999, A3.

Gend en Loos decisions were not crucial. The money at stake in the Dutch case was small, and the Dutch government did not seem to mind paying it. And the Italian government actually won its *Costa v. ENEL* case—its policy was upheld.

This focus on the material impact makes sense especially when one considers the short time horizons of political actors. Rather than using scarce resources to scrutinize every legal decision, politicians usually wait for a legal decision to set off a 'fire alarm'. Not only does such a strategy save political resources,[10] it also allows politicians to take credit and win public support when they do finally address concerns raised by adverse court decisions.

Finally, politicians have a variety of policy objectives, and they must make hard choices about which issues to prioritize. French president de Gaulle actually suggested changing the ECJ's jurisdictional authority in light of the ECJ's *Van Gend en Loos* and *Costa v. ENEL* rulings.[11] And a convention under negotiation in 1968 was held hostage for a number of years over the issue of what type of jurisdictional authority the ECJ should have for this convention.[12] But clearly De Gaulle was unwilling to devote resources to fighting the new ECJ doctrine. France was on the minority side of most of the contentious issues in European integration at the time, and he had to choose his battles carefully. At the time France was focused on winning concessions regarding the Common Agricultural Policy, the shift to qualified majority voting in the Council, and the creation of an independent source of revenue for the EC (Moravcsik 1998: 177–97; Gerbet 1983: 316–20). The French government also seemed to believe that the ECJ's doctrines would not amount to much. As late as 1995 the legal adviser charged with coordinating French positions on European issues argued that the ECJ did not matter until the 1980s because the decisions were principles without any reality.[13]

The different incentives of politicians can explain why member states did not react more strongly to the ECJ's declaration of the direct effect and supremacy of European law.

[10] McCubbins developed this argument with respect to congressional oversight of administrative agencies. The argument is equally applicable to political oversight of courts (McCubbins and Schwartz 1987).

[11] De Gaulle's former Prime Minister Michel Debré mentioned this in the discussion of the Foyer–Debré Propositions de Loi (Rasmussen 1986: 351).

[12] This was the Brussels Convention of 27 Sept. 1968, adopted 3 June 1971. This case will be discussed further later in this chapter.

[13] Interview with the French legal adviser at the *Secrétariat Général de Coordination Interministérielle des Affaires Européennes*, 31 Oct. 1995, Paris.

The ECJ's strategy: playing off the short time horizons of political actors

The incentives for politicians to think in election cycles and to use a 'fire alarm' system of oversight leads to a focus which prioritizes the material and political impact of legal decisions over the long term effects of European legal doctrine. The ECJ understands political incentives, and it plays on them. Knowing that member states were most concerned with the material impact of its decisions, the ECJ made decisions that, while bold in doctrinal rhetoric, had minimal financial and political consequences. Clarence Mann commented on the ECJ's early jurisprudence in politically contentious cases: 'by narrowly restricting the scope of its reasoning, [the ECJ] manages to avoid almost every question in issue' (1972: 413). Stuart Scheingold observed that in Article 173 cases (now Article 230), 'the ECJ used procedural rules to avoid decisions of substance' (1971: 21). Trevor Hartley generalized these observations, identifying a policy style the ECJ uses to develop doctrine:

A common tactic is to introduce a new doctrine gradually: in the first case that comes before it, the Court will establish the doctrine as a general principle but suggest that it is subject to various qualifications; the Court may even find some reason why it should not be applied to the particular facts of the case. The principle, however, is now established. If there are not too many protests, it will be re-affirmed in later cases; the qualifications can then be whittled away and the full extent of the doctrine revealed. (Hartley 1988: 78–9)

The Commission also understood the different incentives of politicians, and was an accomplice in the ECJ's efforts to build doctrinal precedent.[14] According to the Director of the Commission's legal services from 1958 to 1970, the Commission realized that legal means—with or without sanctions—would not have worked to enforce the Treaty if there were no political will to proceed with integration. For this reason, the Commission's legal services did not really try to force member state compliance through infringement cases in the 1960s. Instead it adopted what the director called the 'less worse' solution of compromising on principles but working to help the ECJ develop its doctrine, especially doctrine which national courts could apply.[15] Lawyers for the Commission also advocated broad readings of European law in their arguments before the ECJ (Stein 1981: 25). By making sure that ECJ decisions did not arouse political passions, the judges and the Commission could build a legal edifice without serious political challenge.

---

[14] Indeed, one former Commissioner called the Commission's legal strategy 'informal complicity'. Interview with former EC Commissioner, 9 June 1994, Paris.

[15] Interview with the former director of the Commission's Legal Services, 7 July 1994, Paris.

Shifting the context of governments: forcing them to play by the legal rules of the game

In retrospect, political non-action seems quite short-sighted. But in the 1960s it was very hard to predict what would happen as a result of the Court's declarations. European law supremacy was at that time only a *potential* problem, and the risk of the ECJ running amok was still fairly low given that there were relatively few national court references to the ECJ, and that most national legal systems did not allow for the supremacy of European law over subsequent national law. Indeed, in the 1960s the Italian Constitutional Court and the French *Conseil d'État* rejected a role enforcing European law supremacy,[16] lending support to those who thought the ECJ's supremacy claims would not amount to much. But as political actors focused on other issues, the subject of European law supremacy was debated within national legal communities. Once national courts agreed to send the ECJ preliminary ruling references, and enforce European law supremacy, the dynamic of member state–ECJ relations changed.

Before national courts enforced European law supremacy, it was fairly easy for national governments to avoid unwanted ECJ rulings. ECJ decisions were few and far between, and the Commission could be persuaded to limit the use of the infringement procedure, keeping compliance issues out of court.[17] National governments could also simply ignore the ECJ. ECJ decisions themselves carried no fines or sanctions, and the ECJ had little political legitimacy in the European population at large, so ignoring an ECJ decision was politically safe. Before national courts accepted the supremacy of European law over subsequent national law, national governments could also pass new legislation at home, binding their countrymen and their courts to follow national policy instead of ECJ jurisprudence. Joseph Weiler called this the option of exit from EC legal obligations through non-compliance (Weiler 1991: 2412).

---

[16] *Costa v. ENEL & Soc. Edisonvolta*, Italian Constitutional Court Decision 14 of 7 Mar. 1964, [1964] I Il Foro It. 87 I 465. '*Semoules* decision', Syndicat Général de Fabricants de Semoules de France, *Conseil d'État* decision of 1 Mar. 1968, [1968] Recueil Lebon 149, [1970] CMLR 395.

[17] As discussed above, the Commission's legal services had determined that using infringement suits to challenge national trade barriers would not be an effective means to create the common market. In the first 10 years of the Economic Community, the Commission raised only 27 infringement cases against member states. According to Hjalte Rasmussen, 'Citizens of the several member states, often in vain, drew the attention of the services of the Commission on flagrant breaches of Community obligations' (Rasmussen 1986: 238).

But when national courts started sending cases to the ECJ and applying ECJ jurisprudence, disputes were no longer so easily kept out of the legal realm.[18] Preliminary ruling cases gave the ECJ plenty of opportunities to develop its doctrine further, and allowed European law to expand into more and more policy areas. National courts also referred cases constructed by lawyers to challenge compromises the Commission had accepted, thus forcing into the legal realm disputes that states had tried to keep out of court.[19] Once national judiciaries had accepted European law supremacy, national courts would not let politicians ignore unwanted ECJ decisions, and it became much harder for governments to interpret their way out of compliance.

National court support of ECJ jurisprudence effectively closed the option of exit through non-compliance with an ECJ decision, forcing governments to play by the legal rules of the game in an arena where member states were at an inherent disadvantage vis-à-vis the ECJ. As Joseph Weiler argued:

By the fact of their own national courts making a preliminary reference to the ECJ, governments are forced to juridify their argument and shift to the judicial arena in which the ECJ is preeminent (so long as it can carry with it the national judiciary). When governments are pulled into court and required to explain, justify, and defend their decision, they are in a forum where diplomatic license is far more restricted, where good faith is a presumptive principle and where states are meant to live by their statements. The legal arena imposes different rules of discourse. (Weiler 1994: 519)

The turnover tax struggle of 1966 offers a clear example of how the ECJ could rely on politicians' fixation on the short-term impact of their decisions to diffuse political protests, and how national judicial support shifted the

[18] National courts made 741 references to the ECJ between 1960 and 1979. Even if only 40% of national court references were challenges to national policy (two studies regarding the content of national court references to the ECJ found that about 40% of the references concerned questions about the compatibility of national and European law (Schwartz 1988: 15, 23; Chalmers 2000a: 34)) there would still have been 296 challenges to national policy referred by national courts in this period, nearly 3 times the number of infringement cases raised by the Commission in the same period. Table 1.2 above summarizes the number of cases sent to the ECJ by the Commission, member states, and national courts. Source for national reference rates: ECJ annual reports. Source for Commission cases 1960–95: ECJ's Research and Documentation Division.

[19] e.g. the *Lütticke* case was designed to challenge a deal between the Commission and the German government where the German government lowered its tax on milk powder from 4% to 3%. (See discussion of the turnover tax struggle above, Ch. 3, Round 2.) The *Cassis de Dijon* case also was intended to challenge a Commission deal made with Germany regarding importation of the liqueur Anisette (Alter and Meunier-Aitsahalia 1994: 538). *Lütticke (Alfons) GmbH v. Hauptzollamt Saarlouis*, ECJ Case 57/65, [1966] ECR 205. 'Cassis de Dijon', *Rewe Zentral AG v. Bundesmonopolverwaltung für Branntwein*, ECJ Case 120/78, [1979] ECR 649.

types of responses available to governments. When the ECJ's 1966 *Lütticke* decision[20] created hundreds of thousands of refund claims for 'illegally' collected German turnover equalization taxes, the German Finance Ministry issued a statement: 'We hold the decision of the European Court as invalid. It conflicts with the well reasoned arguments of the Federal Government, and with the opinion of the affected member states of the Community.' It instructed German customs officials and tax courts to ignore the ECJ decision in question—thus the government tried to exit through non-compliance.[21] The decree would have ended the conflict had lower tax courts not refused to follow it. With national courts admitting thousands of challenges to German turnover taxes, with lawyers publishing articles condemning the government's attempts to intimidate plaintiffs and ignore a valid European legal judgment,[22] and with the dangerous possibility that nearly all German turnover taxes could be illegal, the German government asked its lawyers to find a solution (Meier 1994).

The Ministry of Economics' test-case strategy is discussed in Chapter 3. The German government convinced the ECJ to minimize the material impact of its *Lütticke* decision by shifting the legal basis for German turnover taxes to a Treaty article that did not create direct effects.[23] The numerous cases disappeared, but the strategy conceded the ECJ's precedent established in the *Lütticke* case—national laws creating tariff and non-tariff barriers to trade could be challenged through private litigant cases raised in national courts. In addition, since the *Lütticke* case was the first German case raising the issue of European law supremacy, the strategy also conceded the supremacy of European law over national law. National courts' support for the ECJ's *Lütticke* decision had forced the German government to accept a legal decision that it had declared invalid.[24]

The doctrinal precedents inserted into the ECJ's materially benign legal decisions were, in fact, institutional building-blocks that could be applied to

---

[20] ECJ Case 120/78, [1979] ECR 649, *Lütticke* decision.

[21] 7 July 1966 (IIIB.4-V8534-1/66), republished in AWD (1966) p. 327.

[22] The articles include Wendt (1967a; 1967b), Stöcker (1967), Meier (1967a).

[23] The 1966 case concerned turnover taxes that fell under Article 95 of the EEC treaty, and the ECJ decision had been that Article 95 created direct effects. The German government argued that German taxes were actually 'average taxes' that were guided by Article 97 EEC, and that Article 97 did not create direct effects, so that individuals did not have legal standing to challenge German turnover taxes in national courts (Meier 1994; Everling 1967). The ECJ accepted the legal argument and found that Article 97 did not create direct effects. The Federal Tax Court declared that German taxes were 'average taxes', and nearly all of the plaintiffs lost legal standing. See Ch. 3, pp. 83–5, for complete references.

[24] This was the claim made by German Finance Ministry. See n. 21 above.

more polemical cases in the future. Once ECJ doctrine was accepted by national judiciaries, the ECJ became bolder in applying its doctrine, making a series of decisions that surprised and upset different national governments including the *ERTA* (1971), *Charmasson* (1974), *Cassis de Dijon* (1979), and *Factortame* (1990) decisions.[25] For the ECJ and for national courts, most of these decisions were the logical application of existing ECJ jurisprudence. While the ECJ could have used technicalities to avoid upsetting governments, it no longer needed to do so. Indeed, Geoffrey Garrett, Daniel Kelemen, and Heiner Schultz found the more developed and specified the ECJ doctrine, the more the ECJ is willing to apply it against member states (Garrett et al. 1998: 158).

Under the 'legal rules of the game', the means and methods of influence are different. States cannot ignore decisions because they think they are wrong, nor can they rely on national law to avoid European obligations. Furthermore, once a case makes it to court, judges—not politicians, and not the public—are in the powerful position of deciding what to do.

But there were still a number of ways governments could influence court behaviour within the legal rules of the game. These techniques could have been used to challenge the ECJ's assertion of European law supremacy. Member states could have reversed the ECJ's supremacy doctrine by rewriting the contested European legislation to make it clear that European law was not supreme over national law. They could have also rewritten the Court's mandate, limiting access to the European Court and circumscribing its jurisdictional authority to make it harder or politically more dangerous for the ECJ to apply European law supremacy. And they could have used the appointment process to create a court that was more sympathetic to protecting national sovereignty. The next section considers why member states did not use these strategies.

II. Why did national governments not reassert control?

Our sovereignty has been taken away by the European Court of Justice. It has made many decisions impinging on our statute law and says that we are to obey its decisions

---

[25] *Commission v. Council (ERTA)*, ECJ Case 22/70, [1971] ECR 263, [1971] CMLR 335. *Charmasson v. Ministre de l'économie et des finances*, ECJ Case 48/74, [1974] ECR 1383. N. 19 above, 'Cassis de Dijon', *Regina v. Secretary of State for Transport, ex parte Factortame Ltd*, ECJ Case C-213/89, [1990] ECR I-2473.

instead of our own statute law . . . Our courts must no longer enforce our national laws. They must enforce Community law . . . No longer is European law an incoming tide flowing up the estuaries of England. It is now like a tidal wave bringing down our sea walls and flowing inland over our fields and houses—to the dismay of all. (Lord Denning, of the judicial branch of the House of Lords, 1990)

Once national courts accepted a role enforcing European law supremacy, national governments were no longer able to ignore European legal obligations. At this point, national governments had three options—all of which implied mobilizing and expending political resources. (1) They could try to get national courts to reverse their acceptance of European law supremacy; (2) they could amend the Treaty of Rome to make it clear that European law was not supreme to national law, and/or scale back the ECJ's jurisdiction so that it would be less able or willing to use European law to challenge cherished national policies; or (3) they could accept the supremacy of European law but work to influence the ECJ in its application of supremacy doctrine on a case-by-case basis. All three strategies were attempted at different times.

Attempts to stop national courts from accepting European law supremacy

There were a number of attempts to get national courts not to apply European law supremacy, or ECJ jurisprudence. Chapter 4 discussed the French National Assembly's attempt to make it illegal for national courts to set aside French law for any reason (see pp. 156–7). The Aurillac amendment was passed overwhelmingly in the National Assembly, but the government persuaded the Senate not to act, so the amendment never gained force. In Belgium, the parliament attempted to reverse national court acceptance of European law supremacy by subjecting the primacy of European and international law to parliamentary control.[26] There were also examples where parliaments tried legislatively to overturn national court decisions enforcing European law supremacy.[27]

These examples exist, but they are relatively few—perhaps because the difficulty of such an endeavour discourages those who may be inclined to challenge national judges. Three factors tend to sap the will of politicians to proceed in challenging national courts. First, the attempts to politically

---

[26] *Doc. Parl.* 1971–2, Chambre, 200/1 27 Apr. 1972. Discussed briefly in Bribosia (1998: 11).

[27] The turnover tax struggle discussed above is an example. Also, a bill challenging an ECJ interpretation of the Euratom Treaty was proposed in the National Assembly. JO Ass. Nat. Deb. of 1 June 1979, p. 4607. For a summary of political challenges to ECJ authority, see Goldstein (1997: 171).

sanction the judiciary are often seen as unconstitutional and an assault on judicial independence. The legislation enacting the sanction is subject to invalidation on appeal to constitutional bodies,[28] and judges asked to adhere to it can reject it.

Second, there is concern that intimidating national actors because they are faithfully implementing European law can create unwanted consequences. It can be seen as illegitimate: an authoritarian strategy inappropriate in a democratic system. And it can antagonize other European states. It could provoke the Commission or other member states to raise an infringement case. It could weaken a government's bargaining leverage in the Council (why be held hostage to a state that might not follow the rule anyway?). Such concerns led the French government to fight within the Senate to let the Aurillac amendment die so that it was never enacted into law.[29] In Germany in the 1970s, rather than challenging the German Constitutional Court the federal government bought off plaintiffs who threatened to raise European legal disputes bound to provoke conflict.[30]

Perhaps most importantly, it is usually easier for governments to find creative ways to lessen the impact of a contested decision than it is to forge ahead with fights in parliament over the national judiciary.[31] Whether it is because politicians hold deep respect for the national constitution, or because there is considerable domestic political support for judicial independence, or because it would have been difficult for political edicts to become legally enforceable, politicians apparently lacked the will to engage in a constitutional battle with national courts. The failed political attempts to sanction national courts for enforcing European law had the opposite effect to that intended. Rather than stopping national court enforcement of European law, the failed attempts

---

[28]   This holds only where legislation can be appealed to a constitutional body.

[29]   For more on the failed Aurillac amendment, see Ch. 4, pp. 156–7, and Buffet-Tchakaloff (1984: 346), Galmont (1990), Isaac (1980), and Jacqué (1981: 4-14). There are other examples where the executive circumvented the parliament to avoid domestic impediments to its European agenda. See Rasmussen (1986: 352–3) and Buffet-Tchakaloff (1984: 336–41).

[30]   In interviews, members of the German economics ministry also admitted working to circumvent German high court challenges to ECJ authority, because high court challenges created problems with the Commission and undermined German influence in EC negotiations. Interview with the legal adviser for European law at the Federal Ministry for Economic Affairs, 11 May 1993, Bonn.

[31]   To this day French Gaullists continue their efforts to change the French constitution to disallow European law supremacy. They tried to amend the French constitution during the ratification debates for the Maastricht Treaty (Stone 1993: 78). And they continue to devise potential amendments for the constitution (Mazeaud 1996; Berthu 1997). Until the day the Gaullists or the National Front controls the French parliament, however, these efforts are unlikely to succeed.

showed national courts that political bodies would not sanction them if they enforced European law supremacy at home.

Institutional constraints to redefining the ECJ's mandate

Unable to stop national courts from applying ECJ jurisprudence, politicians turned to the European level to try to stop the encroachment of European law on national prerogatives. It is well within the legal rules of the game for member states to change the mandate or jurisdiction of the ECJ, or to specify more clearly the meaning and limitations of European law. Why did member states not make it clear that European law did *not* create direct effects and was *not* supreme to national law? Why not change the preliminary ruling procedure to explicitly state that references cannot concern questions of national law. Or since lower courts more readily send far-reaching questions to the ECJ, why not limit the right of reference to high courts only?

The institutional design of the European Union makes it relatively easy for member states to extract concessions during the initial stage of policy-making, but hard to reform existing policies—especially policies based on founding treaties. George Tsebelis (1995) has shown that the larger the number of actors able to veto legislative outcomes, the more difficult it is to reform policy. In the European Union, every member state is a potential veto player when it comes to amending the Treaty, since such amendments require unanimous consent of the member states. The requirement that amendments be negotiated during an inter-governmental conference (IGC), and be ratified by national parliaments, creates another barrier to amending the Treaty to reverse the ECJ's supremacy doctrine. When new policy is made, however, states can use the veto threat to extract compromises and side-payments from those who want new policies. The existence of multiple veto-players and the inertia created by the status quo have created a 'joint decision trap' in the EC which can make policies that member states agree are sub-optimal nonetheless impervious to reform (Scharpf 1988). The weight of the status quo has been insurmountable as far as reforming the ECJ's jurisdiction under the Treaty of Rome is concerned.

These institutional barriers explain why attempts to expand the ECJ's authority have been blocked at the same time that there have not been serious attacks on the ECJ's authority under the Treaty of Rome. Already in 1968 there was concern that preliminary ruling references from lower courts were compromising national sovereignty. De Gaulle did not mobilize against the ECJ in the 1960s, but France blocked ratification of the Brussels convention on the mutual recognition of national court decisions until a deal was made where the right of reference of national courts was limited to a narrow list of high courts,[32] courts that were expected to be more sensitive to concerns about national sovereignty.[33] In the late 1970s, negotiations over inter-governmental conventions to deal with fraud against the EC and crimes committed by EC employees also stalled over the issue of a preliminary ruling role for the ECJ. Again the terms of the conventions had been agreed to, and this time no national sovereignty was at stake; but the stumbling-block to ratifying the conventions was preliminary ruling authority for the ECJ.[34] France refused to extend preliminary ruling authority for the ECJ at all, while the Benelux countries refused to ratify the agreements without a right of reference for national courts.[35] In the 1980s member states agreed to establish the Treaty on a European Union. The ECJ was excluded entirely from the Common Foreign and Security Policy and Justice and Home Affairs in the original Maastricht Treaty. In the 1990's, the conflict over extending preliminary ruling jurisdiction played itself out again regarding the 1992 Cannes conventions on Europol, the Customs Information System, and the resurrected conventions regarding fraud in the EC.[36] This time Britain refused to extend preliminary ruling authority, while Germany, Italy, and the Benelux parliaments refused to ratify the agreement without preliminary ruling authority for the ECJ.[37] A role for the ECJ in justice and home affairs was

[32] Protocol on the Interpretation by the Court of Justice of the European Communities of the Convention of 27 September 1968 Concerning Judicial Competence and the Execution of Decisions in Civil and Commercial Matters, 3 June 1971, 1262 UNTS 241.

[33] Based on an interview with the director of the EC law section at the German Ministry of Justice who was responsible for these negotiations, 2 Nov. 1995, Bonn.

[34] Based on interviews with Dutch, French, and German negotiators for these agreements, 27 Oct. 1995, Brussels, 30 Oct. 1995, Paris, and 2 Nov. 1995, Bonn.

[35] Based on an interview with the director of the EC law section at the German Ministry of Justice who was responsible for these negotiations; 2 Nov. 1995, Bonn.

[36] Convention Based on Article K.3 of the Treaty of the European Union of 7 February 1992 on the Establishment of European Police Office, 26 July 1995, BPP EC 13 (1995), 1995 OJ (C 316) 2–32; Convention Drawn Up on the Basis of Article K.3 of the Treaty of the European Union on the Use of Information Technology for Customs Purposes, 26 July 1995, BPP EC 18 (1996), 1995 O.J. (L 316) 34–47; Convention on the Protection of the European Communities Financial Interests, 26 July 1995, 1995 OJ (C 316) 48. According to sources within the Legal Services of the Council, France and perhaps Spain are hiding behind the British position, lying low so that the British take the political heat for a position they too support. Interview at the Legal Services of the Council, 27 Oct. 1995, Brussels.

[37] Based on interviews with the director of the EC law section at the German Ministry of Justice who was responsible for these negotiations, 2 Nov. 1995, Bonn, and with the director of the Legal Services of the Council, 26 Oct. 1995, Brussels.

created in the Treaty of Amsterdam (1996), but a compromise was required where member states were allowed to decide for themselves whether their courts would be allowed to make preliminary ruling references, and whether only courts of last instance would have such rights.[38] And with respect to asylum and immigration issues, the right of reference is restricted to courts of last instance.[39]

This pattern reveals a great political discomfort with the role national courts were playing in the European legal system. Institutional constraints meant that sovereignty-jealous states could win concessions regarding new ECJ powers, but got nowhere when they tried to reform existing ECJ authority. The most serious effort to change the ECJ's mandate and power occurred in 1995. In negotiations over the Treaty of Amsterdam, Euro-sceptics forced the British government to pursue a series of proposals to make the ECJ more politically accountable and to limit the cost of ECJ decisions. The most radical proposals involved creating a political appeals process whereby member states could overturn ECJ decisions, and 'clipping the court's wings' by changing its jurisdictional authority.[40] These ideas failed to win even tepid support inside or outside Britain because they violated norms regarding judicial independence.[41] Instead, the British government suggested creating an appeals procedure that would give the ECJ a second chance to reflect on its decision in light of political displeasure. The British also suggested a treaty amendment to limit liability damages in cases where the member state acted in good faith, and an amendment which would explicitly allow the Court to limit the retrospective effect of the its judgments.[42] The British proposals were rejected entirely by the other member states. The Dutch, German, and French legal advisers agreed that the Court's mandate, as it stood in the Treaty of Rome, was not up for renegotiation.[43]

[38] Article 35 TEU (formerly Article K.7), as revised in Treaty of Amsterdam.

[39] Article 68 TEU (formerly Article 73p), as revised in Treaty of Amsterdam.

[40] These suggestions to 'clip the Court's wings' were discussed in an article in the *Financial Times* and in an academic article written by a civil servant in the *Bundesministerium für Arbeit und Sozialordnung*, Mr Clever (Clever 1995; Brown 1995).

[41] Based on interviews in the British Foreign and Commonwealth Office, 10 Nov. 1995, London.

[42] The proposals were put forth in Sept. 1995 in preparatory documents for the 1996 IGC. The author of the paper was David Davis, and it was made available to negotiators.

[43] Based on: interview with the legal adviser at the Permanent Representation of the Netherlands at the European Union, 26 Oct. 1995, Brussels; interview with a former legal adviser at the Department of Justice in the Netherlands, 27 Oct. 1995, Brussels; interview with the Council to the Speaker regarding European Legislation, House of Commons, UK, 8 Nov. 1995, London; interview with a legal adviser in European Affairs at the Foreign and Commonwealth Office,

France and Britain were able to extract concessions with respect to new ECJ powers, but few countries had sympathy for their efforts to reign in the ECJ. While some states shared their frustrations, there was a widespread fear that opening the *acquis communautaire* to renegotiation would be like opening Pandora's box—who knows what troubles would come out, and hard-won progress in integration could be undermined. In addition, small states prefer a strong European legal system. Before the ECJ, political power is equalized, and within the ECJ small states have a disproportionate voice, since each judge has one vote and decisions are taken by simple majority. The small states are not alone in their defence of the ECJ. The Germans from the outset wanted a 'United States of Europe', and for a long time the German government considered a more federal-looking European legal system a step in the right direction.[44]

The difficulty of reforming existing policy, created by the existence of multiple veto actors and the inertia of the status quo, explains why the ECJ's transformation of the European legal system was not reversed, while its legal advances were also not formally enshrined in the Treaty of Rome. Displeasure with the ECJ's activism is reflected, however, in the heated battles over extending ECJ authority to new areas. Member states are hesitant to even replicate the ECJ's existing format with respect to new areas of EU authority.

The credibility gap: the difficulty of influencing ECJ decision-making

National governments had virtually no success reversing national court acceptance of European law supremacy, or in getting their courts not to apply ECJ jurisprudence. Nor have they been able to reverse the ECJ's doctrinal advances at the European level. This leaves member states with the third

9 Nov. 1995, London; interview with a legal adviser in European Affairs at the Foreign and Commonwealth Office, 9 Nov. 1995, London; interview with a political adviser to the Minister of the State, Foreign and Commonwealth Office, 10 Nov. 1995, London; interview with the legal adviser on European Affairs at the Treasury Solicitor's Office, 10 Nov. 1995, London; interview with the legal adviser at the Permanent Representation of France at the European Union, 25 Oct. 1995, Brussels; interview with the legal adviser to the Foreign Ministry in France, 30 Oct. 1995, Paris; interview with the Legal Director at the *Secrétariat Général de Coordination Interministerielle des Affaires Européennes*, 31 Oct. 1995, Paris; interview with the director of the European law section, Ministry of Justice in Germany, 2 Nov. 1995, Bonn.

[44] Interview with the director of the EC law section, Ministry of Justice in Germany, 2 Nov. 1995, Bonn; interview with the legal adviser at the Permanent Representation of the Netherlands at the European Union, 26 Oct. 1995, Brussels; interview with a former legal adviser at the Department of Justice in the Netherlands, 27 Oct. 1995, Brussels.

option: trying to influence how the ECJ applies European law supremacy on a case-by-case basis. Here again national governments have found their tools far more limited than expected.

Neo-realists expected the ECJ to be especially vulnerable to political pressure. As Geoffrey Garrett and Barry Weingast argued:

> Embedding a legal system in a broader political structure places direct constraints on the discretion of a court, even one with as much constitutional independence as the United States Supreme Court. This conclusion holds even if the constitution makes no explicit provisions for altering a court's role. The reason is that political actors have a range of avenues through which they may alter or limit the role of courts. Sometimes such changes require amendment of the constitution, but usually the appropriate alterations may be accomplished more directly through statute, as by alteration of the court's jurisdiction in a way that makes it clear that continued undesired behavior will result in more radical changes . . . *the possibility of such a reaction drives a court that wishes to preserve its independence and legitimacy to remain in the area of acceptable latitude.* (Garrett and Weingast 1993: 200–1; emphasis original)

Since the ECJ is an international court, the authority of which is *not* based on a constitution, and since appointments to the ECJ are renewed every six years, Garrett and Weingast expected the ECJ to be even more cautious than most domestic courts.

The problem with this argument is already apparent. There are certainly political limits to what a court can do, some area of 'acceptable latitude' beyond which courts cannot stray. Indeed, *all* political actors are ultimately constrained to stay within acceptable boundaries. But the institutional constraints of policy reform in the EU, combined with the lack of consensus to change the ECJ's existing mandate, create a credibility gap: political threats against the ECJ simply ring hollow. The ECJ can safely calculate that political controversy will not translate to an attack on its institutional standing; thus it will not need to alter its behaviour in light of a country's political preferences. For these reasons, Mark Pollack calls amending the Treaty the 'nuclear option—exceedingly effective, but difficult to use—and . . . therefore a relatively ineffective and non-credible means of member state control' (1997: 40).[45]

As Garrett and Weingast point out, every six years the Council may choose not to reappoint an ECJ judge (1993: 201). One would think this would allow member states to influence the ECJ. Using appointments to influence

---

[45] Garrett has retreated from this position; most recently note that 'the more difficult it is for new legislation to be passed (for example, by higher voting thresholds or more veto players), the more bureaucracies and courts are able to exercise discretion' (Tsebelis and Garrett 2001).

judicial positions is never a sure thing, but it is an especially weak tool in the EU. While the Council formally chooses judges, there is an understanding that each country will select its own judge. If the appointee is to have any influence within the Court, he or she must have mastery of French, the language of deliberation, and a solid grounding in European law. These requirements limit governments' options. The candidate must also survive complicated political negotiations at the national level, negotiations which include such factors as which party made the previous high judicial or EU political appointment, which judges were denied promotion in a national appointment debate, and which judges would be willing to leave the domestic scene to take up residence in the Grand Duchy of Luxembourg. These domestic political factors tend to take precedence over a judge's interpretative position on European matters.[46]

Once appointed, the threat that the judge will not be reappointed is unlikely to influence judicial positions. ECJ decisions are issued unanimously, so it is hard to pin activism on any particular national appointee. And in practice, ECJ judges are far more likely not to be reappointed because of domestic factors beyond their control (like party change or political infighting) than because of their decisions while on the Court (Rozes 1985: 508). Even if they are not reappointed, after prestigious service at the ECJ former judges usually have a variety of options including national judicial appointment, a government position, or an academic appointment.[47]

Garrett raises another potential political tool of control over the Court—the threat of non-compliance. He asserts that the ECJ fears that non-compliance or a legislative reversal will undermine its legitimacy (Garrett 1995: 179–80).[48] This concern is not as significant as he suggests. While no court wants a decision to be flouted, as Walter Mattli and Anne-Marie

---

[46] Based on interviews with the Italian, Greek, Dutch, Belgian, French, German, British, and Irish judges at the ECJ in the autumn of 1992, plus interviews in France and Germany with academics and court watchers. For more on the background of ECJ appointees, see Kenney (1998). There are a few exceptions where judicial positions on European legal issues seemed to matter. Rumour has it that the appointment of the French judge Grevisse was designed to curb judicial activism. And according to an informed French observer, the French started drawing from the more conservative *Conseil d'État* for appointments to the ECJ in an attempt to reduce activism. (Interview with Marie-France Buffet-Tchakoloff, author of *France devant la Cour de Justice*, 6 June 1994, Paris.) In Germany, Everling was seen as having a greater appreciation of the 'borders' of EC authority, and Zuleeg was not reappointed in part because of the perception that he was too willing to interpret European law expansively.

[47] Garrett now argues that 'the threat of not being reappointed seems not to act as a powerful constraint on their behavior' (Tsebelis and Garrett 2001).

[48] This assumption is reasserted ibid.

Slaughter have argued, it is better for a court to make a legally sound decision which politicians will contest than to be seen as having bent to political pressure (Mattli and Slaughter 1995: 186). Indeed, in most legal systems there remains a significant level of non-compliance: think of the many states in the US where unconstitutional law and policy exist despite US Supreme Court rulings. Clear examples of non-compliance exist, but does this mean that the US Supreme Court curbs its jurisprudence to avoid non-compliance? It is hard to sustain the assertion that in most cases, or even in the most political of cases, the fear of non-compliance shapes the ECJ's jurisprudence.

If member states cannot sway the interpretation of the ECJ, they may still be able to change the European law itself. This would not necessarily be an affront to the ECJ, nor would it necessarily undermine the Court's legitimacy. The political system is supposed to work by having legislators draft and change laws, and courts apply laws. If legislators do not like how the law is applied, the remedy expected by all is that the legislation will be changed. If the legislative change is inappropriate or unconstitutional, most probably courts will not follow it! Furthermore, the reality of the joint-decision trap makes it extremely difficult to reverse the ECJ advances based directly on an EC treaty. In theory it should be easier to change European law based on regulations or directives, since such a change may be possible with qualified majority consent (Tsebelis and Garrett 2001). But surprisingly few of the ECJ's interpretations have provoked legislative action reversing the thrust of the decision.[49] Most ECJ decisions are not reversed because decisions affect member states differently, so there is no coalition of support to change disputed legislation. Also, it takes significant political capital to mobilize the Commission and other states to legislate over a decision. If a member state can accommodate the ECJ's decision on its own, by interpreting it narrowly or by buying off the people the decision affects, such an approach is usually easier than mobilizing other member states to re-legislate. Even in cases where decisions are reversed, the European legal system as an institution remains unchanged. Nothing states have done has touched the doctrines that form the foundation of ECJ's authority: the Supremacy and the Direct Effect

---

[49] The best-known case is the Barber protocol of the Maastricht Treaty (TEU protocol 2) that actually did *not* reverse an ECJ decision, but simply limited the retrospective effects of the decision. This case was exceptional in that it affected the traditional defenders of the ECJ who spearheaded efforts to change European legislation (it was a Dutch proposal with German support). Also unusual is the fact that the decision came down during IGC negotiations, and thus could be easily tacked on as an amendment to a larger agreement in process.

of European law, or the 'four freedoms' (the free movement of goods, capital, labour, and services). These doctrines are protected because they are based on the Treaty.

The key to politicians being able to cow the ECJ into political subservience is the credibility of their threat. If a political threat is not credible, politicians can protest all they want without influencing judicial decisions.[50] After enough time passes, and enough protests or attempts to challenge ECJ jurisprudence lead nowhere, political passivity sets in. Past failures are brought forward as a reason to avoid new attempts to reign in the ECJ. Lawyers advise their governments not to pursue legal arguments or legislative attempts that contravene well-accepted legal tenets. Other negotiating partners reject ideas that seem like regressions in the process of European integration. Inertia undermines the political will to effect change, and passivity is taken as a sign of tacit support.

Of the three potential strategies to challenge European law supremacy, two have proved impossible. Member states have been unable to keep national courts from enforcing European law supremacy, nor have they been able to reverse the ECJ's transformation of the European legal system. Member states instead try to influence the ECJ in its application of European law supremacy, but their tools of influence are limited. Despite the constraints on legislating over ECJ decisions, or cowing the ECJ into quiescence, there are still ways in which member states can influence the process of legal integration. The next section considers where and how this is accomplished.

III. What powers do national governments have over the process of legal integration?

In the framework of the general law of international treaties, the member-states are now, and always have been, the masters of the Community treaties . . . (from the German Constitutional Court's 1987 *Kloppenberg* decision)[51]

National governments decide when to give new powers to European bodies, thus where to expand the reach of European law over national policy. Their

---

[50] Indeed, Garrett has backed away from nearly all of his previous claims about member state control over the ECJ because he sees the difficulty in using the techniques of political control. See Tsebelis and Garrett (2001).

[51] 'Kloppenburg', *Frau Kloppenburg v. Finanzamt Leer* BVerfG, decision 2 BvR 687/85 of 8 Apr. 1987, BVerfGE 75, [1988] 3 CMLR 1. Quote from CMLR, p. 18.

legislative powers in the Council, and their treaty-making powers in inter-governmental conferences, ensure that member states in some respects stay in charge of the overall process of legal integration. But once written, European legal texts take on a life of their own. In theory, member states always have the option of revising the texts should they be unhappy with the outcome. But in practice, changing existent legislation is difficult to do and often politically unfeasible. Because it is very difficult to change the ECJ's jurisdictional authority and mandate, or to overturn ECJ decisions, the ECJ continues to have significant autonomy and decisive influence at the inter-pretive and implementation phases of the policy process. This means that member states are really only the masters of the treaty during the drafting of legislation.

The same factors that allowed the ECJ to transform the European legal system despite the intention of national governments continue to limit member states' ability to control how the ECJ interprets European law. While national governments monitor the European legal process more actively than they did thirty years ago, they still have election-driven incentives and a scarcity of political resources that lead them to focus on the material impact of decisions rather than on their doctrinal implication. The institutional rules that limit the Council's ability to change the ECJ's mandate or to legislate over ECJ decisions still create a credibility gap, undermining governments' ability to cow the ECJ into quiescence. Thus the ECJ can still play on polit-icians' short time horizons, building its doctrine incrementally without arousing a political response. Once ECJ doctrine is accepted by national judiciaries, governments will still find themselves constrained in what they can do by the legal rules of the game.[52] And once the ECJ makes a decision, the existence of multiple veto players combined with the inertia of the status quo will still make it difficult to reverse.

If the ECJ can essentially rewrite European legal texts in the process of interpreting them, and force these interpretations on member states, how can national governments stop the process of legal integration from tram-pling on valued national policies?

National governments can influence ECJ interpretations through their arguments during legal deliberations. While governments failed to prevail in the *Van Gend en Loos* and *Costa v. ENEL* cases, their arguments have swayed the ECJ in subsequent cases. For example, in the turnover tax case discussed

---

[52] If states can keep a dispute out of court, they may not need to follow the legal rules of the game. But any deal reached will have to be as good as what a disputant could win in court, other-wise a legal case will be likely.

earlier the German government succeeded in influencing the ECJ to remove the legal standing of German importing firms so as to eliminate the challenges to German turnover taxes.[53] The key to government influence in such cases will be the plausibility and the legitimacy of their arguments. The ECJ is more interested in shaping future behaviour than in exacting revenge for past digressions, especially if that digression was unintentional. The ECJ can often be convinced to allow a legal exit to governments or to limit the retrospective impact of a decision as long as its legal precedent remains binding for the future. In addition, if a member state can present credible evidence that the cost of a specific interpretation will be disproportionate to the objective at stake, the ECJ is likely to seek a less costly solution.

National governments can also influence how the law is interpreted by carefully drafting European legislation. As mentioned, the joint-decision trap does not apply to the first stage of drafting new legislation, in which states can often block arrangements that do not meet their satisfaction.[54] Having learnt from the past, member states have found clever ways to inoculate new European legislation and new EU areas of authority against unwanted and expansive ECJ interpretations. National governments have added protocols to European treaties that caveat a member state's legal commitment to implement European law. Examples from the Treaty on a European Union include a protocol allowing the Danish to keep their legislation limiting the acquisition of second homes (aimed at the wealthy Germans—protocol 1), one which allowed Portugal to maintain an interest-free credit facility for the regions of Azores and Madeira, and a protocol protecting Irish abortion policy (protocol 17). The process of writing in caveats is not limited to Treaty negotiations. According to an article in the *Economist*, a lot of EC legislation contains secret footnotes. The article comments on a 'confidential' report by the Commission's legal service claiming that 'a handy negotiating tool' has grown 'out of proportion.' For example,

[The 1994] directive on data protection attracted 31 such [exception] statements. Britain secured an exemption for manual filing systems if—work this one out—the costs involved in complying with the directive outweigh the benefits. Germany secured the right to keep data about religious beliefs under wraps. Since these and other statements are not published, Joe Bloggs will know about these manœuverings only by chance or if his government chooses to tell him.[55]

---

[53] Discussed in Sect. II above, and more fully in Ch. 3, Round 2.

[54] Where there is qualified majority voting, a national veto can be surmounted. But the EU still strives to gain unanimous support for its policies, making concessions to create broader support.

[55] 'Seeing Through It', *Economist*, 16 Sept. 1995, p. 59. The directive referred to ultimately became the Parliament and Council Directive 95/46/EC of 24 Oct. 1995 on the Protection of

The extent to which these exceptions are legally binding is unclear, but they reveal an attempt by member states to anticipate and avoid having legal integration undermine valued national policies.

Member states have also sought to limit ECJ activism by formally excluding the ECJ from certain policy areas so as to protect national sovereignty (Burley and Mattli 1993: 74). The most notable examples (mentioned earlier) are the exclusion of the ECJ from the Common Foreign and Security Policy and Justice and Home Affairs (so-called Pillars 2 and 3, now called Titles V and VI) in the Maastricht Treaty. Small states were especially unhappy that the ECJ was excluded from Title VI, and they managed to get aspects of Justice and Home Affairs transferred into the ECJ's realm in the Treaty of Amsterdam, but in a restricted way. For issues of asylum law, migration policy, border controls and the Schengen Agreement, the preliminary ruling system was extended only to the courts of last instance that are less likely to send controversial issues of national policy to the ECJ (Article 68 TEU, formerly Article 73p of the Treaty of Amsterdam).[56] The ECJ was also explicitly denied jurisdiction over domestic issues concerning internal order and security.[57] For issues of policing and judicial cooperation (e.g. fighting terrorism and drug trafficking) states are allowed to choose whether their courts can make preliminary ruling references; thus they can keep the ECJ out of domestic issues by denying the right of reference to national courts.[58] More easily overlooked is the provision which states that the policies adopted under the EU framework with respect to Article 34 TEU (formerly Article K.6 of the Treaty of Amsterdam) will not create direct effects, individual rights which can be claimed in national courts. This restriction makes it possible for individuals to challenge the EU agreements themselves, but not the national implementation of these agreements.[59]

Member states can also shift the terms of legal debate entirely, creating space for interpretive developments more favourable to national sovereignty or national policy. The debate over subsidiarity is an example of this. Added

Individuals with Regard to the Processing of Personal Data and the Free Movement of Such Data, 1995 OJ (L 281) 31–50.

[56] The official explanation for excluding lower courts from sending references is that states were worried about a flood of asylum appeals to the ECJ, but EU officials admit that behind this official stance is a fear of ECJ activism on lower court references.

[57] Article 35, para. 5 TEU (formerly Article K.7 of the Treaty of Amsterdam).

[58] Ibid. para. 3.

[59] For more on how the preliminary ruling system applies regarding the Treaty of Amsterdam, see Sauron (1998).

to the Maastricht Treaty was a 'subsidiarity clause' (Article 5 TEU, formerly Article 3b) that sought to create limits on European authority in the national realm.[60] More than an absolute principle (the clause is actually extremely unclear), the subsidiarity clause implies that the division of member state and EU authority is up for renegotiation. While the concept of subsidiarity was initially decried as overly vague, legally meaningless, and politically unnecessary, the principle of subsidiarity has shifted the political and legal debate. Politicians, citizen groups, and journalists invoke the subsidiarity clause to argue against proposed European legislation. In its *Maastricht* decision, the German Constitutional Court also made it clear that it expects the ECJ to enforce the subsidiarity principle—threatening to find inapplicable European laws and ECJ decisions which go beyond the Treaty's mandate.[61] The ECJ has started to apply the subsidiarity principle, scaling back earlier jurisprudence in acknowledgment of the subsidiarity rights of states.[62] The debate over which policy areas are part of the European realm and which are part of the national realm remains fluid.[63] Over time a defined and accepted division of jurisdictional authority between member states and the Community will develop, but this discourse has opened room for the reach of European law in the national sphere to be limited and even reversed in certain areas.

Finally, by influencing public opinion, national governments can also create a constraint on the ECJ. Studies have found that courts gain legitimacy and the consent of litigants by being perceived as procedurally fair (Gibson and Caldeira 1995). Those with significant knowledge of the ECJ do consider it to be even-handed in its application of European law across member states, and procedurally fair. This is the main reason the ECJ enjoys wide legitimacy among legal scholars and lawyers. Unfortunately for the ECJ, however, the wider public is woefully uninformed. Opinion polls have found

[60] The clause states that outside the areas in which the Community has exclusive authority, the Community shall only take actions if and insofar as policy objectives cannot be achieved by member states. The clause implies that the EC needs a reason to enter a policy domain, and that the reason should be that by virtue of scale or effect a policy is better pursued at the European than at the national level.

[61] *Brunner and others v. The European Union Treaty*, '*Maastricht* decision', BVerfG decision 2 BvR 2134/92 and 2 BvR 2159/92 of 11 Jan. 1994, [1994] 1 EuR 95, [1994] CMLR 57. See CMLR, pp. 106–7. See further Ch. 3 above.

[62] One of the first examples of such a decision is: Criminal proceedings against Keck and Mithouard, ECJ Case 267/91 and 268/91, [1993] ECR-I 6097. For a discussion of the ECJ's subsidiarity jurisprudence, see De Búrca (1998).

[63] The ECJ has yet to draw firm boundaries on state authority. For an excellent discussion of criteria that could be used to draw such boundaries, see Bernard (1996).

that the public lacks enough information to assess whether ECJ decisions are procedurally fair. Analysis of these polls reveals that given the ECJ's relative obscurity as a legal and political institution, ordinary citizens form their opinions about the ECJ based on their feelings about European integration, and based on national legal cultural variables (Caldeira and Gibson 1995; 1997). Even by these criteria, few are willing to give the ECJ the benefit of the doubt. When asked in a 1992 'Eurobarometer' whether it might be better to do away with the ECJ if it started making a lot of decisions that most people disagree with, the vast majority of respondents would not commit to keeping the ECJ (Caldeira and Gibson 1997: 216).[64] Analysis of opinion polls on the ECJ led James Gibson and Greg Caldeira to conclude that the ECJ lacks legitimacy, and actually 'has more enemies than friends' in the general public (Caldeira and Gibson 1997: 221). Anti-European integration groups play on these fears in mobilizing support against the EU. The European Court is sensitive to the public perception of its legitimacy, and has received the message that many European see it as a threat to national sovereignty (Rozes 1985: 508). According to ECJ Justice Mancini, attacks on the ECJ during the ratification debates of the Maastricht Treaty (which clearly resonated in the public) has contributed to the ECJ's 'retreat from activism' (Mancini and Keeling 1995: 408).

IV. National governments and the European rule of law

The whole point of a rule of law is that law constrains government actions to keep them accountable to the law and to higher constitutional norms. If member states had been able to reverse the declaration of European law supremacy and circumvent European legal obligations by passing new domestic legislation, if states could still easily ignore or reject unwanted ECJ decisions, and if states had such influence on the ECJ that the latter could only make decisions congruous with the interests of powerful states, one would have to question if a rule of law really existed in Europe.

It can certainly be disconcerting when European policies that no longer enjoy political support within a country remain resistant to change. Indeed, the best way for any individual government to lock in its policy change may

---

[64] The percentage of respondents committed to the ECJ varied by country, from 21.8% in Ireland to 48.8% in the Netherlands, with the rest of the countries falling between 22 and 34% (Caldeira and Gibson 1997: 216).

be to enshrine it in European law, since European laws are much harder to change than national laws. The difficulty of reforming European laws contributes to the perception that the EC lacks democratic accountability. European law supremacy is in part to blame because it means that policies passed by democratically elected governments can be invalidated by the ECJ, based on an interpretation of the Treaty which member states never intended. This is not a price to be paid for a rule of law. Rather it is a sign that the political system needs to be changed.

The rule of law is more than just forcing governments to respect their legal obligations. The rule of law implies that *law* and *legal considerations* become part of the political process itself, shaping and constraining political decision-making. In an effective rule of law, governments avoid actions and policies that violate the law, not waiting to lose in court to modify their behaviour.

An effective rule of law must also be legitimate, and thus responsive to democratic concerns. The solution is not to increase political control over the ECJ; rather it is to make it less difficult and complex to change European legislation when results are unwanted. Or, states must be allowed to opt out of policies that do not enjoy public support. This is what national courts are trying to do, in part, when they create constitutional limits to European authority in the national realm.

The Transformation of the European Legal System and the Rule of Law in Europe

If the doctrines of direct effect and supremacy are . . . the 'twin pillars of the Community's legal system', the [preliminary ruling] reference procedure . . . must surely be the keystone in the edifice; without it the roof would collapse and the two pillars would be left as a desolate ruin, evocative of the temple at Cape Sounion— beautiful but not of much practical utility. (Judge Federico Mancini and Legal Clerk David Keeling of the European Court of Justice)[1]

The European legal system started out with many of the limitations and weaknesses of most international legal systems. The ECJ had few cases to consider, because the Commission refused to raise infringement suits. Clear violations of European law persisted, as ECJ Justices sat waiting for cases in Luxembourg. When disputes over European law did arise, they were usually resolved out of court, and not necessarily in compliance with European law. Basic principles of the Treaty of Rome were not respected, and member states were not held accountable to their European legal obligations.

The transformation of the European legal system was orchestrated by the ECJ through bold legal interpretations asserting the direct effect and supremacy of European law over national law. Formally states were just as obligated to obey European law before the legal system's transformation. Why did establishing the ECJ's 'twin pillars' of direct effect and supremacy make European law more binding? This chapter explains how the transformation of the European legal system contributed to the emergence of an international rule of law in Europe where violations of the law are brought to

---

[1] Mancini and Keeling (1992: 2–3).

court, legal decisions are respected, and the autonomous influence of law and legal rulings extends to the political process itself.

The transformation of the European legal system created a structural change in the way the legal process works in Europe. It harnessed private litigants to monitor state compliance with European law, and national courts to enforce European law against their governments. Obviously this change increased the number of cases challenging the compatibility of national policy with European law that made it to court. But it did more than this. Once it was institutionalized in national legal systems, the transformation of the European legal system shifted the key interpreters of European law from national governments and their administrators to legal bodies. This changed the way public actors thought about European legal obligations. With private litigants raising cases, it was now more likely that violations of law would be challenged in court. Once in court, governments could not count on their arguments prevailing. In the past, because international law was interpreted narrowly, governments could expect courts to defer to their interpretations. With European law supremacy established, the ECJ was more likely to issue bold rulings departing from the strict letter of the law, regardless of whether they challenged national policies, and national courts were more likely to follow the ECJ. With national policy subject to judicial review, national governments were more vigilant about complying with European law, and legal calculations became a greater part of the political process itself. Policies that clearly violated European law became less desirable because of their legal vulnerability, and the threat of a legal suit became a potent negotiating tool.

Section I shows how the weaknesses of the legal system designed by the Treaty of Rome undermined the authority of the ECJ and state respect for European law. Section II shows how the transformation of the European legal system changed the way the legal process operated, inducing greater respect for European law and extending the shadow of the law into the political process itself. As law and legal decisions increasingly shaped the political process, the ECJ and national courts have become important political players in Europe. Section III explains how the transformation extended the influence of law and courts into the political process of European integration.

I. The vicious circle of international law: weak legal mechanisms combined with poor compliance

The legal process plays an important role in promoting greater compliance with the law. The legal process seeks to replace the situation where actors interpret rules by themselves in a self-interested way, with a depoliticized deliberative process that holds actors accountable to a disinterested interpretation of the rules. But simply designating or creating a third-party institution to interpret legal rules will not be enough to ensure that states actually *are* held accountable to disinterested interpretations of the rules. Many international legal bodies remain underused, allowing states de facto to interpret the rules on their own and escape accountability. Furthermore, to create a legal process overseen by a legal institution is to create an expectation that law will be applied equally to all involved. But if legal institutions are not used, or are ignored, their existence can serve to undermine respect for law. Where the judicial process is weak and non-compliance is high, a vicious circle can set in.

If the judicial process is seen as anaemic or illegitimate, legal bodies are likely to be avoided, excluded from disputes, or ignored. Even if a case does go to court, judges are likely avoid rulings that will be flouted so as not to expose the real fragility of the law and the legal process. Where there are no appeals to neutral third parties, actors are able to interpret the rules on their own, in a self-interested way. The more law is flouted, the more law is instrumentalized to justify state actions, the less legitimate law and the judicial process are in the eyes of individuals or governments and the less states and individuals believe in the sanctity of law or the rule of law. When violations of law are not pursued, and when violators can talk their way out of being condemned, the cost of violating law depreciates. The more people or governments cheat and get away with it, the less there is a sense of reciprocity, and the less willing even generally law-abiding individuals and governments are to abide by the rules. Respect for the law is eroded, and the rule of law becomes a sham. Stanley Hoffmann stated the problem well:

[The] normative order itself, when practice contradicts it blatantly and repeatedly, usually ends up collapsing—which means that the law ceases to be taken seriously. A violation is no longer perceived as such, nor are the provisions of the law any longer seen as conferring genuine rights and duties: we are merely in the realm of rhetoric, not of norms. . . . For any normative order to deserve being called by that name, it must partake both of the realm of 'oughts' and of the empirical one: it must be *at least in part* a set of some rules *of* actual behavior; it must not only ask for, but actually inspire, some practice. Otherwise it withers away. (Hoffmann 1987: 375)

Turning to the case of the EC in the 1960s, compliance with the Treaty of Rome was problematic. At the time there were so many exceptions and tolerated violations of European law, with every state protecting its market and creating advantages for national producers and workers, that there was in fact no Common Market. Violating European law had few consequences. And evaluating the compatibility of national policy with European law was not a regular part of national policy-making processes, by which I mean that governments and legislatures did not regularly consider whether proposed or existing policy violated European law when they decided what national policies to create or change. This is not to say that member states went out of their way to violate European rules, or that states never changed a policy because it conflicted with European law. But with all countries protecting their markets, and with significant domestic support for the national protections, the fact that national policy violated European law was not in itself enough to provoke a change. In an organization as complex as a national government, one needs compliance with European rules to be a priority lest inattention, inertia, or the weight of competing interests lead to numerous violations of the law. The Treaty of Rome envisioned that the Common Market would be complete by 1970. Instead by 1970 the process of European integration was at a virtual standstill, and national barriers to trade were rampant. It was clear to all that states were not being held accountable to their obligations under European law.

The EC's legal system was of little help. The system created in the Treaty of Rome relied on member states or the Commission to bring violations of European law to the ECJ. States virtually never brought cases against other states. While the Commission did investigate complaints brought to its attention, it was very willing to make compromises that kept the issue out of court. It certainly did not help that the Common Market's legal system had no enforcement mechanisms. The most the ECJ could do was declare that a member state had failed to fulfil its legal obligations. Such a ruling could embarrass a member into compliance. But if a state was determined to continue its policy, bringing a legal suit could actually be counterproductive. More than exposing the state's action as a violation of European law, it would reveal that the emperor (the EC's nascent legal system) had no clothes. A compromise between the Commission and the violating state might only lead to partial improvement, but it brought with it voluntary compliance by the state and was therefore usually preferable. Because raising infringement suits would not help, and could even hurt, the commission adopted what the director called the 'less worse' solution of compromising on principles but working to help the ECJ develop its doctrine, especially doctrine which national courts could apply.[2]

The lack of enforcement mechanisms was not the only problem. Entrusting prosecution to an essentially political body meant in practice that enforcement of European law became a lower priority. According to the director of the Commission's legal services from 1958 to 1970, the Commission believed that legal means—with or without sanctions—would not have worked to enforce the Treaty if there were no political will to proceed with integration.[3] In their view, aggressively enforcing the Treaty before common policies had been constructed to replace national policies was a losing strategy. Thus the Commission focused on building support for new common rules, and creating a positive will to proceed with the Common Market.

The Commission's strategy may well have made sense. But it was a not a strategy to win the support of those private actors who wanted European rules to be followed, nor was it useful in discouraging states from violating European law. What private litigants and member states observed was that there were almost no infringement cases raised—indeed, only ten such cases were ruled upon by the ECJ in the first ten years of the Community's legal system. There were clear violations of the law, but litigants who appealed to the Community process for legal justice were disappointed. Because the deals reached between member states and the Commission allowed violations of European law to persist, they contributed to the perception that the Community was not serious about adhering to the Treaty of Rome, or to the Treaty's commitment to build a common market. According to Rasmussen,

The implicit or explicit invitations which the Commission was given to commence [infringement] proceedings were too often either rejected or neglected. To observers outside the Commission, the reluctance to file suit yielded an impression of weakness and of imperfect safeguards ensuring it a real independence. This behavior was hardly conducive to a high level of State compliance with Community Law. (Rasmussen 1986: 238)

Not only did the legal system not enhance compliance with European law, but the Commission's unwillingness to use the infringement process arguably undermined respect for European law. It allowed states to use creative interpretations of the rules to justify behaviours that were potentially

---

[2] Interview with the former director of the Commission's Legal Services, 7 July 1994, Paris.
[3] Ibid.

illegal. And fewer suits meant fewer ECJ decisions, denying the ECJ the opportunity to develop its reputation or a web of legal precedent. Indeed, without any authoritative body contradicting the states' arguments, rather than constraining the actions of states European law could be used to justify market barriers. The lack of Commission action was like the *Good House-keeping* seal of approval—it showed that national actions must in fact be legal. This was the German government's claim when its turnover equalization tax system was legally challenged. The government claimed that since the Commission had not challenged the German law in question, it must mean that the law did not violate European law.[4]

National courts were no help either. Even before the transformation of the European legal system, national courts could hear private litigant challenges to national policy based on European law. But in the 1960s national courts were unlikely to give much satisfaction to private litigants. National courts usually decided European legal issues without a reference to the ECJ, and with a heavy supposition that national rules were acceptable. In France the *Conseil d'État* refused even to question the compatibility of French law with European law, or to make a reference to the ECJ.[5] In Germany the Federal Tax Court helped orchestrate a legal exit for the government that allowed German turnover taxes to escape scrutiny.[6] In Italy the Constitutional Court ruled that the fact a national law violates an international treaty might be of consequence at the international level, but was of no consequence at the national level, and thus there was no point in examining whether the law in question violated European law.[7] Indeed, the national practice of *lex posterior derogat legi prior* (the last law passed trumps previous laws) provided a convenient means for

---

[4] *Lütticke (Alfons) GmbH v. Hauptzollamt Saarlouis*, ECJ Case 57/65, [1966] ECR 205. See further Ch. 3 above, Round 2.

[5] See above, Ch. 4, Round 1, for a discussion of French jurisprudence regarding European law in the 1960s.

[6] The Federal Tax court did get the ECJ's opinion on the issue. The ECJ left it to national courts to determine if turnover taxes were 'average taxes' not subject to private litigant challenges. The Federal Tax court issued the guidelines that allowed most turnover taxes to be classified as average taxes and therefore escape scrutiny. See above Ch. 3, Round 2, for more on the turnover tax struggle. *Firma Molkerei-Zentrale Westfalen-Lippe GmbH, Trockenmilchwerk in Lippstadt*, BFH reference to the ECJ of 18 July 1967, Case VII 156/65, [1967] 4 EuR 360. BFH decision in Case VII 156/65, 11 July 1968, [1968] CMLR 300. *Firma Molkerei-Zentrale Westfalen-Lippe GmbH, Trockenmilchwerk in Lippstadt*, ECJ Case 28/67, [1968] ECR 143.

[7] The law in question was passed subsequent to the Treaty, which was the main reason the Constitutional Court refused to evaluate its compatibility with European law. It said: 'the violation of a treaty, even if it results in responsibility by the State at the international level, does not detract from the validity of any conflicting Law.' *Costa v. ENEL & Soc. Edisonvolta*, Italian Constitutional Court Decision 14 of 7 Mar. 1964, [1964] CMLR 425, [1964] I Il Foro It. 87 I 465.

governments to avoid European legal obligations should they wish; all they had to do was pass a new law at the national level.

The reluctance of national courts to displace government policy in favour of European law made potential litigants less willing to risk bringing a case. There really was no point in trying to use the French or Italian legal system to challenge national law since it was clear that the highest court would accord primacy to national law, at least with respect to national laws passed subsequent to European law. While the prospects were not so bleak in the other member states, given how few judges knew anything about European law, a European legal strategy was novel and risky. This was the conclusion Stuart Scheingold drew in 1971:

> The picture with respect to the recognition of the authority of the Court of Justice and the supremacy of Community law is a mixed one . . . in most matters there has been a real reluctance by national courts to use Article 177 . . . only in Holland can the primacy of Community law be taken for granted. Elsewhere, the status of Community law and the willingness to use Article 177 remain in doubt. (Scheingold 1971: 34)[8]

The Commission's failure to pursue violations of the law, combined with the unwillingness of most national courts to scrutinize the compatibility of national law with European law, contributed to the perception that European law was usually ignored in other countries. This became another reason not to comply. Indeed, national judges at times voiced concern that they did not want to disadvantage their nationals vis-à-vis other nationals, either by not applying or by applying European law. Concern about reciprocity was important. It was the idea behind the French constitution's provisions that explicitly condition the supremacy of international law on the reciprocal adherence by other states (Article 55), a requirement that French courts have refused to relax with respect to European law.[9]

The weaknesses of the European legal system fed upon itself. The lack of enforcement mechanisms discouraged the Commission from raising cases, and the lack of Commission cases allowed states to interpret the rules for themselves. The refusal of national courts to enforce European law or refer cases to the ECJ discouraged would-be litigants. Lacking cases, the ECJ was unable to develop jurisprudence, and the lack of ECJ jurisprudence left states significant latitude to interpret European law on their own. And the lack of

---

[8] Mann's analysis in 1972 came to a similar conclusion.

[9] See above, Ch. 4, Round 5, for more on the reciprocity clause as it applies to European law.

any enforcement mechanisms discouraged the ECJ from making unpopular rulings against member states.[10]

National governments did not appear unhappy with this situation. They seemed to like being able to maintain protectionist policies *and* claim they were committed to building a Common Market. Indeed, some governments seemed to expect legal bodies to defer to them in interpreting European law. Governments, after all, had negotiated the treaties. Thus they knew what they meant. One sees this assumption, for example, in the German Finance Minister's order to tax authorities and tax courts to ignore the ECJ's ruling in the *Lütticke* case because 'it conflicts with the well reasoned arguments of the Federal Government, and with the opinion of the affected member states of the Community'.[11] The implication was that legal decisions that conflict with well-reasoned arguments by the government, or with the opinion of affected member states, should not be made or accepted. This was also the assumption of the French government, according to the French legal scholar Marie-France Buffet-Tchakaloff:

The French position on the juridical front is theoretically quite simple: strict and literal interpretation of treaties with respect to the authority of the community, a large and extensive conception of national authority that should prevail whenever there is ambiguity and, a fortiori, in the absence of express legal dispositions. (1984: 187)

National governments may have liked the weak enforcement mechanisms of the legal system, but that is not the point. The mandate of the ECJ is to 'ensure that in the interpretation and application of the Treaty the law is observed' (Article 220 EEC). Not only was the original European legal system unable to do this, it arguably contributed to disregard for the Treaty of Rome.

Where there is a rule of law, governments are not above the law. Public actors are held accountable to third-party interpretations of the rules, and these interpretations are not simple reflections of governments' wishes and opinions. While the weak European legal system was hardly the only reason states were not complying with the Treaty of Rome, neither was the European legal system a helpful solution to deal with the problem of non-compliance.

---

[10] As discussed in Ch. 5 above, the ECJ avoided rulings with material and political consequences in the 1960s. Only after doctrine was established and accepted within national judiciaries would the ECJ strip away the exceptions and apply its full force to the case. See Ch. 5 regarding the ECJ's strategy of playing off the short time horizons of politicians.

[11] 7 July 1966 (IIIB.4-V8534-1/66), republished in AWD (1966), p. 327.

The growing power and authority of the ECJ contributed to a greater respect for European law by member states. Some have even argued that the ECJ not only held states accountable, but also became an important motor of the political process of European integration, advancing integration through legal construction. What is clear is that the stronger and more authoritative the European legal system, the more cases private litigants raised, the more cases national courts referred, and the more the Commission became willing to use infringement suits to promote compliance and to help advance the agenda of European integration. How did the transformation of the European legal system lead to this reversal of fortune?

II. The virtuous circle: how effective legal systems enhance the rule of law

A weak judicial system begets a weak rule of law, which in turn undermines the influence and authority of the legal process, the independence of judges, and respect for legal rules. An effective legal system can set up a virtuous circle, building respect for the law. It does this first of all by providing an authoritative and neutral interpretation of the rules, so that states or individuals are less able to use self-interested interpretations to interpret their way out of compliance. The neutral interpretations form a body of legal precedent, which serves as a guide to states and individuals indicating what types of behaviour are and are not in violation of the law. Legal rulings (and the sanctions which go along with them) signal the consequences that can be expected if violations of the law are caught. The expectation that violations of the law are likely to be caught with a resulting negative consequence encourages greater respect for the rules. As Louis Henkin has argued:

Much law is observed because it is law and because its violation would have undesirable consequences. The effective legal system, it should be clear, is not the one which punishes the most violators, but rather that which has few violations to punish because the law deters potential violators. He who does violate is punished, principally to reaffirm the standard of behavior and to deter others . . . In international society, too, law is not effective against the Hitlers and it is not needed for that nation which is content with its lot and has few temptations. International law aims at nations which are in principal law abiding but which might be tempted to commit a violation if there were not threat of undesirable consequences. (Henkin 1993: 34)

The more rules are respected by all, the greater the willingness of citizens and governments to play by the rules (Keohane 1984: 214). Coercion may still be needed to dissuade some violators, but among generally law-abiding actors the sense that there is a reciprocal respect for the rules helps promote compliance.

The acceptance of the direct effect and supremacy of European law by national courts created key links which changed member states' strategic calculations, increasing national governments' incentives and willingness to bring national policy into accordance with European law. The net effect of the two doctrines was to empower sub-state actors to police their government's compliance with European law and get their cases heard by the ECJ. To state an obvious point—allowing private litigant access increases the number of actors who can raise legal challenges, and thus the number of cases a court has to hear. Just as important, however, is that private litigants tend to be less sensitive to the political concerns of governments, more willing to question the limit of state authority, and more willing to challenge the status quo. Private litigants brought cases that national governments and the Commission had declined to pursue, giving the ECJ a chance to rule on legal issues the Commission and states did not or would not raise.

The numerous references to the ECJ on a variety of substantive and legal issues allowed it to expand the reach and scope of European law, and to practise its well-known incremental style of decision-making. The ECJ used cases involving less controversial issues to develop legal principles. Often it did not apply these principles to the case at hand, or it implied that the principle could be qualified to protect national interests. But in subsequent cases the ECJ whittled away the exceptions. Once the ECJ's legal principle had gained support in national legal communities, it applied the jurisprudence more boldly (Hartley 1994: 78–9). A number of scholars have focused on this incremental decision-making, arguing that it was essential to the ECJ's strategy of building legitimacy and support (Weiler 1991; Burley and Mattli 1993; Helfer and Slaughter 1997). Once the ECJ had this support, it was more willing boldly to challenge national policies. Indeed, Geoffrey Garrett, Daniel Kelemen, and Heiner Schultz find support for the hypothesis that the clearer the ECJ's precedent, the more willing the ECJ is to apply its jurisprudence in polemical cases, ruling against states (Garrett et al. 1998).

The larger number of cases reaching the ECJ had a positive synergistic effect. A by-product of more cases was the emergence of a denser web of legal precedent. As Robert Keohane, Andrew Moravcsik, and Anne-Marie Slaughter argued,

A steady flow of cases . . . allows a court to become an actor on the legal and political stage, raising its profile in the elementary sense that other litigants become aware of its existence and in the deeper sense that interpretation and application of a particular legal rule must be reckoned with as a part of what the law means in practice. Litigants who are likely to benefit from interpretation will have an incentive to bring additional cases to clarify and enforce it. Further, the interpretation or application is itself likely to raise additional questions that can only be answered through subsequent cases. Finally, a court gains political capital from a growing caseload by demonstrably performing a needed function . . . (Keohane *et al.* 2000: 482)

The more the ECJ developed its jurisprudence, the less room there was for states to offer their own self-interested interpretation of the rules. And greater certainty about how the ECJ and national courts would decide heightened private litigant incentives to bring cases, and government incentives to settle out of court in compliance with European law. And as Keohane, Moravcsik, and Slaughter imply, the cases helped the ECJ to develop its reputation, show how it was useful, and therefore enhance its legitimacy.

The transformation had other important implications. Originally national governments could simply pass new legislation to avoid an ECJ decision. Once national courts had accepted European law supremacy, they refused to allow their governments to avoid European legal obligations by relying on national legislation. They also became less willing to rely on government interpretations of European rules. Thus, for example, acceptance of the supremacy of European law came hand and hand with German tax court's refusals to accept the German Finance Ministry's order to ignore the ECJ's *Lütticke* decisions.[12] And once the *Conseil d'État* accepted a role enforcing European law supremacy, it then overturned its previous ruling supporting a national law setting tobacco prices that had been twice condemned by the ECJ,[13] and granted itself the authority to interpret treaties without recourse to the French Foreign Ministry.[14]

While national governments appeared to be willing to ignore ECJ jurisprudence,[15] ignoring their own courts was a different matter entirely.

---

[12] Referred to in n. 6 above, and discussed at length in Ch. 3, Round 2, and in Ch. 5.

[13] '*Arizona Tobacco*', *Société Arizona Tobacco, Conseil d'État* decision of 28 Feb. 1992, [1992] Recueil Lebon 78, [1993] 1 CMLR 253. Sociétés Rothman et Philip Morris, *Conseil d'État* decision of 28 Feb. 1992, [1992] Recueil Lebon 78, [1993] 1 CMLR 253.

[14] *GISTI decision, Conseil d'État* decision of 29 June 1990, [1990] Rev. gen. droit int. pub. 879–911. See Buffet-Tchakaloff (1991).

[15] The Commission reports on failures of states to comply with ECJ decisions. Notable examples where states seemed quite willing to ignore the ECJ include the *Lütticke* case discussed above in Ch. 3 and earlier, the famous sheep-meat war between France and Germany (Rasmussen 1986: 313; Buffet-Tchakaloff 1984: 367), and the tobacco decisions discussed earlier (see n. 13 above).

Citizens might trust their government when it says that an international tribunal's ruling is unsound, and they may actually prefer having national interest take precedence over an international obligations. But few governments want to claim a right to ignore their own courts, and few citizens want their governments to have such a right. The rule of law means that governments follow the law. In a rule-of-law society, governments follow their courts regardless of whether European or national law is at stake. National court rulings created a negative consequence for governments for violating European law.

National court enforcement also shifted the types of responses available to governments faced with legal challenges to national policy. Chapter 5 showed how national court enforcement forced governments to play by the legal rules of the game. Those rules allow governments to try to influence judges to rule in their favour by presenting legal and policy justifications in court. The rules also allow governments to use their legislative power to rewrite laws at the European level should they be unhappy with how courts are applying them. Ignoring a court is outside of these rules, and national courts will ensure that their governments do not ignore the ECJ. Threatening a court is not part of these rules, but it happens. Chapter 5 showed why political threats against the ECJ are politically very difficult to carry out, and thus tend to ring hollow. In practice, with national courts enforcing ECJ decisions, governments had two options: change national policy, or change European policy. The first option was easier, and in most cases the only politically feasible alternative. In this way, national court enforcement increased compliance with European law.

The transformation of the European legal system replaced the vicious circle of a weak legal system and weak compliance by a virtuous circle that made it harder for states to interpret their way out of compliance with European law and made it more likely that states would avoid actions which violated European law. It did this by increasing the chance that national policy would be challenged, by helping to create a dense web of ECJ legal precedent, and by harnessing national courts to apply ECJ jurisprudence and thus creating the expectation of undesirable consequences for violations of European law. Once ECJ decisions were more authoritative and enforceable on their own, the Commission became more willing to make use of the infringement procedure to pressure states to comply with European law. Commission infringement suits against member states exploded in the 1980s. The court went from hearing 27 infringement cases in the 1960s to 70 in the 1970s, 646 in the 1980s, and

861 in the 1990s.[16] Once ECJ decisions were enforceable, the ECJ became more willing to issue decisions with material and political consequences. The enforceability of ECJ rulings also increased the incentive for private litigants to challenge national policies in national courts. The denser web of precedent signalled how the ECJ would resolve disputes. And when the legal outcome was clear, the fact that national courts would enforce ECJ decisions gave governments a greater incentive to avoid the intermediary steps and simply accept that national policy had to change.

The change in state behaviour did not come overnight, nor did it immediately emerge when national courts started to enforce European law supremacy. It came at different times in different contexts as different national actors came to recognize that illegal national policies would be challenged, that they would lose in the ECJ, that national courts would enforce ECJ jurisprudence, and thus that maintaining the policies would ultimately be politically unsustainable. Table 6.1 summarizes how the changes in the European legal system created through the direct effect and supremacy helped reverse the vicious circle undermining the influence of European law and ECJ decisions over state behaviour.

III. Extending the influence of law and courts into the political process

The transformation of the European legal system not only increased compliance with European law, it also extended the shadow of the law into the political process itself. European law is increasingly brought into national political debates by political parties, statesmen, and interest groups which use legal arguments to bolster their position. By raising the spectre that a policy proposal may be challenged before the ECJ, domestic groups can help delegitimize policy proposals with which they disagree. The clearer the meaning of European law, the clearer the web of ECJ precedent, the more likely law is to shape political negotiation (Mnookin and Kornhauser 1979).[17] If the

---

[16] See Table 1.2, p. 15 above.

[17] In a study of bargaining in the shadow of divorce law, Mnookin and Kornhauser (1979) argued that uncertainty about how the case may be decided influences the extent to which bargaining takes place in the shadow of the law. The less legal precedent exists, the higher the uncertainty and the less likely litigants are to settle out of court in the shadow of the law. The preferences of the actors, transaction costs in bringing a legal suit, and strategic calculations of actors also mattered.

Table 6.1. How the transformation of the European legal system facilitated the emergence of a rule of law

Original European legal system	The vicious circle of a weak legal system and weak compliance	Transformation of European legal system	The virtuous circle of a stronger legal system and greater compliance (or how the transformation solved the problems of the original system)
Only the Commission and states can raise infringement suits	*ECJ has few cases to bear.* ECJ cannot develop dense web of precedent. States can interpret European law on their own, to defend their policies. Hard for ECJ to practice incremental style of decision-making.	Direct effect of European law allows private litigants to draw on European law in national courts to challenge national policies.	*Private litigants police member state compliance. National courts become a source of many cases for ECJ.* States cannot use political pressure to keep legal issues out of court. ECJ can practice incremental style of decision-making to build support for its jurisprudence. Private litigants gain awareness of ECJ jurisprudence, and bring more cases exploring legal gaps. ECJ can develop denser web of legal interpretation so that states and private litigants can predict how the ECJ will decide. ECJ precedent makes it harder for states to defend their self-interested interpretations of European rules.
National courts deferring to their governments, deciding European law cases differently,	*Not clear how national courts will resolve European legal issues. National government can rely on national systems to avoid European legal obligations.* Uncertainty discourages private litigants from raising cases. Contradictions between national court and ECJ rulings undermine legitimacy and authority of ECJ.	Supremacy of European law means that governments cannot escape European legal obligations by passing new laws at national level.	*National court acceptance of ECJ jurisprudence enhances the legitimacy and authority of ECJ rulings.* Knowing that national courts will apply ECJ jurisprudence even when a decision will create significant material and political consequences. The clearer and better defined the ECJ's precedent, the more willing the ECJ is to apply precedent to rule against national governments. Coordinated interpretation helps convince citizens and states

and enforcing last law passed.	Little incentive for national courts to enforce European law in a way that is not reciprocated and thus potentially disadvantages national actors vis-à-vis actors in other states.	Judicial rivalries promote a convergence in national legal interpretation around doctrines consistent with ECJ jurisprudence.	that they are being held accountable to the same rules, thus increasing the willingness to comply with European law and ECJ decisions.
	States have incentive to push for their interpretation until the last national appeal is lost.		Knowledge that the national courts apply the ECJ's jurisprudence decreases government's incentive to delay compliance and creates an incentive to avoid policies that conflict with European law.
	Perception that all countries are protecting their markets. Member states do not want unilaterally to stop discriminatory policies.		
ECJ decisions are purely declaratory.	*ECJ decisions can be ignored without cost.*	National courts enforce ECJ decisions and European law over conflicting national policy. National governments cannot avoid European legal obligations by passing legislation at the national level.	*National courts make European law enforceable. There is an expectation that violations of European law will create undesirable consequences.*
	Commission and states less willing to use infringement process since ECJ decisions are easy to ignore.		National court enforcement creates a negative consequence for violations of European law because governments do not want to be seen ignoring their own courts.
	ECJ has fewer cases to hear, leading to a sparse web of precedent.		Commission more willing to raise cases against member states since ECJ decisions will be enforceable at national level.
	Most compliance issues resolved diplomatically, not necessarily in compliance with European law.		Greater incentive for private litigants to raise a suit in a national court.
	Perception that states are above the law, and that the rule of law in Europe is a sham.		Diplomatic negotiation is more likely to occur in the shadow of the law with the knowledge that parties will not accept a worse deal than what they can win in court.

government insists on forging ahead with the policy, it will be seen as a deliberate attempt to avoid a European legal obligation, and will be an invitation for a legal challenge. The fear that a national or European policy might contravene European law and lead to an unwinnable suit leads governments to censor themselves, avoiding policies that they know are going to be challenged in front of the ECJ or at a minimum taking into account European law concerns and writing policies so as to minimize the likelihood of a loss in court.[18] Actors may still choose compromises that do not comply with the letter of the law, but the compromise will probably be much closer to what could be won in court, otherwise someone may challenge the deal in court.

The European legal process is also becoming a tool for actors trying to influence the political process, both domestic and European (Harlow and Rawlings 1992). Private litigants appeal to the European legal system in the hopes that the ECJ will invalidate a national rule they do not like. One noteworthy example of how litigation strategies have been used to influence policy involves the issue of equal pay. Combining victories before the ECJ with grass-roots organization and political pressure, equality actors in the UK forced a conservative British government to lift the cap on sex discrimination awards, compensate women dismissed from the British military because they were pregnant, grant benefits for part-time workers, and equalize pension benefits for men and women (Alter and Vargas 2000: 463–6). European law strategies have also included challenges to the ban on Sunday trading in Britain (Rawlings 1993),[19] the coordinated attack on the German turnover equalization tax system in the 1960s (Meier 1994), and challenges to the denial of workplace benefits to same-sex partners.[20] And European law has been a useful ally of pro-choice advocates seeking to spread information in Ireland about abortion services in the UK.[21]

Legal strategies also figure in institutional politics at the European level. Community institutions and member states challenge the procedures through which a policy is made when they believe they were excluded from the policy-making process, or that a different adoption procedure would create a different policy outcome. Rulings in these cases can influence policy

---

[18] Indeed, many European governments ask their legal advisers to review proposed policy to ensure its compatibility with European law.

[19] *Council of the City of Stoke-on-Trent and Norwich City Council v. B & Q plc*, ECJ Case C-169/91, [1992] ECR I-6635. For an analysis, see Rawlings (1993).

[20] *Grant (Lisa Jacqueline) v. South-West Trains Ltd.*, ECJ Case C-249/96, [1998] ECR I-621.

[21] *Society for the Protection of Unborn Children Ireland v. Grogan*, ECJ Case 159/90, [1991] ECR I-4685, [1991] 3 CMLR 849.

outcomes, and in a more enduring way influence the rules through which policies are adopted and thus the distribution of political power in the policy-making process. As Susanne Schmidt has shown, the Commission uses the European legal system as a tool to change state preferences (and thus votes) and to prod the Council to pass legislation that might otherwise have never existed (Schmidt 2000). The Council also uses the legal system to stymie the Commission, and keep it from assuming powers it claims (Schmidt 2000; Meunier and Nicolaidis 1999: 488–93).

The heightened role of law in the political process has also meant more power and influence for the European Court of Justice. The ECJ has emerged as a Constitutional Court for Europe, able to practice judicial review of European law and national law, referee the political rules of the game, impart new meanings to existing laws, and help define the borders of European and state authority. While some of these powers were part of its original mandate, they have been greatly enhanced by the transformation of the European legal system.[22]

Its authority to conduct judicial review of European and national law gives the ECJ considerable influence over present and future policy. When the Court rules against the validity of European or national law, it eliminates a policy option and forces political bodies to reopen negotiations on the issue. Certainly the ECJ has a greater influence if the law in question is invalidated. But even if the law in question is not invalidated, the decision still has an influence. The decision will typically indicate why certain policies are valid while others are invalid, and thereby provide a signal about what types of policy or legal language will or will not be acceptable in the future. Legislators who do not want their policies to be invalidated will heed these signals. Indeed, in some areas of policy knowing the position of the ECJ has become as important as knowing the position of member states.[23]

---

[22] Under its original mandate, the ECJ could assess the validity of European laws and Commission actions, answer interpretive questions about the law, hear infringement cases against member states, and review claims that European policy was made in a flawed way. Considering how few cases the ECJ had, these powers were more impressive on paper than they were in practice. The transformation of the European legal system gave the ECJ the power to review the compatibility of national law with European law in cases referred by national courts, and thus provided the ECJ with many more cases in which to exercise these powers. The interaction between national courts and the ECJ led to the development of legal doctrine that expanded the bases upon which the ECJ could find European law to be invalid. Now the ECJ can assess the validity of European law with respect to basic rights of citizens. And political–legal developments have introduced a principle of subsidiarity that enhances the role of the ECJ in deciding on the borders of national and European authority.

[23] There are numerous debates where the ECJ's opinion has been decisive, such as the debate regarding the Commission's authority in international trade negotiations, or its opinion about the

Its power of interpretation also gives the ECJ significant influence in the political realm. It can use legal decisions to create interpretations of existing law that alters the meaning and application of the law. The Council can always redraft European law if they do not like how the ECJ is interpreting it. But, as Chapter 5 showed, changing the law is not easy.[24] If member states lack enough consensus to legislate a change, the European Court may be able de facto to alter European policy through legal interpretation. The ECJ has clearly expanded the meaning of the requirement of equal pay for men and women far beyond what member states intended when they drafted Article 141 (formerly Article 119) of the Treaty of Rome and the subsequent equal-pay directives of the 1970s. Member states clearly did not intend European law to mean that national pension schemes with different retirement ages for men and women were illegal,[25] or that prohibitions on women serving in military roles involving the use of arms were illegal.[26] Nor did states expect the free movement of services to affect Ireland's anti-abortion policy.[27] These ECJ rulings, and others, went well beyond what the drafters of European law intended, and beyond what politicians at the time understood European law to mean.[28]

The European Court is also able to influence European politics by provoking political responses. It can provoke relegislation at the European level to reverse an ECJ ruling. And through its rulings, the ECJ can introduce ideas into the policy realm. An example is the ECJ's famous *Cassis de Dijon* ruling.[29] The ruling did not itself impose a policy of mutual recognition of product standards, but it stimulated a Commission response and provoked political mobilization by groups opposing the Commission's policy. The political mobilization led to a consensus in favour of a modified form of

---

validity of Europe's banana regime, or its opinion about the legality of affirmative action policies in a member state.

[24] To change the Treaty requires new intergovernmental negotiations, unanimous consent of all national governments, and ratification of the new text by national parliaments in all member states. Changing secondary law is easier, but if member states are divided it may still be difficult.

[25] *Barber (Douglas Harvey) v. Guardian Royal Exchange Assurance Group*, ECJ Case 262/88, [1990] ECR I-1889. Note that the Barber Protocol of the Treaty on a European Union limited the retrospective effects of this ruling, but it did not alter the requirement that national pension laws should change.

[26] The Court relied on Council Directive 76/207 EEC rather than Article 119 for this decision. *Kreil (Tanja) v. Bundesrepublik Deutschland*, Case C-285/98, [2000] ECR.

[27] N. 21 above.

[28] For more on the ECJ's role in the issue of equal pay, see Mazey (1995; 1998), Harlow (1992).

[29] *'Cassis de Dijon', Rewe Zentral AG v. Bundesmonopolverwaltung für Branntwein*, ECJ Case 120/78, [1979] ECR 649.

mutual recognition that was enshrined into the Single European Act (Alter and Meunier-Aitsahalia 1994).

The ECJ is not the only court gaining influence in the transformed European legal system. The transformation of the European legal system also increased the influence of national courts in the process of European integration. The cases involving European law allowed national courts to see how the process of European integration was affecting the domestic administrative, political and legal order. As Chapters 3 and 4 showed, in order to counter what appeared to be an unchecked transfer of power to the Community by national governments and an unchecked willingness of the ECJ to decide separation of power issues in favour of the European Community, supreme courts reinterpreted national constitutional provisions creating constitutional limits to European law within the national legal order. By positing possible constitutional limits to the validity of European law, supreme courts positioned themselves to serve as a second review, a national-level review, of the validity of European law. Their goal is to influence ECJ decision-making and their governments' behaviour at the European level. Chapters 3 and 4 showed how national courts have used this power to influence the political process. The German Constitutional Court has defined the role the government has to play in protecting the legislative rights of state governments, and in challenging European policies that arguably violate the German constitution. It essentially crafted the strategy of the German government with respect to the EC's broadcasting directive and banana regulation (see Chapter 3, Round 5). The German Constitutional Court has also created leverage over the ECJ using its threats to review the 'applicability' of European law in the national realm as a means to influence the ECJ to take into account the German Constitutional Court's human-rights jurisprudence, and German court's interpretations on the limits of European authority. The French *Conseil Constitutionnel* has created a role for itself reviewing national ratification statutes for European treaties and framework agreements for the Schengen accord. And the French *Conseil d'État* has created a role reviewing proposed European secondary law, allowing it to frame how the impact of proposed laws are assessed within the French government and the parliament.[30]

The fact that statesmen, interest groups, Community institutions, and private litigants can use European law to pressure governments does not mean

[30] See above, Ch. 4, Round 5, for more on these developments. This chapter also explain why French courts are less involved in and less able to influence European policy and politics than their German counterparts.

that they *will* use European law to this end. The ECJ must wait for cases to be raised before it can enter political debates. Potential beneficiaries can lack the organization, knowledge, or resources to mobilize to gain advantages through European law. They may also lack the will to use European law and European legal arguments to advance their goals. A variety of political factors will shape whether or not European law is invoked in the political process, and thus how European law comes to influence policy and politics. I have addressed this issue at length elsewhere (Alter 2000; Alter and Vargas 2000).

There will also still be times when ECJ jurisprudence and European law will be ignored, and when the threat of a legal case will not lead states to change national policy. European law and ECJ jurisprudence might be genuinely unclear and contestable, and a state might really believe that it can win its case. There may be a consensus among political actors that compliance with European law is unattractive, leading a policy to be adopted (and remain unchallenged) even though it violates European law. There are also reasons why a state might persist with a national policy even though the policy probably violates European law. The legal process is very slow, and states can decide to delay compliance until the legal process runs its course (this may be especially attractive if an election is in the offing or the government coalition is in jeopardy). States might also believe that at the end of the day they will be able to get away with their violation by negotiating a settlement which removes the dispute from court and keeps the national policy intact. A state might also know that it will lose in court, but hope that a court ruling against it will create a negative political reaction that might give it political leverage to renegotiate the European policy. And, a government might decide in any case that compliance is simply too costly. It might be willing to pay the cost of a negative ruling, and even pay any fine that emerges, because doing so seems preferable to changing national policy.

These types of situation should not be interpreted as signs that a rule of law does not exist. Within even the most effective legal system some violations of the law will persist. But if there are too many clear examples where those with the power to do so refuse to enforce the law, respect for the law and the rule of law itself will be eroded. The key will be balance. The most visible violations of the law and the most visible violators of the law need to be challenged to avoid the perception that rules can be violated with impunity. But not every violation and violator needs to be caught—indeed, trying to catch everything would quickly overwhelm any legal system.

IV. Conclusion

The transformation of the European legal system made possible the emergence of an international rule of law in Europe where violations of the law are brought to court, legal decisions are respected, and the autonomous influence of law and legal rulings extends to the political process itself. The European legal system can be used to force national governments to respect their European legal obligations, making European legal appeals a potent source of leverage for private litigants, groups, and the Commission to influence national and European policy. These actors help to ensure that governments are not above the law. And the threat of legal suit by these actors leads national governments to take European legal concerns into account during the policy-making process, before a violation of the law occurs.

My point is not that an international rule of law is good for the world order, or for European politics. On the one hand it seems good that states should be held accountable to their agreements at the international level. But the constraining nature of European law imparts a political bias into national policy. The political bias may please those who like freer trade, but it displeases those who prefer national autonomy and the national policies that create barriers to trade. And certainly not all are happy about the heightened political role of the ECJ. Many Europeans are quite troubled that an unaccountable international legal body can overturn a national law that was passed through democratic means.

My main point is that the rule of law changes the nature of the political process, and expands the number of actors involved in the political process. The transformation of the European legal system has turned the ECJ into probably the most influential international legal body in existence. It has empowered private actors to challenge national policies that arguably conflict with European law. It has provided the Commission, the Council, and member states with a tool they can use in the policy-making process. Furthermore, law has become an instrument of political negotiation, used to delegitimize policy options and increase the bargaining leverage of actors who favour a solution more compatible with European law.

The transformation was created by legal actors—judges, litigants, and lawyers—using the legal method to construct an institution of governance, a piece of a supra-state, built upon legal norms. Their phenomenal success in increasing political accountability to international laws has inspired European judges and international lawyers to think more creatively about how law can be used to constrain political actors and states at home and abroad.

As late as the 1970s and early 1980s the European experience appeared to be quite exceptional. But in the late 1980s and in the 1990s there have been signs of a broader trend towards international law influencing state behaviour. The European Court of Human Rights is increasingly active in European human rights issues. The new World Trade Organization dispute resolution system has been hearing a number of cases with broad implications for national policy. And there are new international tribunals being created—such as the Yugoslav and Rwandan war crimes tribunals and the new International Criminal Court tribunal. These developments beg the question of what, if anything, the European experience implies about how to make international law, and these new international legal mechanisms, more effective in shaping state behaviour.

The European legal system has some unique attributes. Access to the European Court is far wider than for most international legal bodies, with states, the European Commission, and private litigants empowered to use the European legal system to challenge European and national policy. The wide access gives the ECJ more opportunities to influence national policy, and the numerous cases have allowed the ECJ to develop European law incrementally, a strategy that has been important in building support for its jurisprudence and enhancing the effectiveness of the European legal system. The preliminary ruling system is also unique. As Federico Mancini noted, the preliminary ruling system is the keystone of the European legal system. It provides a means for private litigant cases to reach the ECJ, and it connects the ECJ to national courts, coordinating how they interpret and enforce European law. It is hard to underestimate how much the preliminary ruling mechanism has mattered in developing the ECJ's web of legal precedent, building legitimacy and support for the ECJ, and creating a national source of pressure to comply with European law. But there are still lessons that can be drawn.

This book has examined the European legal system as a system of international law, presenting a before and after picture of a system that started with many of the weaknesses of other international legal systems, but overcame these weaknesses. This chapter has shown how the structural change in the legal process created by the transformation of the European legal system made the emergence of an international rule of law possible. In other words, the design of the legal system—which actors can raise legal challenges, whether states can keep disputes from reaching a legal body where they will be subject to the legal rules of the game, the number of cases a legal body hears, and how the law is enforced—contributes to whether states become subjugated to the law.

Ultimately the transformation of the European legal system tells us the most about the process of European integration itself. Until recently the process of legal integration has been portrayed by legal scholars and neo-functionalist analysis as one of ever-expanding ECJ authority based on the mutual empowerment of the ECJ and sub-national actors, and the inability of political actors to influence the legal process. This study has painted a significantly different picture. While the European legal system empowers some, the supremacy of European law, in combination with the expanding substantive authority of the ECJ, by its very nature undermines the influence, authority, and independence of some national courts. As Chapters 3 and 4 showed, in order to protect their own independence, influence, and authority, the highest national courts created constitutional barriers to the expansion and influence of European law in the national realm. They also created constitutional limits to what their governments could agree to at the European level, to help ensure that their governments do not transfer away too much sovereignty, further eroding the influence of sub-national actors. National judicial limits significantly constrain national government autonomy *and* the ECJ's autonomy. National courts can influence the ECJ, and as Chapter 5 showed, so can national governments.

The experience of national judges in the process of European integration is in many ways a microcosm of the political process of European integration. The more integration proceeds, the more European powers encroach on the prerogatives of national actors, including national administrations, national parliaments, national judges, and regional and local governments. This encroachment is welcomed by those who find that appealing to the European level allows them to circumvent national political barriers and thus enhances their power and influence. But it provokes a protective response from those who feel constrained and uncomfortable with the growing European authority, and who see their influence, independence, and authority diminished. The only way to check the increasing transfer of power to the European level—a transfer facilitated by the actions of those gaining by appealing to the European level to promote their objectives—is to be part of the political decision-making process. Boycotting the process of integration means that domestic actors have no influence in the process of European integration. Participating in the process of European integration means that domestic actors can have some influence.

Thus a wider circle of national actors become involved participants in the process of European integration. But they do not necessarily work to increase European power. Even those gaining by European integration are fair-weather friends, appealing to the European level when it is useful and challenging European policy when national options seem more appealing. Those who want to protect national prerogatives become part of the Euro-game, working to check and limit the expansion of European powers at the expense of national sovereignty. The backlash engendered by the successes of European integration redirects the process of European integration. Certain transfers of authority may be locked in by institutional arrangements, but in the future European integration can be curtailed, stopped, and even reversed, so that integration is not necessarily ever-expanding, driven by a one-way ratchet towards increasing EC authority.

REFERENCES

Interviews

The Commission

Representative of the Legal Services of the Commission, 11 Jan. 1994 (Brussels).
Former Commissioner from the 1960s–80s, 9 June 1994 (Paris).
Former Director of the Legal Services of the Commission (1958–70), 7 July 1994 (Paris).
Director of Academic Affairs, 11 July 1994 (Brussels).
In the Directorate General for Employment, Industrial Relations and Social Affairs, 26 Oct. 1995 (Brussels).

The Council

Legal Adviser, Legal Services of the Council, 25 Oct. 1995 (Brussels).
Director of the Legal Services of the Council, 26 Oct. 1995 (Brussels).
Legal Adviser, Legal Services of the Council, 27 Oct. 1995 (Brussels).

European Court of Justice

ECJ Justice from Italy, 26 Oct. 1992 (Luxembourg).
ECJ Justice from Ireland, 25 Oct. 1992 (Luxembourg).
ECJ Justice from Belgium, 28 Oct. 1992 (Luxembourg).
ECJ Justice from Greece, 29 Oct. 1992 (Luxembourg).
Former ECJ Justice from Luxembourg, 3 Nov. 1992 (Luxembourg).
ECJ Justice from the Netherlands, 16 Nov. 1992 (Luxembourg).
ECJ Justice from the UK, 16 Nov. 1992 (Luxembourg).
ECJ Justice from France, 16 Nov. 1992 (Luxembourg).
ECJ Justice from Germany, 18 Nov. 1992 (Luxembourg).
Former ECJ Justice from Germany, 8 Nov. 1993 (Bonn).
Former ECJ Justice from France, 7 July 1994 (Paris).
Registrar at the Court of First Instance, 7 Nov. 1995 (Luxembourg).

France

Treasurer of the *Commission pour l'Étude des Communautés Européennes*, 14 May 1994 (Paris).
Researcher specializing on the *Conseil Constitutionnel*, 18 May 1994 (Paris).
President of the *Association des Juristes Européens*, 26 May 1994 (Paris).
French lawyer specializing in EC law litigation, 26 May 1994 (Paris).
Secretary-General of the *Conseil Constitutionnel*, 30 May 1994 (Paris).

Conseiller d'État, 30 May 1994 (Paris).

French professor of law specializing in EC Law, 6 June 1994 (Paris).

Former judge at the *Conseil Constitutionnel*, 20 June 1994 (Paris).

Former head of the Legal Services at the Foreign Ministry in France, 20 June 1994 (Paris).

Former judge at the *Conseil Constitutionnel*, 23 June 1994 (Paris).

Former judge at the *Cour de Cassation*, 24 June 1994 (Paris).

Judge at the *Conseil d'État*, 27 June 1994 (Florence).

Secretary-General of the *Conseil d'État*, 5 July 1994 (Paris).

Judge at the *Conseil d'État*, 7 July 1994 (Paris).

French lawyer licensed to practise before the *Conseil d'État* and the *Cour de Cassation*, 7 July 1994 (Paris).

French professor specializing in EC Law (by correspondence), 11 July 1994.

Conseiller d'État, 11 July 1994 (Paris).

French professor specializing in European law, 12 July 1994 (Paris).

Legal adviser at the Permanent Representation of France at the European Union, 25 Oct. 1995 (Brussels).

Legal Adviser to the Foreign Ministry in France, 30 Oct. 1995 (Paris).

Legal Director at the *Secrétariat Général de Coordination Interministérielle des Affaires Européennes*, 31 Oct. 1995 (Paris).

Judge at the *Conseil d'État*, 21 July 1998 (Paris).

Germany

German lawyer specializing in European law, 26 Apr. 1993 (Cologne).

Legal adviser for European law at the Federal Ministry for Economic Affairs, 11 May 1993 (Bonn).

Former legal adviser for European law at the Federal Ministry for Economic Affairs, 8 Nov. 1993 (Bonn).

German lawyer specializing in European law, 8 Nov. 1993 (Cologne).

German law professor specializing in international law and European law, 9 Nov. 1993 (Bonn).

Legal correspondent at the *Frankfurter Allgemeine Zeitung*, 15 Nov. 1993 (by correspondence).

Legal adviser for European law at the Federal Ministry for Economic Affairs, 6 Dec. 1993 (Bonn).

Legal correspondent from *Der Spiegel*, 8 Dec. 1993 (Karlsruhe).

Judge at the Federal Constitutional Court of Germany, 8 Dec. 1993 (Karlsruhe).

Clerk to a judge at the Federal Constitutional Court of Germany, 8 Dec. 1993 (Karlsruhe).

German lawyer specializing in European Law, 10 Jan. 1994 (Cologne).

Original secretary for the *Wissentschaftliche Gesellschaft für Europarecht*, 11 Jan. 1994 (Brussels).

Founding member of the *Wissentschaftliche Gesellschaft für Europarecht*, 26 Jan. 1994 (Hamburg).

Former president of a lower tax court in Hamburg, 27 Jan. 1994 (Hamburg).

Director of the EC law section, Ministry of Justice in Germany, 17 Feb. 1994 (Bonn).

Former judge at the Federal Tax Court, 21 Feb. 1994 (Munich).

Federal Tax Court judge from the 7th senate, 21 Feb. 1994 (Munich).

Federal Tax Court judge from the 5th senate, 22 Feb. 1994 (Munich).

Lower tax court judge in Munich, 22 Feb. 1994 (Munich).

Former clerk at the Federal Tax Court (1967–72), 22 Feb. 1994 (Fussen).

Former lower tax court judge from Munich, 22 Feb. 1994 (Fussen).

Secretary of the *Wissentschaftliche Gesellschaft für Europarecht*, 3 June 1994 (Brussels).

Director of the EC law section, Ministry of Justice, 2 Nov. 1995 (Bonn).

Legal adviser at the Ministry of Economic Affairs, 6 Jan. 1996 (by correspondence).

Legal advisers representing national governments other than France and Germany

Legal adviser at the Permanent Representation of the Netherlands at the European Union, 26 Oct. 1995 (Brussels).

Former legal adviser at the Department of Justice in the Netherlands, 27 Oct. 1995 (Brussels).

Council to the Speaker regarding European Legislation, House of Commons, UK, 8 Nov. 1995 (London).

Legal adviser in European affairs at the Foreign and Commonwealth Office, UK, 9 Nov. 1995 (London).

Legal adviser in European Affairs at the Foreign and Commonwealth Office, UK, 9 Nov. 1995 (London).

Political adviser to the Minister of State, Foreign and Commonwealth Office, 10 Nov. 1995 (London).

Legal adviser on European Affairs at the Treasury Solicitor's Office, UK, 10 Nov. 1995 (London).

Negotiators of the Treaty of Rome

Negotiator of the legal section of the Treaty of Rome from Luxembourg, 3 Nov. 1992 (Luxembourg).

Negotiator of the legal section of the Treaty of Rome from France, 7 July 1994 (Paris).

Negotiator of the legal section of Treaty of Rome from France, 23 June 1994 (Paris).

Books and Articles

Anon., Die Kommission Kritisiert Das Bundesverfassungsgericht, *Frankfurter Allgemeine Zeitung*, 21 Dec. 1974.

Anon., Rapport Français. 1997. Cahier de Conseil Constitutionnel 4 (Second Semester). http://www.conseil-constitutionnel.fr/cahiers/ccc4/ccc4aver.htm

Abraham, R. 1989. *Droit international, droit communautaire et droit français: Le Politique, l'économie, le social.* Paris: Hachette.

Alter, K. J. 1996. The European Court's Political Power. *West European Politics* 19(3): 458–87.

—— 1998. Explaining National Court Acceptance of European Court Jurisprudence: A Critical Evaluation of Theories of Legal Integration. In Slaughter et al. (1988: 225–50).

—— 2000. The European Legal System and Domestic Policy: Spillover or Backlash? *International Organization* 54(3): 489–518.

—— and S. Meunier-Aitsahalia. 1994. Judicial Politics in the European Community: European Integration and the Pathbreaking *Cassis de Dijon* decision. *Comparative Political Studies* 24(4): 535–61.

—— and J. Vargas. 2000. Explaining Variation in the Use of European Litigation Strategies: EC law and UK Gender Equality Policy. *Comparative Political Studies* 33(4): 316–46.

Armstrong, K. 1995. Regulating the Free Movement of Goods: Institutions and Institutional Change. In *The New Legal Dynamics of the European Union*, ed. J. Shaw and G. More. Oxford: Clarendon press, 165–91.

—— 1999a. Governance and the Single European market. In *The Evolution of European Union Law*, ed. P. Craig and G. De Búrca. Oxford: Oxford University Press, 745–89.

—— 1999b. New Institutionalism and European Union Legal Studies. In *Lawmaking in the European Union*, ed. P. Craig and C. Harlow. London: Kluwer Law International, 89–110.

Ball, C. 1996. The Making of a Transnational Capitalist Society: The Court of Justice, Social Policy, and Individual Rights under the European Community's Legal Order. *Harvard International Law Journal* 37(2): 307–88.

Bańkowski, Z., and E. Christodoulidis. 1998. The European Union as an Essentially Contested Project. *European Law Journal* 4(4): 341–54.

—— and A. Scott. 1996. The European Union? In *Constitution, Democracy and Sovereignty*, ed. R. Bellamy. Aldershot: Avebury Press, 77–95.

Barak, A. 1989. *Judicial Discretion.* New Haven, Conn.: Yale University Press.

Barnard, K., and E. Sharpston. 1997. The Changing Face of Article 177 References. *Common Market Law Review* 34(5): 1113–71.

Bebr, G. 1973. Case Law Review: Note on the Frankfurt Verwaltungsgericht's *Internationale Handelsgesellschaft* Decision. *Common Market Law Review* 10(1): 96–9.

—— 1983. The Rambling Ghost of 'Cohn-Bendit': *Acte Clair* and the Court of Justice. *Common Market Law Review* 20: 439–72.

Benvenisti, E. 1993. Judicial Misgivings Regarding the Application of International Law: An Analysis of the Attitude of National Courts. *European Journal of International law* 4(2): 159–83.

Berman, G., R. Goebel, W. Davey, and E. Fox. 1993. *Cases and Materials on European Community Law*. St Paul, Minn.: West.

Bernard, N. 1996. The Future of European Economic Law in the Light of the Principle of Subsidiarity. *Common Market Law Review* 33: 633–66.

Berthu, G. 1997. Le Contrôle de l'Europe par la constitution française. Strasbourg: Parlement Européen, Groupe Europe des Nations.

Betten, R., and S. van Thiel. 1986. Direct Effect of Sixth VAT Directive Denied: Kloppenburg Revisited. *European Taxation* (Jan.): 22–5.

Blankenburg, E. 1996. Changes in Political Regimes and Continuity of the Rule of Law in Germany. In *Courts, Law and Politics in Comparative Perspective*, ed. H. Jacob, E. Blankenburg, H. Kirtzer, D. M. Provine, and J. Sanders. New Haven, Conn.: Yale University Press, 249–316.

Boigel, A. 1995. Les Transformations des modalités d'entrée dans la magistrature: De la nécessité sociale aux vertus professionnels. *Pouvoirs* 74: 27–40.

Bonichot, J.-C. 1989. Convergences et divergences entre le Conseil d'État et la Cour de Justice des communautés européennes. *Revue française de Droit Administratif* 5(4): 579–604.

Boulouis, J. 1975. Note. *L'Actualité juridique: Droit administratif* 12: II Jurisprudence, 569–74.

Bribosia, H. 1995. Direct Applicability and the Primacy of European Community Law in the Belgian Legal Order. Fiesole, Italy: European University Institute.

—— 1998. Report on Belgium. In Slaughter et al. (1998: 1–41).

Brown, K. 1995. Government to demand curb on European Court. *Financial Times*, 2 Feb., p. 9.

Buffet-Tchakaloff, M.-F. 1984. *La France devant la cour de justice des communautés européennes*. Aix-en-Provence: Presses Universitaires d'Aix-Marseille.

—— 1991. L'Interprétation des traités par le Conseil d'État: L'Arrêt Gisti. *Revue Générale de Droit International Public* 1: 190–24.

Bulmer, S. 1998. New Institutionalism and the Governance of the Single European market. *Journal of European Public Policy* 5(3): 365–86.

Burley, A.-M., and W. Mattli. 1993. Europe before the Court. *International Organization* 47(1): 41–76.

Caldeira, G., and J. Gibson. 1995. The Legitimacy of the Court of Justice in the European Union: Models of Institutional Support. *American Political Science Review* 89(2): 356–76.

——— 1997. Democracy and Legitimacy in the European Union: The Court of Justice and Its Constituents. *International Social Science Journal* 152 (June): 209–24.

Caporaso, J., and J. Keeler. 1995. The European Union and Regional Integration Theory. In *The State of the European Union*, ed. C. Rhodes and S. Mazey. Boulder, Colo.: Lynne Rienner/Longman, 29–62.

Cappelletti, M. 1989. *The Judicial Process in Comparative Perspective*. Oxford: Clarendon Press.

Cappelletti, M. and D. Golay. 1986. The Judicial Branch in the Federal and Transnational Union: Its Impact on Integration. In *Methods, Tools and Institutions: Political Organs, Integration Techniques and Judicial Process*, ed. M. Cappelletti, M. Seccombe, and J. Weiler. Berlin: Walter de Gruyter, 261–348.

Cassia, P., and E. Saulnier. 1997. L'Imbroglio de la Banane. *Revue du Marché Commun et de l'Union Européenne* 411: 527–44.

Chalmers, D. 1997. Judicial Preferences and the Community Legal Order. *Modern Law Review* 60(2): 164–99.

—— 2000a. The Positioning of EU Judicial Politics within the United Kingdom. *West European Politics* 23(3): 169–210.

—— 2000b. A Statistical Analysis of Reported Decisions of the United Kingdom Invoking EU Laws 1973–1988. Jean Monnet Paper, Harvard Law School, 1/2000.

Chevallier, R.-M. 1965. Note on the Shell-Berre decision of the *Conseil d'État*. *Common Market Law Review* 3(1): 100–7.

Claes, M. 1995. Judicial Review in the European Communities: The Division of Labour between the Court of Justice and National Courts. In *Judicial Control: Comparative Essays on Judicial Review*, ed. R. Bakker, W. A. Heringa, and F. Stroink. Antwerp: Maklu Uitgevers, 109–31.

—— and B. De Witte. 1998. Report on the Netherlands. In Slaughter et al. (1998: 171–94).

Clever, P. 1995. EuGH-Rechtsprechung im Sozialbereich- Kritik, aber auch hoffnungsvolle Zuversicht. *Zeitschrift für Sozialhilfe und Sozialgestezbuch* 34(1): 1–14.

Cohen-Jonathan, G. 1975. Observations: Cour constitutionnelle allemande et règlements communautaires. *Cahiers de Droit Européen* 11: 173–206.

Combarnous, M. 1995. La Réforme du contentieux administratif: du décret du 30 septembre 1953 à la loi du 31 décembre 1987. *L'Actualité Juridique: Droit administratif* 50 (2 June 1995): 175–82.

Conant, L. 2000. Europeanization and the Courts: Variable Patterns of Adaption among National Judiciaries. In *Transforming Europe: Europeanization and Domestic Change*, ed. J. Caporaso, M. Green Cowles, and T. Risse-Kappen. Ithaca, NY: Cornell University Press, 97–115.

Conseil Constitutionnel. 1997. *Rapport Français*. Cahier de Conseil Constitutionnel 4 (2nd semester). http://www.conseil-constitutionnel.fr/cahiers/cc4/ccc4aver.htm

Conseil d'État. 1992. Rapport Public. Paris: Conseil d'État.

Constantinesco, L. 1968. Anmerkung zur Semoules Entscheidung des Conseil d'États. *Europarecht* 3: 318–30.

Cox, A. 1987. *The Court and the Constitution*. Boston: Houghton Mifflin.

Craig, P. 1992. Once Upon a Time in the West: Direct Effect and the Federalization of EEC Law. *Oxford Journal of Legal Studies* 12(4): 453–79.

—— 1998. Report on the United Kingdom. In Slaughter et al. (1998: 195–226).

Dadomo, C., & Farran, S. 1996. *French Legal System*. London: Sweet & Maxwell.

Darras, J., and O. Pirotte. 1976. La Cour Constitutionnelle fédérale allemande a-t-elle mis en danger la primauté du droit communautaire? *Revue Trimestrielle de Droit Européen* 12: 416–38.

Dauvergne, A. 1989. 'Mutation' au Conseil d'État. *Le Point*, 23 Nov. 1989.

De Búrca, G. 1998. The Principle of Subsidiarity and the Court of Justice as an Institutional Actor. *Journal of Common Market Studies* 36(2): 217–35.

—— 1999. Direct Effect, Supremacy and the Nature of the Legal Order. In *The Evolution of EU Law*, ed. P. Craig and G. De Búrca. Oxford: Oxford University Press, 177–214.

Dehaussy, J. 1990. La Supériorité des normes internationales sur les normes internes: à propos de l'arrêt du Conseil d'État du 20 octobre 1989, Nicolo. *Journal du Droit International* 117: 5–33.

Dehousse, R. 1998. *The European Court of Justice: The Politics of Judicial Integration*. New York: St Martin's Press.

de Laubadère, A. 1965. Note sur l'ârret Shell-Berre. *L'Actualité Juridique: Droit Administratif* (July–Aug.): 440–4.

Denning, Lord. 1990. Introduction to The European Court of Justice: Judges or Policy makers? London: Bruges Group.

De Soto, J. 1964. Note sur arrêt Shell Berre. *Journal du Droit International* 89(4): 800–6.

De Witte, B. 1984. Retour à 'Costa': La primauté du droit communautaire à la lumière du droit international. *Revue Trimestrielle de Droit Européen* 20: 425–54.

Donner, A. 1968. *The Role of the Lawyer in the European Communities*. Evanston, Ill.: Northwestern University Press.

Downs, A. 1967. *Inside Bureaucracy*. Boston: Little, Brown.

Druesne, G. 1975. La Primauté du droit communautaire sur le droit interne: L'Arrêt de la Cour de Cassation du 24 Mai 1975. *Revue du Marché Commun*: 378–90.

Dutheillet de Lamothe, O., and Y. Robineau. 1979. Chronique générale de jurisprudence administrative française. *L'Actualité Juridique: Droit Administratif* 3: 27–34.

Ehlermann, C. 1975. Primauté du droit communautaire mise en danger par la Cour Constitutionnelle fédérale allemande. *Revue du Marché Commun* 181: 10–19.

Eising, R., and B. Kohler-Koch. 1999. Governance in the European Union: A Comparative Assessment. In *The Transformation of Governance in the European Union*, ed. B. Kohler-Koch and R. Eising. London: Routledge, 267–85.

Eleftheriadis, P. 1996. Aspects of European Constitutionalism. *European Law Review*, 21 Feb., 32–42.

Errera, R. 1987. French Courts. In *Article 177 EEC: Experiences and Problems*, ed. H. Schermers, C. Timmermans, A. Kellermann, and S. Watson. Amsterdam: Elsevier Science, 78–108.

Everling, U. 1967. Sprachliche Mißverständnisse beim Urteil des Gerichtshofes der Europäischen Gemeinschaften zur Umsatzausgleichersteuer. *Außenwirtschafts-dienst des Betriebs-Beraters* 5 (15 May): 182–4.

Everling, U. 1996. Will Europe Slip on Bananas? The Bananas Judgment of the European Court of Justice and National Courts. *Common Market Law Review* 33: 401–37.

Favoreau, L. 1988. Dualité ou unité d'ordre juridique: Conseil Constitutionnel et Conseil d'État participent-ils de deux ordres juridiques différents? In *Conseil Constitutionnel et Conseil d'État*. Paris: Librairie Général de Droit et de Jurisprudence, 145–89.

——and P. Loïc. 1975. Les 'Suites' de la décision du 15 janvier 1975: L'Arrêt de la Cour de Cassation du 24 mai 1975. *Revue de Droit Public et de Science Politique* 81: 1335–43.

Fitzpatrick, B., J. Gregory, and E. Szyszczak. 1993. Sex Equality Litigation in the Member States of the European Community: A Comparative Study. Commission of the European Union DG V. V/407/94, Oct. 1993.

Folsom, R. 1995. *European Union Law*, 2nd edn. St Paul, Minn.: West Publishing.

Foster, N. G. 1994. The German Constitution and EC Membership. *Public Law* (autumn): 392–408.

Foubert, P. 1996. Case c-68/95 T, *Port GmbH & Co. v. Bundesanstalt für Landwirtschaft und Ernahrung*. *Columbia Journal of European Law* 3: 125–31.

Fourré, J., and W. Wenner. 1965. Der EWG-Vertrag in der Gerichtspraxis (Artikel 37 und 177). *Außenwirtschaftsdienst des Betriebs-Beraters* 6 (15 May 1965): 149–52.

Friedrich, K. 1985. Bundesfinanzhof contra Europäischen Gerichtshof. *Recht der Internationalen Wirtschaft* 10 (Oct.): 794–6.

Galmont, Y. 1990. Le Conseil d'État et le contrôle de la conformité des lois aux traités. MS.

Garrett, G. 1992. The European Community's Internal Market. *International Organization* 46(2): 533–60.

——1995. The Politics of Legal Integration in the European Union. *International Organization* 49(1): 171–81.

——D. Kelemen, and H. Schulz. 1998. The European Court of Justice, National Governments and Legal Integration in the European Union. *International Organization* 52(1): 149–76.

——and B. Weingast. 1993. Ideas, Interests and Institutions: Constructing the EC's Internal market. In *Ideas and Foreign Policy*, ed. J. Goldstein and R. Keohane. Ithaca, NY: Cornell University Press, 173–206.

Genevois, B. 1987. Le Conseil Constitutionnel et le principe de séparation des autorités administratives et judiciaires. *Revue Française du Droit Administratif* 3(2): 287–99.

——1988a. Le Droit international et le droit communautaire. Paper read at Conseil Constitutionnel et Conseil d'État, Palais du Luxembourg, Paris: Librairie Général de Droit et de Jurisprudence, 191–217.

——1988b. Le Juge de l'élection, le traité et la loi. *Revue Française de Droit Administratif* 4(6): 908–16.

——1989. Note. *Revue Français du Droit Administratif* 5(5): 824–33.

Gerbet, P. 1983. *La Construction de l'Europe*. Paris: Imprimerie Nationale.

Gibson, J., and G. Caldeira. 1995. The Legitimacy of Transnational Legal Institutions: Compliance, Support, and the European Court of Justice. *American Journal of Political Science* 39(2): 459–89.

Glendon, M. A., M. W. Gordon, and C. Osakwe. 1985. *Comparative Legal Traditions.* St Paul, Minn.: West.

Goldstein, L. F. 1997. State Resistance to Authority in Federal Unions: The Early United States (1790–1860) and the European Community (1958–1994). *Studies in American Political Development* 11 (spring): 149–89.

Golub, J. 1996a. Modelling Judicial Dialogue in the European Community: The Quantitative Basis of the Preliminary References to the ECJ. Fiesole, Italy: European University Institute. RSC 96/58.

—— 1996b. The Politics of Judicial Discretion: Rethinking the Interaction between National Courts and the European Court of Justice. *West European Politics* 19(2): 360–85.

Haas, E. 1985. *The Uniting of Europe.* Palo Alto, Calif.: Stanford University Press.

—— 1975. *The Obsolescence of Regional Integration Theory.* Berkeley, Calif.: University of California Press.

Haas, P. M. 1992. Introduction: Epistemic Communities and International Policy Coordination. *International Organization* 46(1): 1–36.

Harding, C. 1992. Who Goes to Court in Europe: An Analysis of Litigation against the European Community. *European Law Review* 71(2): 104–25.

Harlow, C. 1992. A Community of Interests? Making the Most of European Law. *Modern Law Review* 55 (May): 331–51.

—— and R. Rawlings. 1992. *Pressure Through Law.* London: Routledge.

Harmsen, R. 1993. European Integration and the Adaptation of Domestic Constitutional Orders: An Anglo-French Comparison. *Journal of European Integration* 17(1): 71–98.

Hartley, T. 1986. Federalism, Courts and Legal Systems: The Emerging Constitution of the European Community. *American Journal of Comparative Law* 34: 229–47.

—— 1988. *The Foundations of European Community Law,* 3rd edn. Oxford: Clarendon Press.

—— 1994. *The Foundations of European Community Law,* 4th edn. Oxford: Clarendon Press.

—— 1996. The European Court, Judicial Objectivity and the Constitution of the European Union. *Law Quarterly review* 112: 95–109.

Helfer, L., and A.-M. Slaughter. 1997. Toward a Theory of Effective Supranational Adjudication. *Yale Law Journal* 107(2): 273–391.

Henkin, L., R. C. Pugh, O. Schachter, and H. Smit. 1993. *International Law: Cases and Materials,* 3rd edn. St Paul, Minn.: West.

Herdegen, M. 1995. After the TV Judgement of the German Constitutional Court: Decision-Making Within the EU Council and the German Länder. *Common Market Law Review* 31: 1369–84.

Hilf, M. 1975. Auswirkung auf die Gemeinschaftsrechtsordnung. *Zeitschrift für aus-ländisches öffentliches Recht und Völkerrecht* 35(1): 51–66.

——1988. Der Justizkonflict um EG-Richtlinien: gelöst. *Europarecht* 23(1): 1–19.

Høegh, K. 1999. The Danish Maastricht Judgement. *European Law Review* 24 (Feb.): 80–90.

Hoffmann, S. 1987. Reaching for the Most Difficult: Human Rights as a Foreign Policy Goal. In *Janus and Minerva: Essays in the Theory and Practice of International Politics*, ed. S. Hoffmann. Boulder, Colo.: Westview Press, 370–93.

Horn, N., H. Kötz, and H. G. Leser. 1982. *German Private and Commercial Law: An Introduction*. London: Oxford University Press.

Hubac, S., and Y. Robineau. 1988. Droit administratif: vues de l'intérieur. *Pouvoirs* 46: 113–26.

Hummings, N. M. 1975. European National Laws. *Journal of Business Law*: 326–9.

Ipsen, H. P. 1975. BVerfG versus EuGh re 'Grundrechte'. *Europarecht* 1/2 (Jan.–June): 1–19.

——1990. 'Europarecht': 25 Jahrgänge 1966–1990. *Europarecht* 25(4): 323–39.

Isaac, G. 1980. A propos de l' 'amendement Aurillac': Vers une obligation pour les juges d'appliquer les lois contraires aux traités? *Gazette du Palais* II: Doctrine: 583–5.

Jacobs, F., and Karst, K. 1986. *The 'Federal' Legal Order: The USA and Europe Compared—A Juridical Perspective*. New York: Walter de Gruyter.

Jacqué, J.-P. 1981. The Individual member States' Community Obligations: Faithful Implementation or Realization of Unilateral Goals with a Particular View to EC-Member States' Court's Defiance of the European Court of Justice, France. Paper read at Conference on Individual Member States' Community Obligations, ed. H. Rasmussen. Copenhagen: manuscript on file with author and at *ECJ* Library.

Jeantet, F.-Ch. 1976. La Cour de Cassation et l'ordre juridique communautaire. *La Semaine Juridique, Juris-Classeur Périodique*, Édition Commerce et Industrie 4; Études et Commentaires 11962: 45–50.

Joerges, C. 2000. Interactive Adjudication in the Europeanisation Process? A Demanding Perspective and a Modest Example. *European Review of Private Law* 1: 1–16.

Kapteyn, P. J. G. 1979. National Courts: Conseil d'État (Assemblée), Decision of 22 Dec. 1978, *Cohn-Bendit. Common Market Law Review* 16: 701–3.

Kenney, S. 1998. The Judges of the European Communities. In *Constitutional Dialogues in Comparative Perspective*, ed. S. Kenney, W. Reisinger, and J. Reitz. London: Macmillan.

Keohane, R. 1984. *After Hegemony*. Princeton, NJ: Princeton University Press.

——A. Moravscik, and A.-M. Slaughter. 2000. Legalized Dispute Resolution: Interstate and Transnational. *International Organization* 54(3): 457–88.

King, G., R. Keohane, and S. Verba. 1994. *Designing Social Inquiry: Scientific Inference in Qualitative Research*. Princeton, NJ: Princeton University Press.

Kokott, J. 1998. Report on Germany. In Slaughter et al. (1998: 77–131).

Kommers, D. 1989. *The Constitutional Jurisprudence of the Federal Republic of Germany.* Durham, NC: Duke University Press.

Kovar, R. 1975. La Primauté du droit communautaire sur la loi française. *Cahiers de Droit Européen* 11(5–6): 636–64.

——1979. Observations. *La Semaine Juridique-Juris Classeur Périodique* II. Jurisprudence 19158.

Lachaume, J.-F. 1990. Une victoire de l'ordre juridique communautaire: l'arrêt Nicolo consacrant la supériorité des traités sur les lois postérieures. *Revue du Marché Commun* 336: 384–94.

Laderchi, P. R. 1998. Report on Italy. In Slaughter et al. (1998: 147–70).

Ladeur, K.-H. 1997. Towards a Legal Theory of Supranationality: the Viability of the Network Concept. *European Law Journal* 3(1): 33–54.

Lagneau-Devillé, A. 1983. Influences du pouvoir exécutif sur les prérogatives du juge en France, sous la Vème République. In *Fonction de juger et pouvoir judiciaire*, ed. P. Gérard, F. Ost, and M. Van de Kerchare. Brussels: Faculté Universitaire Saint-Louis, 469–92.

Lagrange, M. 1968. Note sur arrêt Semoules. *Recueil Dalloz-Sirey* 15: 286–9.

——1971. The European Court of Justice and National Courts: The Theory of the *Acte Clair*: A Bone of Contention or a Source of Unity? *Common Market Law Review* 18: 313–24.

Lecourt, R. 1964. Le Rôle du droit dans l'unification européenne. *Gazette du Palais*: 49–54.

——1965. La Dynamique judiciaire dans l'édification de l'Europe. *France Forum* 64: 20–2.

——1973. L'Europe méconnue: Les Français et la Cour de Justice. *Le Monde* (29 Nov.), 5–6.

——1976. *L'Europe des juges*. Brussels: Émile Bruylant.

——1991. Quel eut été le droit des communautés sans les arrêts de 1963 et 1964? In *Mélanges en hommage à Jean Boulouis: L'Europe et le droit.* Paris: Dalloz, 349–61.

Lenaerts, K. 1992. Some Thoughts about the Relation between Judges and Politicians. *University of Chicago Legal Forum* 93–133.

Long, M. 1994. The European Community and EC Law: The Responses Given by the *Conseil d'État*. Paris: Mentor Group Conference, Conseil d'État.

Loschak, D. 1972. *Le Role politique du juge administratif français.* Paris: Librairie Générale de Droit et de Jurisprudence.

Lowi, T. 1969. *The End of Liberalism.* New York: Norton.

MacCormick, N. 1993. Beyond the Sovereign State. *Modern Law Review* 56(1): 1–18.

Maher, I. 1994. National Courts as European Community Courts. *Legal Studies* 14(2): 226–43.

——1998. Community Law in the National Legal Order: A Systems Analysis. *Journal of Common Market Studies* 36(2): 237–54.

Mancini, F. 1989. The Making of a Constitution for Europe. *Common Market Law Review* 24: 595–614.

Mancini, F. 1998. Europe: The Case for Statehood. *European Law Journal* 4(1): 29–42.

——and D. Keeling. 1992. From CILFIT to ERTA: The Constitutional Challenge Facing the European Court. *Yearbook of European Law* 11: 1–13.

——1994. Democracy and the European Court of Justice. *Modern Law Review* 57(2): 175–90.

——1995. Language, Culture and Politics in the Life of the European Court of Justice. *Columbia Journal of European Law* 1(2): 397–413.

Manin, P. 1991. The *Nicolo* case of the *Conseil d'État*: French Constitutional Law and the Supreme Administrative Court's Acceptance of the Primacy of Community Law over Subsequent National Statute. *Common Market Law Review* 28: 499–519.

Mann, C. 1972. *The Function of Judicial Decision in European Economic Integration.* The Hague: Martinus Nijhoff.

Marks, B. A. 1989. A Model of Judicial Influence on Congressional Policy Making: *Grove City College v. Bell* (1984). Dissertation, University of Washington.

Marks, G., L. Hooghe, and K. Blank. 1996. European Integration from the 1980s: State-centric v. Multi-level Governance. *Journal of Common Market Studies* 34(3): 341–78.

Mattli, W., and A.-M. Slaughter. 1995. Law and Politics in the European Union: A Reply to Garrett. *International Organization* 49(1): 183–90.

——1998. Revisiting the European Court of Justice. *International Organization* 52(1): 177–209.

Mayer, F. 2000. *Kompetenzuberschreitung und Letztentscheidung: Das Maastricht Urteil des Bundesverfassungsgerichts und die Letztentscheidung uber Ultra vires-Akte in Mehrebenensystemen.* Munich: Beck.

Mazard, R. 1971. Rapport de M. le Conseiller Mazard. *Recueil Dalloz Sirey* 14: Jurisprudence 221–2.

Mazeaud, P. 1996. Rapport d'information par la délégation de l'Assemblée Nationale pour l'Union Européenne. Paris: Assemblée National.

Mazey, S. 1995. The Development of EU Equality Policies: Bureaucratic Expansion on Behalf of Women? *Public Administration* 73 (winter): 591–609.

——1998. The European Union and Women's Rights: From the Europeanization of National Agendas to the Nationalization of a European Agenda? *Journal of European Public Policy* 5(1): 131–52.

McCubbins, M., and T. Schwartz. 1987. Congressional Oversight Overlooked: Police Patrols Versus Fire Alarms. In *Congress: Structure and Policy*, ed. M. McCubbins and T. Sullivan. Cambridge: Cambridge University Press, 409–25.

Meier, G. 1967a. Aktuelle Fragen zur Umsatzausgleichsteuer. *Außenwirtschaftsdienst des Betriebs-Beraters* 3 (15 Mar. 1967): 97–101.

——1967b. Zur Aussetzung der Einsprüche gegen Umsatzausgleichsteuer-bescheide. *Außenwirtschaftsdienst des Betriebs-Beraters* 2 (15 Feb. 1967): 75–7.

——1970. Anmerkung. *Außenwirtschaftsdienst des Betriebs-Beraters* 5 (May): 233–4.

—— 1975. Verfassungsbeschwerde gegen Verordnungen der EWG-Anmerkung. *Europarecht* 1/2 (Jan.–June): 168–9.

—— 1994. Der Streit um due Umsatzausgleichsteuer aus integrationspolitischer Sicht. *Recht der Internationalen Wirtschaft* 40(2): 149–51.

Menzel. 1981. *Bonner Kommentar*. Bonn.

—— and C. Tomuschat. 1981. Art. 24. In *Bonner Kommentar*, 56–84.

Merryman, H. 1996. The French Deviation. *American Journal of Comparative Law*, 44, 109–19.

Meunier, S., and K. Nicolaidis. 1999. Who Speaks for Europe? The Delegation of Trade Authority in the EU. *Journal of Common Market Studies* 37(3): 477–501.

Micklitz, H. & Reich, N. 1996. Public Interest Litigation Before European Courts. Baden-Baden: Nomos.

Millett, T. 1990. *The Court of First Instance of the European Communities*. London: Butterworths.

Mnookin, R., and L. Kornhauser. 1979. Bargaining in the Shadow of the Law: The Case of Divorce. *Yale Law Journal* 88: 950–97.

Möhring, P. 1965. Rechtsvereinheitlichung und Rechtsgarantien im EWG-Bereich. *Neue juristische Wochenschrift* 18(48): 2225–30.

Moravcsik, A. 1998. *The Choice for Europe*. Ithaca, NY: Cornell University Press.

Morris, P. E., and P. W. David. 1987. Directives, Direct Effect and the European Court: The Triumph of Pragmatism. *Business Law Review* (Apr.): 85–8 and 116–18, (May): 35–6.

Murphy, W. 1964. *Elements of Judicial Strategy*. Chicago: Chicago University Press.

Niskanen, W. 1971. *Bureaucracy and Representative Government*. Chicago: Aldine Atherton.

Olsen-Ring, L. 2000. Einflüsse der Maastricht-Entscheidung des Bundesverfassung-gerichts auf die Rechtsprechung des Obersten Gerichtshof Dänemarks. In *Deutschen Zwischen Europäsierung und Selbstbehauptung*, ed. M. Knodt and B. Kohler-Koch. Mannheim: Campus.

Pache, E. 1995. Das Ende der Bananenmarktordnung? *Neue juristische Wochenschrift* 1/2: 95–103.

Pacteau, B. 1996. Procédure administrative contentieuse, retour à la loi, et après. *Revue Française de Droit Administratif* 12(1): 5–9.

Page, E. 1985. *Political Authority and Bureaucratic Power*. Knoxville: University of Tennessee Press.

Parris, H. 1966. The *Conseil d'État* in the Fifth Republic. *Government and Opposition* 2(1): 89–104.

Peers, S. 1999. Banana Split: WTO Law and Preferential Agreements in the EC Legal Order. *European Foreign Affairs Review* 4: 195–214.

Pellet, A. 1997. Le Conseil constitutionnel, la souveraineté et les traités. *Cahier de Conseil Constitutionnel* 2 (2nd Semester). www.conseil-constitutionnel.fr/cahiers/ccc4/ccc4somm.htm

Pescatore, P. 1969. Die Menschenrechte und die europäische Integration. *Integration*: 103–36.

—— 1973. Community Law and the National Judge. *Law Guardian* (Jan.).

—— 1981. Les Travaux du 'groupe juridique' dans la négociation des traités de Rome. *Studia Diplomatica (Chronique de Politique Etrangère)* 34(1–4): 159–78.

Pescatore, P. 1983a. The Doctrine of 'Direct Effect': An Infant Disease of Community Law. *European Law Review* 8(3): 155–77.

—— 1983b. La Clarence du législateur communautaire et le devoir du juge. In *Gedächtnisschrift für L.-J. Constantinesco*. Cologne: Carl Heymanns, 559–80.

—— 1986. References for Preliminary Rulings under Article 177 of the EEC Treaty and Cooperation between the Court and National Courts. Luxembourg: European Court of Justice.

Pierson, P. 1996. The Path to European Integration: A Historical Institutionalist Perspective. *Comparative Political Studies* 29(2): 123–63.

—— and S. Leibfried. 1995. *European Social Policy: Between Fragmentation and Integration*. Washington, DC: Brookings Institution.

Pirotte-Gerouville, J. 1976. La Primauté du droit international et la spécificité de l'ordre communautaire dans l'affaire Jacques Vabre. *Revue Trimestrielle de Droit Européen*: 215–28.

Pollack, M. 1997. Delegation, Agency and Agenda Setting in the EC. *International Organization* 51(1): 99–134.

Provine, D. M. 1996. Courts in the Political Process in France. In *Courts, Law and Politics in Comparative Perspective*, ed. H. Jacob, E. Blankenburg, H. Kritzer, D. M. Provine, and J. Sanders. New Haven, Conn.: Yale University Press, 177–248.

Putnam, R. 1988. Diplomacy and Domestic Politics: The Logic of Two Level Games. *International Organization* 42(3): 427–61.

Questiaux, N. 1995. Administration and the Rule of Law: The Preventative Role of the French *Conseil d'État*. *Public Law* (summer): 247–58.

—— 1998. Implementing EC Law in France: The Role of the French *Conseil d'État*. In *Lawmaking in the European Union*, ed. P. Craig and C. Harlow. London: Kluwer Law International, 479–97.

Radamaker, D. 1988. The Courts in France. In *The Political Role of Law Courts in Modern Democracies*, ed. J. Waltman and K. Holland. London: Macmillan, 129–52.

Rasmussen, H. 1984. The European Court's *Acte Clair* Strategy in CILIT, or *Acte Clair*, of Course! But What Does It Mean? *European Law Review*: 242–59.

—— 1986. *On Law and Policy in the European Court of Justice*. Dordrecht: Martinus Nijhoff.

—— 1998. Denmark's Maastricht-Ratification Case. *Irish Jurist* 33: 77–101.

Rawlings, R. 1993. The Eurolaw Game: Some Deductions from a Saga. *Journal of Law and Society* 20: 309–40.

Rendel, M. 1970. *The Administrative Functions of the French Conseil d'État*. London: Weidenfeld & Nicolson.

Riegel, R. 1974. Bundesverfassungsgerichtsbeschluß Anmerkung. *Neue juristische Wochenschrift* 48: 2176–7.

——1976. Das Grundrechtsproblem als Kollisionsproblem im europäischen Gemeinschaftsrecht. *Bayerische Verwaltungsblätter* 12 (15 June 1976): 354–60.

Robertson, A. H. 1966. *European Institutions: Cooperation, Integration, Unification*, 2nd edn. New York: Praeger.

Rozes, S. 1985. Independence of Judges of the Court of Justice of the European Communities. In *Judicial Independence: The Contemporary Debate*, ed. S. Schetreet and J. Descenes. Dordrecht: Martinus Nijhoff, 501–11.

Rupp, H. H. 1970. Die Grundrechte und das Europäische Gemeinschaftsrecht. *Neue juristische Wochenschrift* 9: 353–9.

——1974. Zur bundesverfassungsgerichtlichen Kontrolle des Gemeinschaftsrechts am Maßtab der Grundrechte. *Neue juristische Wochenschrift* 48: 2153–6.

Ruzié, D. 1975. Note. *Journal de Droit International* 4: 805–8.

Sabourin, P. 1993. Le Conseil d'État au droit communautaire. *Revue de Droit Public et de la Science Politique en France et à l'Étranger* (Mar.–Apr.): 397–430.

Sauron, J.-L. 1998. Le Renvoi préjudiciel de l'article 177 du traité instituant la Communauté Européenne: Crise ou renouveau? *Petites Affiches* 66 (June): 8–14.

Scharpf, F. 1988. The Joint-Decision Trap: Lessons from German Federalism and European Integration. *Public Administration* 66 (autumn): 239–78.

Scheingold, S. 1971. The Law in Political Integration: The Evolution and Integrative Implications of Regional Legal Processes in the European Community. Cambridge, Mass.: Harvard University Center for International Affairs.

Schepel, H., and R. Wesseling. 1997. The Legal Community: Judges, Lawyers, Officials and Clerks in the Writing of Europe. *European Law Journal* 3(2): 165–88.

Scheuner, U. 1975. Der Grundrechtsschutz in der Europäischen Gemeinschaft und die Verfassungsrechtsprechung. *Archive des Öffentlichen Rechts* 100(1): 30–52.

Schmidt, S. 2000. Only an Agenda Setter? The European Commission's Power over the Council of Ministers. *European Union Politics* 1(1): 37–61.

Schockweiler, F. 1991. L'Emprise du droit communitaire sur les pouvoirs du juge national. *Bulletin du Cercle François Laurent*: 51–76.

Schoettl, J.-E. 1998. Traité de Amsterdam. *L'Actualité Juridique: Droit Administratif* (Feb.): 135–47.

Schwartz, J. 1988. *Die Befolgung von Vorabentscheidungen des Europäischen Gerichtshofs durch deutsche Gerichte*. Baden-Baden: Nomos.

Seidel, M. 1987. Article 177 EEC: Experiences and Problems: Germany as a Member State. In *Asser Institute Colloquium on European Law Session XV*, ed. H. Schermers, C. Timmermans, A. Kellermann, and W. J. Stewart. Amsterdam: Elsevier Science, 239–58.

Shapiro, M. 1980. Comparative Law and Comparative Politics. *Southern California Law Review* 53: 537–42.

——1981. *Courts: A Comparative Political Analysis*. Chicago: University of Chicago Press.

Shapiro, M. 1999. The European Court of Justice. In *The Evolution of European Union Law*, ed. P. Craig and G. De Búrca. Oxford: Oxford University Press, 321–49.

Shaw, J. 1994. European Union Legal Studies in Crisis? Towards a New Dynamic. Fiesole, Italy: European University Institute. RSC 95/23.

Simon, M. 1976. Enforcement by French Courts of European Community Law, II. *Law Quarterly Review* 92: 85–92.

Slaughter, A.-M., A. Stone Sweet, and J. Weiler (eds.). 1998. *The European Courts and National Courts*. Oxford: Hart.

Smith, Gavin. 1990. *The European Court of Justice: Judges or Policy Makers?* London: Bruges Group.

Soulas de Russel, D., and U. Engels. 1975. L'Intégration de l'Europe à l'heure de la décision de la Cour Constitutionnelle fédérale du 29 mai 1974. *Revue Internationale de Droit Comparé* 23(2): 377–84.

Stack, J. F., Jr. 1992. Judicial Policy-Making and the Evolving Protection of Human Rights: The European Court of Human Rights in Comparative Perspective. *West European Politics* 15(3): 137–55.

Stein, E. 1981. Lawyers, Judges and the Making of a Transnational Constitution. *American Journal of International Law* 75(1): 1–27.

Stein, T. 1986. National Courts: Note on Decision of *Bundesfinanzhof* of 25 April 1985. *Common Market Law Review* 23: 727–36.

Stirn, B. 1995. Tribunaux administratifs et cours administratives d'appel: un nouveau visage. *L'Actualité Juridique: Droit Administratif* (20 June 1995): 183–9.

Stöcker, H. A. 1967. Einzelklagebefugnis und EWG-Kommissionsentscheidung: Alternative oder kumulierter Rechtsschutz in Umsatzausgleichsteuersachen. *Der Betrieb* (40): 1690–2.

Stone, A. 1990. The Birth and Development of Abstract Review: Constitutional Courts and Policymaking in Western Europe. *Policy Studies Journal* 19(1): 81–95.

—— 1992. *The Birth of Judicial Politics in France: The Constitutional Council in Comparative Perspective*. New York: Oxford University Press.

—— 1993. Ratifying Maastricht: France Debates European Union. *French Politics and Society* 11(1): 70–88.

—— and T. Brunnel. 1998. The European Court and the National Courts: A Statistical Analysis of Preliminary References, 1961–95. *Journal of Public European Policy* 5(1): 66–97.

Stone Sweet, A. 2000. *Governing with Judges*. Oxford: Oxford University Press.

—— and T. Brunnel. 1998. Constructing a Supranational Constitution: Dispute Resolution and Governance in the European Community. *American Political Science Review* 92(1): 63–80.

Streinz, R. 1994. Das Maastricht-Urtile des Bundesverfassungsgerichts. *Europäische Zeitschrift für Wirtschaftsrecht* 11: 329–33.

Tallberg, J. 1999. Making States Comply: The European Commission, The European Court of Justice, and the Enforcement of the Internal Market. Dissertation, University of Lund.

Tatham, A. 1991. Effect of European Community Directives in France: The Development of the Cohn-Bendit Jurisprudence. *International Comparative Law Quarterly* (Oct.): 907–19.

Torrelli, M. 1968. La Cour Constitutionnelle fédérale allemande et le droit communautaire. *Revue du Marché Commun* 112: 719–23.

Touffait, A. 1975. Les Jurisdictions judiciaires françaises devant l'interprétation et l'application du droit communautaire. In *La France et le communautés européennes*, ed. J. Rideau, P. Gerbet, M. Torrelli, and R. M. Chevallier. Paris: Librairie Générale de Droit et de Jurisprudence, 823–5.

Tsebelis, G. 1995. Decision Making in Political Systems: Veto Players in Presidentialism, Parliamentarism, Multicameralism and Multipartyism. *British Journal of Political Science* 25: 289–325.

——and G. Garrett. 2001. The Institutional Determinants of Supranationalism in the European Union. *International Organization* 55(2): 357–90.

Van der Groeben, H. 1985. *The European Community: The Formative Years*. Brussels: Commission of the European Communities.

Vedel, G. 1992. Schengen et Maastricht. *Revue Française de Droit Administratif* 8(2): 173–80.

——1987. L'Attitude des jurisdictions françaises envers les traités européens. Saarbrücken: Europa-Institut der Universität des Saarlands.

Vincur, J. 1998. The Tour—and France—Are Catching Up to Life. *International Herald Tribune*, Paris, 31 July 1998, 1 and 20.

Volcansek, K. 1986. *Judicial Politics in Europe*. New York: Peter Lang.

Voss, R. 1987. Federal Republic of Germany National Report. In *Article 177 EEC: Experiences and Problems*, ed. H. Schermers, C. Timmermans, A. Kellermann, and J. S. Watson. Amsterdam: Elsevier Science, 239–52.

Waelbroeck, M. 1967. Observations: L'Applicabilité directe de l'article 95 du traité CEE. *Cahiers de Droit européen* 2: 184–94.

Weiler, J. H. H. 1995. The State 'über alles': Demos, Telos and the German Maastricht Decision. Fiesole, Italy: European University Institute. RSC 95/19.

Weiler, J. 1981. The Community System: The Dual Character of Supranationalism. *Yearbook of European Law* 1: 257–306.

——1991. The Transformation of Europe. *Yale Law Journal* 100: 2403–83.

——1994. A Quiet Revolution: The European Court of Justice and Its Interlocutors. *Comparative Political Studies* 26(4): 510–34.

——1999. The Constitution of the Common Market Place: The Free Movement of Goods. In *The Evolution of EU Law*, ed. P. Craig and G. De Búrca. Oxford: Oxford University Press, 349–77.

——and N. Lockhart. 1995. 'Taking Rights Seriously' Seriously: The European Court and Its Fundamental Rights (Part 1). *Common Market Law Review* 32: 51–95.

Weill, C. 1978. Les députés RPR votent avec la gauche contre le gouvernement. *Le Matin*, 1 Dec. 1978.

Weiss, F. 1979. Self Executing Treaties and Directly Applicable EEC Law in French Courts. *Legal Issues in European Integration* 1: 51–84.

Wendt, P. 1967a. Kein Rechtsschutz im Umsatzausgleichsteuer-Sachen? *Der Betrieb* 48: 2047–8.

——1967b. Ungeklärte Fragen im Streit um die Unmsatzausgleichsteuer. *Außenwirtschaftsdienst des Betriebs-Beraters* 9 (Sept.): 348–54.

Wenner, W. 1964. Anmerkung zur Entscheidung des französischen Conseil d'État zu Artikel 177 des EWG-Vertrages. *Recht der Internationalen Wirtschaft* 8: 261–2.

Wincott, D. 1995. The Role or the Rule of the Court of Justice: An 'Institutional' Account of Judicial Politics in the European Community. *Journal of European Public Policy* 2(4): 583–602.

Zoller, E. 1992. *Droit des relations extérieures*. Paris: Presses Universitaires de Paris.

Zuleeg, M. 1971. Fundamental Rights and the Law of the European Communities. *Common Market Law Review* 8: 446–61.

——1975. Das Bundesverfassungsgericht als Hüter der Grundrechte gegenüber der Gemeinschaftsgewalt. *Die Öffentliche Verwaltung* 1–2: 44–6.

——1993. Bundesfinanzhof und Gemeinschaftsrecht. In *75 Jahre Reichsfinanzhof-Bundesfinanzhof*, ed. Präsident des Bundesfinanzhofs. Bonn: Stollfuß, 115–30.

INDEX

Learning Resources
Centre